Bereavement Camps for Children and Adolescents

Bereavement Camps for Children and Adolescents is the first book to describe in detail how to create bereavement camps for children and adolescents. It is a comprehensive how-to guide, offering practical advice on planning, curriculum building, and evaluation. Readers will find a step-by-step plan for building a nonprofit organization, including board development and fundraising, such as grant writing, soliciting businesses, and holding special events, as well as valuable information on nonprofit management and volunteer recruitment. The appendices include a variety of sample forms and letters.

Irene Searles McClatchey, PhD, MSW, LCSW, developed a healing camp for bereaved children and adolescents, Camp MAGIK, in 1995. She is actively involved with the camp and has published extensively on its efficacy.

Jane S. Wimmer, PhD, MSW, is retired from a career in child welfare and college teaching. She is a volunteer with Camp MAGIK.

D1202721

Bereavement Camps for Children and Adolescents

Planning, Curriculum, and Evaluation

IRENE SEARLES McCLATCHEY
JANE S. WIMMER

Routledge
Taylor & Francis Group

NEW YORK AND LONDON

First published 2018
by Routledge
711 Third Avenue, New York, NY 10017

and by Routledge
2 Park Square, Milton Park, Abingdon, Oxon, OX14 4RN

Routledge is an imprint of the Taylor & Francis Group, an informa business

Library of Congress Cataloging-in-Publication Data
Names: McClatchey, Irene Searles, author. | Wimmer, Jane, 1945–
    author.
Title: Bereavement camps for children and adolescents : planning,
    curriculum, and evaluation / by Irene Searles McClatchey and
    Jane S. Wimmer.
Description: New York, NY : Routledge, 2018. | Includes bibliographical
    references and index.
Identifiers: LCCN 2017018425 | ISBN 9781138284388 (hardback) |
    ISBN 9781138284395 (pbk.)
Subjects: LCSH: Bereavement in children. | Bereavement in
    adolescence. | Grief therapy. | Camps.
Classification: LCC BF723.G75 M33 2018 | DDC 155.9/37083—dc23
LC record available at https://lccn.loc.gov/2017018425

ISBN: 978-1-138-28438-8 (hbk)
ISBN: 978-1-138-28439-5 (pbk)
ISBN: 978-1-315-21381-1 (ebk)

Typeset in Dutch823BT
by Apex CoVantage, LLC

To all campers who come so bravely to camp to share their stories and give each other support.

To Jim McDonald, whose passionate support of Camp MAGIK keeps the magic going.

To our beautiful families, who renew us with their love.

And in memory of our fathers, Karl Erland Harry Erlandson and James M. Shoemaker, who left us too young.

■ *Contents*

Foreword

One of the courses I teach is titled *Children, Adolescents, Death, and Loss*. This graduate-level course draws Art Therapy, Mental Health Counseling, and Guidance and Counseling students as well as occasional School Administration or Education students. One of the emphases of the class is that children and adolescents do much better in "natural settings"—for example, play, music, or other expressive therapies—than in a traditional counseling model. Even when the most empathic adult says to a child, "let's talk," the child's defenses inevitably are aroused and the child wonders what he or she did wrong.

Camps are one of the most effective natural settings for a child. I still fondly recall going to my local Boy's Club Winter Camp as a child and adolescent. I remember going from the Metro-North train that took us from New York City—being then loaded in an open air truck that delivered us from the train in Brewster to a fire-heated cabin in the Carmel woods. I can recite the invariant menu offered weekend after weekend, year after year—grilled cheese sandwiches that welcomed us to camp and a closing meal of beef stew that made the pizza store next to the Brewster train station a must stop before the return home. Some of my fondest memories of that era rest in that camp as well as some of my oldest and most enduring friendships. Those readers who had similar camp experiences—whether winter or summer—can recall those magic moments of camp.

Bereavement camps offer children new friendships and the opportunity to enjoy themselves as well as a place to safely express their thoughts and have their feelings validated. That is why bereavement camps offer such a powerful vehicle of support for bereaved children and that is why Irene Searles McClatchey and Jane S. Wimmer's book *Bereavement Camps for Children and Adolescents: Planning, Curriculum, and Evaluation* is such a welcome addition to the literature. The authors offer a rare combination of solid academic credentials with the practical experience of running such a camp. This book offers "everything you wanted to know about grief camps and were afraid—or did not know enough—to ask." It begins by firmly rooting readers in the grief experience of children and adolescents and the interventions that help with the nuts and bolts of running a camp, then moves from inception to funding to curriculum to evaluation—the complete package.

One of the most positive aspects of the book is that though the authors have considerable experience in one camp model, they fully discuss the plethora of models and curricula available. Now that such a sourcebook is available, it seems irresponsible to plan or run a grief camp without a well-worn copy of *Bereavement Camps for Children and Adolescents: Planning, Curriculum, and Evaluation* by one's side.

Perhaps it is my own previous camp experiences—both as camper and counselor many, many years ago—that attract me to the model. Yet the truth is that camps can offer much to children struggling with loss. For children or adolescents who have lost a parent or a sibling, the world can seem very lonely. After all, as one adolescent boy reminded me "your friends want to hang. You don't want to be known as the kid whose dad died." In a grief camp setting you are, he stated, with "kids who get it." For a child or adolescent, the validation and support of peers is a critical gift. Children and adolescents realize they are not alone in their grief. "Normal" takes on a new meaning.

Grief camps also offer children and adolescents not only support but also education to understand their grief and tools to help them cope—and even grow—with their grief. The projects that are done in camp often make important points: that feelings, be they of anger, sadness, guilt, or whatever, are normal and natural; there is help available; and there are others who do understand the pain of grief. Moreover, camps remind that love never dies and the bonds that one has with people who died can never really be severed.

But camps do two things even better perhaps than any other intervention. In the fun of daily activities they reinforce that even as we encounter loss in life, there can still be joy, that even in the midst of grief, we can still take pleasure and have fun. Children and adolescents are reminded that there are good days and bad days on the roller coaster of grief. That understanding offers promise to sustain them in the tough days that may still be ahead.

And there is one more critical lesson in the relationships that children and adolescents make with one another and with their counselors: They are reassured that even in loss they can still love again—creating new bonds even as they grieve.

Kenneth J. Doka, PhD
Professor, Graduate School, The College of New Rochelle
Senior Consultant, The Hospice Foundation of America

Preface

When I first sat down to write how Camp MAGIK originated, I started out with my usual impersonal and reserved tone. Born and raised in Sweden, culturally I am reserved and protective of my privacy. I realized, however, that at camp, I have invited thousands of children to open up and share their stories, and that it would not hurt for me to do the same . . . so here is my story:

This Sunday started out as any other, except it was an unusually warm August day for Sweden. I was staying with a friend and his family for the weekend before having to return to school in a couple of weeks. This day my friend was going to take me out on his boat. I was very excited. Being a farmer's daughter, boating was not one of the things I got to do routinely, if ever. After a great day in the sun, boating and swimming, we returned to my friend's home. I was supposed to get on the bus that afternoon for my trip back home, but my friend and I had decided that I was going to call home to tell my parents that I had missed the bus, and that I would stay there another night. Back at my friend's home I dialed my parents' number. My mother answered the phone. She sounded tired. "Darling, I have tried to reach you all day. Is your friend or his father there? I want to talk to them." This was odd, and I knew something was wrong. I gave the phone to my friend, and from his short responses—"aha," "yes," "I am so very sorry"—I gathered something was definitely wrong. After he hung up the phone, my friend told me softly that early that morning my father had died suddenly. My mother had ten children, of which I and my twin sister were the youngest, and had desperately tried to reach one of us throughout the day. She had been unable to reach anybody, and at 5 in the evening I was the first one to speak with her that day. In spite of my friend's attempt to be gentle, I attacked him, hitting him with my closed fists, yelling at him that he was lying. After my friend and his father took me to the emergency room to get a sedative shot, I slept unexpectedly soundly that night, waking up thinking that it was all a nightmare. It was not. I was devastated. I actively grieved for a long time, with extreme feelings of guilt. I had not always been a pleasant daughter. My own adolescent angst spilled over into my relationship with my parents; heated arguments about anything and everything were common. When my father died, I knew I had somehow contributed to his death. I also knew that my own time on this earth was soon to be finished. Today, I realize I was experiencing posttraumatic stress symptoms, but at the time I did not know this. I spent ten years of deep grieving before finding a knowledgeable therapist who could help me move forward.

Twenty years later I lived in the United States and was working as a social worker at a hospice. I met families through my work where a young parent died and I was heartbroken not to know where to refer children for bereavement support or counseling. Adding to my sadness was my own experience of losing my father and knowing the impact that the loss of a parent could have on a young person. Seeing children in hospice lose their parents made me want to help in ways that I wished I had been helped. But there were no resources. I asked myself to be the resource.

I started by creating a support group for children and adolescents of hospice patients. The group format was a closed eight-week group meeting on a weeknight. Children signed up, typically anywhere from six to eight members. However, to my frustration, it was obvious that it took some time for the participants to trust each other enough to share freely. Each session started with socialization and it took time before the participants would open up. I racked my brain to figure out how I could help the children trust each other enough to share on a deeper level. The camp idea came to me.

I needed funding and approached the director of the hospice where I worked. I was very fortunate—as a former pediatric nurse, she was immediately on board. Next came the question of what to call the camp. I sent an announcement to family, colleagues, and friends asking for suggestions, offering a $25 gift certificate for the winning name. One anonymous submission that caught my eye was Camp MAGIC. The person submitting the proposed name suggested that GIC stood for Grief In Children but was unsure about the other letters. I showed the suggestion to other social workers at the hospice, one of whom suggested that the C at the end be replaced by a K for Kids. Another social worker then proposed that the acronym stand for Mainly About Grief In Kids. The camp name was born. I later found out that it was submitted by my younger daughter. The name described perfectly what I planned it to be—the focus was mainly grief among kids, but time would also be spent on other things, such as typical camp activities. Then I needed a campsite.

After a brief search, we chose a campsite outside Atlanta. We sent word about the planned camp to hospice families. Seventeen children came to the first three-day, two-night camp. The activities planned included various "grief" group activities, such as feeling identification, coping skills, letter writing to the persons they had lost, and a balloon release of their messages, following the four tasks of grieving according to Worden (1996). Everyone worked as a volunteer. We formed four different groups based on age, and each group had a social worker as a group lead-counselor and a second volunteer as co-counselor. The four social workers were hospice social workers, and the co-counselors were hospice volunteers.

This first camp cost less than $5,000 and was paid for by the hospice's foundation. Part of the foundation's mission was to provide education around death, dying, and bereavement. The camp fell under this mission. From here camp evolved into its current existence following the trajectory described here. Within a year, two camps a year were held with more than 50 participants in each session. When I left the hospice in 2000, the camp became its own freestanding nonprofit. Within two more years, there were three camps annually and a parent/guardian camp. Within 13 years we were serving more than 200 campers a year. Each camp now serves 65–75 campers and anywhere from 15 to 30 parents/guardians. Ten counseling groups each hold 6–8 campers matched according to age and developmental levels. The groups are led by social workers, who are hired based on their training and experience in working with bereaved youth. Each group has two co-counselors, who are recruited from graduate and undergraduate programs in social work, human services, and counseling. A small number of co-counselors are teachers or other community members interested in childhood grief, often due to their own experiences. Increasingly, many former campers are now participating as co-counselors, several of whom have chosen to study and work in the helping professions.

After a few initial camp sessions, I decided to measure the outcome of the camp. I specifically wanted to know how children were impacted in regard to grief symptoms and posttraumatic stress symptoms, since many of the campers had experienced a traumatic death of a parent or sibling, such as murder and suicide. To my dismay, in spite of positive satisfaction surveys and anecdotal reports from campers and families, the outcome measures showed that camp actually increased posttraumatic stress symptoms. Horrified, I researched posttraumatic stress disorder (PTSD) interventions. From my readings, I inferred that the grief work done at camp stirred up sufficient emotions to remind the campers of the traumatic loss and camp did not address these symptoms of trauma. These results led to the evolution of the current curriculum, wherein the first part of camp is dedicated to trauma-focused interventions and the second part is dedicated to grief activities. Evaluations of camp since the institution of trauma interventions consistently show that camp decreases PTSD and complicated grief symptoms, and increases positive behaviors and emotional and cognitive growth. We are constantly reviewing what we do at camp. The curriculum is dynamic and open to change as we go along and learn more about childhood grief. Our current curriculum is shared in Chapter 6.

Irene (Rene) Searles McClatchey

Reference

Worden, J. W. (1996). *Children and grief: When a parent dies*. New York, NY: The Guilford Press.

Acknowledgments

We approach acknowledgments with gratitude to a number of people:

Kenneth J. Doka, PhD, who supported the beginning effort of the book and saw us to completion by agreeing to write the Foreword.

Jackson P. Rainer, PhD, with special thanks, who believed the time had come for this book to be written, assisted with its start, and kindly edited the entire draft at the book's completion.

Betsy (M. E.) Vonk, PhD, MSW, and Pamela Awtrey Harrington, MSW, who helped with the launch of this book.

Emma Domby, who assisted with research, and Alexa Mellman who, with Emma, diligently attended to minute details.

Steve King, PhD, MSW, who reviewed the family therapy section in Chapter 3.

Susan Anderson and Edna Bacon at ArtReach Foundation, who reviewed the section on art therapy in Chapter 3.

The Moyer Foundation and Bethany Gardner, Lisa Willis, and Jocelyn Matics, who assisted with information for this book and who dedicate their time to the needs of bereaved children.

Anna Moore and Dylan Ford, who helped us navigate the world of publishing.

John B. McClatchey, PhD, who constantly supported us and who did the final read-through.

All of the bereavement camps that responded to our requests for information. These are listed with their websites in Appendix F.

Introduction

Why Write This Book?

Adults across the ages and across cultures respond to the needs of orphaned children. This book about the intervention of bereavement camps is an attempt to illuminate one aspect of that response. With more and more agencies establishing or wanting to create healing camps for bereaved children, it is important that what is planned is indeed doing what it is designed to do. Very little research has been done on bereavement camps, while more and more children and adolescents who have had a significant loss will attend one. Outcome studies on camp are mixed, and different models have been studied. In *Adolescent Encounters with Death, Bereavement, and Coping*, Balk and Corr (Eds., 2009) discuss a variety of aspects of adolescent bereavement. In the chapter on "Camps and Support Groups for Adolescents," Orloff, Armstrong, and Remke (2009, pp. 291–308) give details on several specific camp programs. They begin their discussion with a statement that summarizes the issue of insufficient research in discussing camps and programs for bereaved adolescents:

> Much of what is known about these programs comes from descriptions in various publications (e.g., Creed, Ruffin, & Ward, 2001; Klontz, Bivens, Leinart, & Klontz, 2007; LoCicero, Burkhart, & Gray, 1998; Martinuik, 2003; Neibors et al., 2004; Schachter, 2007; Schachter & Georgopoulos, 2008; Summers,

1993), conversations between care providers, and comments from participants or other anecdotal information. Much less is known about the long-term therapeutic value or demonstrated efficacy of such services (e.g., Currier, Holland, & Neimeyer, 2007; Forte, Hill, Pazder, & Feudtner, 2004). This fact often makes it difficult for providers to determine best practices when designing and implementing their own specialized services for ill and bereaved adolescents.

(p. 291)

The purpose of the book is to help others establish camps for bereaved children and teens in their geographical locations, and to encourage high quality programs and ongoing evaluations. This book supports the philosophy of The Dougy Center, the National Center for Grieving Children and Families in Portland, Oregon, that grief is a natural response to death, and that each child grieves in his or her own unique way. Each child also takes the time he or she needs to heal; there is no set time limit (The Dougy Center, 2004). Interventions are used to guide the child or adolescent through the process, provide education on natural reactions, normalize these reactions, and give suggestions for healthy coping skills.

Outline of Chapters

This book is divided into nine chapters: Chapter 1, "Bereavement Camp Background"; Chapter 2, "Theories of Childhood and Adolescent Grief"; Chapter 3, "Interventions for Bereaved Children and Adolescents"; Chapter 4, "Nonprofit Organization and Administration"; Chapter 5, "Critical Components of Camp"; Chapter 6, "Camp MAGIK and Other Models"; Chapter 7, "Evaluation"; Chapter 8, "Outcomes of Camp Interventions"; and Chapter 9, "Former Campers Returning as Volunteers." Chapters 1, 5, 6, 8, and 9 focus on bereavement camps. Chapters 2, 3, 4, and 7 describe theories and skills that are transferable to many different types of programs or nonprofit organizations.

In Chapter 1 the reader gets background information on the reasons for children's bereavement camps and learns about the issue of parental death and the bereavement camp modality of intervention. The chapter includes individual case stories of four children impacted by parental death. It also provides a history and brief statistics on parental death worldwide and in the United States. It gives the rationale for the camp setting as a background for work with bereaved children, describes a history of bereavement camps, and discusses childhood grief resources.

Chapter 2 describes theories of childhood grief. In order to successfully meet the needs of bereaved children and adolescents, it is necessary to be aware of current knowledge of how death impacts them. The chapter discusses culture as the milieu of grief and differentiates between bereavement, mourning, and grief. The reader gets a historical background of childhood bereavement recognition and an understanding of child and adolescent developmental stages. Theories and approaches include trauma and grief, complicated and prolonged grief, persistent complex bereavement disorder, multidimensional grief theory, trauma-informed care, posttraumatic growth, and neuropsychological findings related to childhood trauma.

Chapter 3 describes various interventions and settings for treatment of children after the death of a parent or sibling. Each child has individual needs and styles, and there is no one treatment modality that meets the needs of all children. Interventions include play therapy, art therapy, grief therapy, and cognitive-behavioral therapy. In addition, the reader gets an extensive description of trauma-focused cognitive-behavioral therapy. Settings include individual therapy, family therapy, home-based family therapy, groups, and bereavement camps. The chapter gives special consideration to children with disabilities in the camp setting and addresses the use of communication technology and Internet resources in the grieving process.

Chapter 4 walks the reader through important elements of establishing a nonprofit organization to run a bereavement camp. Although this chapter uses bereavement camps as a focus, its content can be generalized to other organizations. The reader gets advice on board development, creating a mission statement, and strategic planning. Guidelines include areas of funding, such as the elevator speech, marketing materials, grant writing, solicitation from individuals and businesses, and special events. The reader can find samples of a Letter of Proposal and a Logic Model to use for bereavement camps. In addition, the chapter stresses the importance of involvement with the community and community partnerships.

Chapter 5 focuses on the practical aspects of running a bereavement camp for children and adolescents. The chapter describes the important decisions and considerations to make and steps to take when first planning a bereavement camp. These include the decision on what type of camp to run; site selection; insurance; volunteer recruitment, screening, training, and supervision; medical staff, medications, and policies; and transportation. The reader will get advice on how to recruit campers, the importance of assessing campers for readiness, how to handle check-in, and the importance of follow-up after camp.

Chapter 6 depicts several camp models and curricula to help establish new camps and give ideas to those who run current camps. The chapter is designed to give various perspectives to anyone currently running bereavement camps and helpful details to those in the first stages of planning a new camp. Models include a therapy camp based on Camp MAGIK, a psycho-educational camp lead by professional counselors, and a psycho-educational camp lead by trained volunteers. In addition, the reader gets a detailed description of the Camp Erin program elements for its national camps together with an outline of a Camp Erin camp.

Chapter 7 presents basic knowledge that is useful in determining if bereavement camps are meeting the needs of the children and adolescents they serve. The chapter stresses the importance of evaluation to ensure quality programming. The chapter defines and discusses evidence-based practice, and clarifies the complex issues of confidentiality and evaluator conflict of interest. Topics include what and who should be studied, by whom, and why. In addition, the chapter discusses types of evaluation and research, and gives the reader useful examples of each of the following: surveys, qualitative evaluations, quantitative evaluations, mixed methods evaluations, and action research.

Chapter 8 gives insight into what is known about the impact of bereavement camps by presenting bereavement camp research conducted between 2000 and 2017. The chapter includes information about current evaluation methods gleaned from contact with 76 of more than 350 children's bereavement camps located in the United States and Canada. In addition, the chapter reviews published research on camp outcomes, grouped according to the methodology used. The chapter includes a presentation of a large-scale longitudinal study being conducted in 38 camps in the Camp Erin and Comfort Zone Camp systems, and ends with a description of nine studies by this book's first author, Rene McClatchey.

Chapter 9 puts the reader in touch with the human ability to find meaning after devastating loss. Six volunteers—four who came to camp as youth, and two adults who are parents of former campers— share their powerful stories of major losses of loved ones, how they survived and learned to heal.

Sundry Comments

Each chapter ends with a brief list of recommended readings and a list of references. The recommended readings give readers the opportunity to expand their knowledge with suggested sources.

In this book the term "parent" refers to a child's parent or adult caregiver. No distinction is made between parent, grandparents, legal guardian, and other caregiving relationships.

References

Balk, D. E., & Corr, C. A. (2009). *Adolescent encounters with death, bereavement, and coping*. New York, NY: Springer.

Orloff, S. F., Armstrong, D., & Remke, S. S. (2009). Camps and support groups for adolescents. In D. E. Balk & C. A. Corr (Eds.), *Adolescent encounters with death, bereavement, and coping* (pp. 291–308). New York, NY: Springer.

The Dougy Center (2004). *Helping children cope with death*. Portland, OR: Author.

1

Bereavement Camp Background

When you walk into camp you feel like a burden has been lifted off your shoulders, because these people are really there for you. They are there for you and it's a bonding experience with the other people, too. You feel like you are alone in this but you are really not. There are other people who are going through the same thing and camp brings those people together, to feel wanted and to feel as if their lives are not over. This is just the beginning.
—16-year-old camper (McClatchey & Wimmer, 2012)

The goal of this chapter is to introduce the reader to the issue of parental death and to the bereavement camp modality of intervention. The chapter begins with individual case stories of children and families impacted by parental death. In our descriptions, adjustments have been made to protect campers' identities. Next, a brief worldwide perspective is given followed by information on orphaned children in the United States. The authors provide a rationale for the camp setting as a background for work with bereaved children, including a history of bereavement camps. The chapter concludes by revisiting the four case stories.

Meet Some Campers

Bree, 17, asked her mother not to go talk to her husband, Bree's father. She had witnessed her father beat her mother many times. Her mother was in deep despair each time. She felt she owed her husband one more visit to explain her reasons for wanting a divorce, especially since he was begging her to stay. Bree pleaded with her mother, "Mom, you decided to divorce him. He knows why. Please don't go." Before midnight, Bree was awakened by her older sister who gently told her that their mother would not come home anymore. Her father had killed their mother and had been arrested.

Marius, 14, and his father were shooting hoops late one Saturday evening. Marius's father suddenly grabbed his chest and slumped to the ground. Marius knew immediately what was going on. He had just received training in CPR at his high school. He worked diligently to resuscitate his father while his mother was calling 911. Marius only gave up his efforts as the ambulance's emergency medical technicians took over. He stood in the driveway feeling like a failure, watching the ambulance drive off with his parents into the dark night. He was never to see his father again.

Amber, 11, was being tucked in bed by her mother on the warm summer evening. Everyone was on vacation from school, and her older sisters had joined them in her bedroom. As they were discussing their day and making plans for the next day, they heard footsteps coming up the stairs. Her father emerged in the doorway holding a gun in one hand and a bottle of alcohol in the other. He slowly raised the hand with the gun, aimed, and shot Amber's mother, sisters, and then Amber. Her father slowly walked back downstairs. In the deafening quiet Amber realized that she was still alive, even if her leg was aching. She pulled herself along the floor into the hallway to summon help. When she got to the hallway, she heard, then saw, her father coming back up the stairs still holding the gun. She knew she was about to be killed. Terrified, she locked eyes with her father who lifted his gun and aimed it at Amber. He changed his mind, and pointed the gun to his temple. With one loud boom, he killed himself. She and her oldest sister were the only survivors.

Morgan, 10, rushed off the school bus and ran to his house to tell his dad about the excellent grade he had received on his book project. Morgan lived with his dad and his father's on-again off-again girlfriend. That day Morgan did not expect her to be at his house. He grabbed the key under the flowerpot and let himself in. His dad was not home, which was a bit unusual, since his shift at the hospital ended at 3 o'clock in the afternoon and he generally was home to greet Morgan. Morgan fixed himself a snack and proceeded to play games on his computer. He was really absorbed in the games and did not realize how late it was until he started feeling hunger pains. It was 8:30 and dad was still not home. Now, this was odd as it was 30 minutes until Morgan's bedtime. He picked up the phone and dialed his father's cell phone number. He let it ring and ring with no answer. He did this several times before he called his paternal grandfather, Robert. Hearing that Morgan's father was not home, his grandparents immediately came over. Together they called his father's work, friends, and acquaintances. Nobody had seen or heard from him that afternoon. Finally, Robert began calling hospital emergency rooms and got the news that two young men had been brought in with gunshot wounds that day and that the ER personnel were trying to locate relatives. Not until Robert and his wife arrived at the ER were they informed of the death of not only Morgan's father, but also their other son, Morgan's uncle. Morgan was anxiously waiting for them to come back home, and his excitement of seeing his grandparents return quickly changed into devastation as he heard the news.

The Global Perspective on Parental Death

Around the globe, children have coped with the death of parents from before the time of recorded history. In England between 1700 and 1750 the rate of death for women at childbirth was 10.5 per 1,000 and between 1800 and 1850, maternal deaths in childbirth were 5.0 per 1,000 (Chamberlain, 1999, Table 1). The maternal mortality rates for 2010 statistics reflect a worldwide high in maternal deaths in Southern Sudan with 20.54 per 1,000. The varied numbers can be viewed from the perspective of Sweden with 4 per 100,000 (.004 per 1,000) and the United States with 21 per 100,000 (.021 per 1,000) (U.S. Government, n.d.).

Often the deaths of these women of childbearing age leave children within the family unit orphaned. In the 21st century, wars, civil unrest, disease, and natural disasters continue to bring grief to many children daily. Statistics from 2014 produced by the U.S. Agency for International Development (U.S. Government, 2016) show that there were 140 million orphans under the age of 18 worldwide. In most instances, cultural practices and extended family are the only resources available to help children cope with their grief. In cases of displaced persons and refugees, many children are left with no one—no family, no extended family, no community.

The AIDS epidemic has been a highly visible phenomenon bringing attention to grandparents raising orphaned grandchildren. It is estimated that 17 million children worldwide have experienced the death of one or both of their parents to AIDS. Approximately 90% of these children live in Sub-Saharan Africa (U.S. Government, 2014, para.1). This crisis is huge and the reactions of orphaned children vary widely; several researchers have documented the difficulties children face. Bhargava (2005), studying AIDS orphans in Ethiopia, found family financial well-being to be the strongest predictor of school participation and social and emotional adjustment. Cluver, Orkin, Boyes, Gardner, and Nikelo (2012) found that AIDS orphan status and caregiver sickness in South Africa caused "worsening in mental health symptoms over a four-year period" (p. 863) in youth and "increased depression, anxiety, and posttraumatic stress symptoms" (p. 857) regardless of family income. In Uganda, Atwine, Cantor-Graae, and Bajunirwe (2005) found that AIDS orphans had higher scores on depression and other mental health difficulties than a control group and that orphans who had access to support groups had better outcomes. They note the need for increased mental health services for this population and a lack of these services in most low-income countries.

The U.S. Perspective

Millions of children in the United States are impacted by parental death. Statistics from the Social Security Administration death benefits indicate that in 2014 approximately 1.9 million children under the age of 18 received payments based on the death of a parent (SSA, n.d.). This number does not reflect the additional children who did not qualify for Social Security survivors' benefits. Bereaved children's grief reactions include mental, emotional, physical, behavioral, and spiritual responses (DeSpelder & Strickland, 2014). Although most children and adolescents bounce back from grief without professional intervention, childhood grief can have serious consequences if not addressed. These include short- and long-term effects including acting-out behavior; difficulties in school; developmental delays; higher rates of substance abuse, depression, and deviance; increased risk of mortality into early adulthood; and numerous other social and psychological issues (Berk, 2010; Berg,

Rostila, Saarela, & Hjern, 2014; Dopp & Cain, 2012; Ellis, Dowrick, & Lloyd-Williams, 2013; Li et al., 2014; McClatchey, Vonk, & Palardy, 2009).

Although the landscape is slowly changing, there are still few resources available to children and adolescents who have experienced a loss. Most programs involve either individual counseling or support group meetings at a grief center, such as offered by Judi's House in Denver, Colorado; Hope House in Astoria, Oregon; Kate's Club in Atlanta, Georgia; or The Alcove Center for Grieving Children & Families in Margate, New Jersey. Other resources for bereaved children and adolescents are provided by local hospices that are mandated by Medicare to provide bereavement services to the patient's family for up to one year after the death of a patient, however the family unit is defined by the patient.

One fairly new setting for addressing childhood bereavement is the camp setting. In the last 20 years, more than 350 healing camps, or grief camps, for bereaved children have been established and this number increases every year. Why are so many grief organizations interested in the camp setting?

Why a Camp Setting?

Until the current age of industrialization, nature was used for subsistence (Keniger, Gaston, Irvine, & Fuller, 2013). Today nature is for enjoyment and leisure (Fuller & Irvine, 2010). Keniger et al. (2013) describe three ways in which people interact with nature: indirect, incidental, and intentional. The indirect way includes viewing nature in pictures or through a window. The incidental way includes encountering nature while doing some other activity, such as driving through the countryside to visit somebody. The intentional way includes using nature for recreation, for example, canoeing, hiking, or gardening. The use of the camp setting for interventions with bereaved children would fall in the third category.

There are several noted benefits to spending time in nature. Nature provides free therapy without any side effects and improves cognitive functioning (Berman, Jonides, & Kaplan, 2008). Interacting with nature improves attention and memory (Berto, 2005). The camp setting has been credited with being a safe and caring environment that fosters honesty, trust, and respect. At the same time, the setting is not conducive to bullying (American Camp Association [ACA], 2005).

Outcome studies have shown that the camp setting helps camp-ers make new friends and collaborate with others (ACA, 2005). Camp also helps foster teamwork among campers (Garst & Bruce, 2003). It helps increase independence among campers (ACA, 2005), and boosts self-esteem (Readdick & Schaller, 2005). Other positive outcomes from camp participation include strengthened values and social competence (Thurber, Scanlin, Scheuler, & Henderson, 2007). There is also a correlation between the camp experience and spiritual development among campers (Henderson, Oakleaf, & Bialeschki, 2009).

The camp environment lends itself particularly well to sup-porting grieving children. Children do not generally tolerate strong feelings for long periods of time, so alternations between grief activ-ities and various camp activities, such as canoeing, hiking, archery, and kick-ball, provide needed relief from grief processing. Campers get the message that it is acceptable and desirable to have fun even though they are grieving. The camp setting also helps campers bond during the various recreational activities, which may help build trust for sharing during various grief activities. The most powerful impact of camp may be, however, the opportunity to meet other children and adolescents who have had similar experiences, which normal-izes the bereaved campers' situations.

Bereavement Camp History

One of the first bereavement camps in the United States still operating is Grief Camp, which is part of the Amanda the Panda program of HCI Care Services and Visiting Nurse Services of Iowa. It is a free weekend camp that started in 1982. Currently, there are two weekend camps a year. The Grief Camp began with children and teens but now also incorporates adults. Shortly thereafter, in 1988, El Tesoro de la Vida Grief Camp, part of Camp Fire USA First Texas Council, held its first session. This is a week-long sleep-away camp for children aged 6–17 and is fee-based. Ninety percent of the week is spent participating in traditional camp activities while the remaining 10% helps campers deal with their grief. In 1989 Shannon's Hope Camp was begun by Bridges (formerly Hospice of Charleston) in South Carolina. The camp was named in honor of a teen who died in 1988, is currently held twice each year, and uses a weekend for-mat in a beachfront setting. Children attending are aged 6–15. Camp HOPE in Wisconsin also began in 1989, in memory of the founders' daughter. The camp serves teens and younger children with a parallel camp experience for parents. Camp HOPE is free of charge and weekends are scheduled variously in the spring, fall, and winter.

Other camps emerged throughout the United States in the early 1990s, and these have evolved in many different ways. The following is not a complete history of bereavement camps from the 1990's onwards, but rather a representative sample. In 1990, Delaware Hospice's Camp New Hope began with Saturday workshops, and by 1991 the first camp, with 12 campers, was held. The New Hope program has evolved with multiple services, and two free four day camps are now held each summer. Camp Evergreen was created by Hosparus Hospice in Kentucky in 1992. Although during the early years the focus was on children, the program changed to a family camp in 2004. Center for Hospice Care, serving eight counties in North Central Indiana, also calls its program Camp Evergreen. This annual free camp program started as a weekend camp in 1994 for 7–14-year-old bereaved youth. It has been modified to serve more children and currently offers a weekend camp for teens aged 13–17 and a day-long camp for children aged 6–12. Hospice Atlanta, a division of Visiting Nurse Health System, created Camp STARS (Share Together As Real Support) and held its first camp, free of charge, for bereaved children in 1994 in Georgia. The program is now community funded and family focused, and includes two family camps a year serving 160 to 220 participants in each camp. Losses grieved might include parents, siblings, or extended family members. Camp MAGIK (Mainly About Grief In Kids) was begun in 1995 and offers a free weekend camp three or four times a year for bereaved campers aged 6–17. It also serves the children's parents/guardians in a parallel camp during the weekend. Camp MAGIK is one of the few freestanding nonprofit organizations that is not affiliated with a hospice program or bereavement center; it is funded primarily through private donations and through The Moyer Foundation's Camp Erin program.

Many other camps came into being over the next 20 years. Although there are independent, freestanding camps, many more are affiliated with hospice organizations or bereavement centers. Some of the largest groups are either networks of camps, such as The Moyer Foundation's Camp Erin; camps affiliated with a national hospice organization, such as Camp I Believe and Camp Kangaroo; or camps run in various locations with one camp model and organization, such as Comfort Zone Camp. The vast majority of the camps are free of charge to participating campers.

The Moyer Foundation, out of Seattle, Washington, and Phil-adelphia, Pennsylvania, was founded in 2000 by Major League Baseball pitcher Jamie Moyer and his wife Karen with an original mission to support children in distress. Two years later, in 2002, The Moyer Foundation launched Camp Erin, a national network of weekend bereavement camps for children and teens aged 6–17. Camp Erin was established in honor of Erin Metcalf, a teenage fam-ily friend who died from cancer at age 17. When hospitalized, Erin often expressed concern for the other children in the hospital as well as her own family and friends. At the time of this writing, Camp Erin is the largest bereavement camp program in the country, with 48 Camp Erin locations in the United States and Canada. It has served more than 21,500 bereaved children and teens. The Moyer Founda-tion partners with bereavement programs in hospitals, hospices, and bereavement centers to establish Camp Erin locations and provides best practices, funding, research, program evaluation, and ongoing support. In addition to national standards, the Camp Erin curricu-lum is shaped by each partner organization to meet the needs of the local community. The Moyer Foundation offers continued care to campers and their families through newsletters, social media, and personalized support from The Moyer Foundation Resource Center.

Comfort Zone Camp was started in 1998 by author Lynne Hughes. This camp is designed to serve children and teens who have experienced the death of a parent, guardian, or sibling. Comfort Zone uses the little buddy/big buddy system, where campers are matched with an adult volunteer who serves as the camper's mentor, friend, and "anchor." Comfort Zone is an independent organization that is headquartered in Richmond, Virginia, but holds programs in Cal-ifornia, Massachusetts, New Jersey, North Carolina, and Virginia. Each age range has its own specific curriculum, but this curriculum is uniform for each separate age group throughout the various loca-tions. The organization offers to partner with other organizations. It presents four camp models: a one-day camp for aged 5–17, a three-day weekend program for aged 7–18, young adult programs for aged 18–26, and a four-hour family program that incorporates the entire family. Comfort Zone Camp's curriculum is based on Positive Youth Development, is strengths based, and is aimed at helping camp-ers develop healthy coping skills and resilience. The model devel-oped by Comfort Zone Camp uses psycho-educational grief groups, cognitive-behavioral, and trauma-focused cognitive-behavioral ther-apy, play therapy, and art therapy. Groups are led by professional therapists.

Two different hospices sponsor large national camp programs. Camp I Believe is affiliated with Kindred Gentiva. Most recently, Camp I Believe ran 17 programs with sites in 11 states. Each local hospice organization creates its own program, but the components are similar throughout the system. Most are overnight weekend camps, but a few are day camps. The longest-running camp in the group is the camp in Happy, Texas, which was begun in 2003. Another model of support for camps affiliated with a national hospice organization is Camp Kangaroo, which is affiliated with Seasons Hospice and Palliative Care. Camp Kangaroo was established in 2012 to help children journey through grief. This weekend camp program is currently available in ten sites across the United States, with more planned. It is psychotherapy and creative arts therapy based.

Experience Camp, a week-long overnight camp, started in 2009 at Camp Manitou in Maine under the name "Manitou Experience." After opening additional camps in California (2013) and New York (2015), the name of the camp changed to Experience Camps to reflect the national scope of the organization. Under the direction of professional bereavement staff, campers work through their grief by creating bonds with other youth who have been through similar experiences and by participating in traditional camp activities, like team sports and talent shows.

With a different mission, Tragedy Assistance Program for Survivors (TAPS) runs Good Grief Camp for children and teens who have lost a parent, stepparent, or sibling who died while on military active duty. The camp was first started in 1994 and helps campers learn coping skills and how to normalize their feelings. These weekend camps pair the child or teen with an active duty service member who serves as the child's or teen's mentor in the grieving process.

Another model for bereavement camps is the Outward Bound program for grieving teens and young adults. The Outward Bound philosophy of growth through challenging wilderness expeditions is well established. The teen grief program, Heroic Journey, began in 2006 and provides an opportunity for participants to share the common bond of the death of a loved one. The program adds grief-related group conversations, rituals, and ceremonies to the normal Outward Bound activities. Donors, including New York Life Foundation, make it possible for Outward Bound to provide the experience at a cost that is lower than most of its other programs and in some cases at no cost. Programs are available in several states across the country.

Far-Reaching Childhood Grief Resources

There are several outstanding far-reaching resources for professionals, community volunteers, and others who support or work with bereaved children and adolescents, including those working with bereavement camps.

National Alliance for Grieving Children

National Alliance for Grieving Children (NAGC) was established in 2004, growing out of the Symposium for Childhood Grief that had been started in 1997 by a group of professionals working with bereaved children and adolescents. NAGC is spearheaded by a dedicated group of child bereavement specialists. NAGC's mission is to promote "awareness of the needs of children and teens grieving a death and provides education and resources for anyone who wants to support them" (NAGC, 2016). The organization serves as a network for bereavement professionals and community volunteers who work with bereaved youth. NAGC holds an annual conference and frequent educational webinars where members and others share ideas, information, and the latest research on childhood bereavement. The organization's website provides valuable information to not only professionals in the field but also caregivers of bereaved children and adolescents. Included on the website is an international database of bereavement support programs across the United States and the world, as well as information about childhood grief. An important part of the work of NAGC is to spread awareness and public sensitivity about childhood grief and the needs of bereaved children and teens. The organization now has more than 700 members, and more than 450 professionals attend the annual conference. NAGC receives its funding from grants, corporate donations, products created such as an activity book for use by bereaved families, symposium registrations, and memberships.

The Moyer Foundation

The Moyer Foundation holds a bi-annual conference on bereavement camps, The National Bereavement Camp Conference, where professionals and volunteers working with bereavement camps, or who are considering starting a bereavement camp, gather to collaborate, learn, and exchange ideas related to bereavement camp best practices. In addition, The Moyer Foundation's Resource Center provides a comprehensive online library of carefully curated resources for children and families affected by grief and addiction. Families, educators, and other care providers are provided a personalized set of resources, including articles, videos, activities, and referrals. Furthermore, The Moyer Foundation provides funding for the establishment of Camp Erin locations across the United States and Canada.

New York Life Foundation

The New York Life Foundation supports programs that benefit young people, primarily through two distinct focus areas: childhood bereavement (beginning in 2008) and educational enhancement for middle school children (beginning in 2013). Since 2008 the Foundation has made a strategic commitment to support and raise awareness of grieving children and their families. It is the largest corporate funder in the emerging grant-making area of childhood grief support. The Foundation also encourages and facilitates the community involvement of employees and agents of New York Life by supporting engagement in local philanthropic engagement, integrating their financial investments with sustained, company-wide philanthropic activity through volunteer programs, fundraising, and team grant opportunities.

The Foundation funds a diverse range of distinct grief-related nonprofits, underwriting bereavement camps, youth community groups, tragedy assistance for military families, university research, and more. In addition to supporting nonprofit partners and organizations, the Foundation has also sought to better understand the issue of childhood bereavement through the development of a series of groundbreaking surveys. In collaboration with its partners, it has created several educational resources and awareness initiatives informed by the survey results. Highlights include:

1. Coalition to Support Grieving Students: The Foundation leads a pioneering collaboration among leading K–12 professional organizations to produce the first-ever educator-specific grief resources and training materials.
2. A Child In Grief: This is an online bereavement resource for parents, families, educators, and community members that

provides articles, tips, and stories for those coping with the loss of a loved one. The site also offers the National Bereavement Resource Guide, a continuously updated national directory of local resources for children and families.
3. Shared Grief Project: This is a multimedia site designed to bring hope to grieving children by sharing the stories of respected athletes and other celebrities who experienced childhood loss.

Since 2008, the New York Life Foundation has committed more than $35 million to support bereaved children (L. Siegel, personal communication, March 15, 2017).

Revisiting Campers

Bree was a very hesitant participant in the camp sessions. Although she was sharing her narrative, she was shy and not actively participating in the typical camp activities. According to her counselor at camp, she was carrying guilt and feeling she should have known to warn her mother not to meet up with her father. Her father had been abusive towards her mother for years, and Bree was glad that her mother finally decided to divorce her father so that she and her sister could live quietly with their mother. When their father wanted to meet up with their mother just to "settle things," Bree had a foreboding sense that something bad "was going down." Although she had begged her mother not to go see her father, she felt she had not been insistent enough and had regretted it ever since. In groups, using cognitive-behavioral therapy, Bree learned the difference between regret and guilt, and realized her lack of power in preventing her father from killing her mother. Although she has not been able to forgive her father, she has succeeded in forgiving herself. She frequently visits her mother's grave but three years after the murder of her mother, she has not yet visited her father in jail. She has graduated from college with a degree in criminal justice and hopes one day to go to law school.

Marius was ambivalent about coming to camp but it was evident that his mother was desperate for any help she could get for her son. She described him as a high-achieving teen who did not talk about what had happened. He had become angry at home, was in frequent fights with his siblings, and had received multiple in-school suspensions. Marius did not share in the first couple of counseling sessions, but gradually warmed up to his fellow campers and counselors. On Saturday evening he was the big star in the talent show, singing a rap song. Before he left camp, he described the night scene with his father's heart attack and his emotions around it in detail. Two months later, when the camp director made a follow-up visit to his home, Marius told him that camp had been a turning point. The words this expressive and intelligent young man used were:

> Counseling sessions opened me up a lot, moved me along a lot. Camp gave me the ability to feel. I was an emotional wreck before camp, just trying to trudge through the world without feeling because it hurt so bad. It was exhausting. Camp kind of just made me lay it all out there.

His mother agreed that camp had changed not only her son, but also his relationship with her. Six years later camp continues to receive an annual donation from the family.

Before **Amber** came to camp there were many phone calls between the camp director and Amber's grandparents—on both sides. She and her older sister lived with her maternal grandparents, who insisted that Amber's coming would just "stir things up." According to them, Amber was doing well and was not really affected by the tragedy. Amber's paternal grandparents had a different viewpoint. They were "torn apart" and felt that Amber's reaction was not natural. However, since they were not the temporary guardians of Amber (her other grandparents were) they had no voice. They did ask if they could come to the parent/guardian session of camp to process their own losses even if they could not convince Amber's maternal grandparents to let Amber attend. They were offered the adult session but did not give up on the possibility of bringing Amber to camp.

Eventually the camp director's conversations with the maternal grandparents, together with their discussions with the paternal grandparents, convinced them to let Amber come to camp. At camp, Amber was in good spirits outwardly. She shared her story freely in group sessions without showing any sad or upset feelings. Her camp counselor felt that she was guarded and could not let any emotions in. This lasted most of camp. In her last session, she was able to share a bit of sadness around missing her mother. Needless to say, her counselor was concerned about her. Amber asked the camp director if she knew of anybody she could see after camp who would understand her situation. The camp director referred her to one of the counselors at camp who, in her life outside of volunteering for camp, works in private practice. It was here that Amber was finally able to get in touch with her emotions.

Morgan was a sweet 10-year-old boy whose father and uncle had been shot at random at a gas station where they stopped after work. When the camp director made her first assessment call to his home, she spoke with Morgan's grandfather Robert. Looking at the completed application form she confirmed that Robert also planned to come to camp for the adult session. For some reason the grandfather's response touched her: "Yep, I am coming. That's my boy, and wherever he goes, I go." The two of them arrived at camp, Robert with a labored walk, and assisted by a cane. It was obvious he was not in good health. Morgan was a lively 10-year-old who immediately settled in with his new friends at camp. He was social and had no problems sharing his story and participating in the group sessions. Robert, from whom Morgan may have received his outgoing personality, was excited to meet everyone. He processed deep grief emotions in the adult session over the loss of his two sons. His bright spot was Morgan and the bond between the two was undeniable.

Robert sent emails for a while after camp, either expressing his gratitude for camp, or sending the camp director links to articles he had read in regards to grief that he wanted to share with her. After a while, the emails stopped. She did not think anything of it. Robert and Morgan had attended one of the fall camp sessions. The following fall the camp received a camp application for Morgan, but camp does not take repeat campers because of the waiting lists. Camp emailed the referring school counselor to let her know. That is when the director found out that Robert had died a couple of months earlier. He had become ill with pneumonia and was hospitalized, but the treatments did not work. The director immediately contacted Morgan's home and for the first time talked to Robert's wife. She explained that Morgan was in "bad shape." The additional loss had triggered several emotional outbursts. The director also spoke with Morgan, who told her, "I believe I have to go to that camp again." Morgan attended camp for a second time for a different loss. His grandmother attended the adult group session. This time around in camp Morgan was a little leader, nudging his fellow campers to open up and talk about their losses. He told his new friends that "it helps." In spite of so many devastating losses, Morgan was able to reach out and help others in need. His grandmother, hearing from other parents and guardians at camp of financial struggles, ended up—with the assistance of other parents in the group—creating a nonprofit organization that now serves as a clearing-house for financial support for struggling widows.

Recommended Reading

Camp MAGIK
http://campmagik.org

National Alliance for Grieving Children
https://childrengrieve.org

New York Life Foundation
www.newyorklife.com/foundation

The Moyer Foundation
https://moyerfoundation.org/

References

American Camp Association (ACA). (2005). *Directions: Youth development outcomes of the camp experience*. Martinsville, IN: American Camp Association.

Atwine, B., Cantor-Graae, E., & Bajunirwe, F. (2005). Psychological distress among AIDS orphans in rural Uganda. *Social Science and Medicine, 61*, 555–563.

Berg, L., Rostila, M., Saarela, J., & Hjern, A. (2014). Parental death during childhood and subsequent school performance. *Pediatrics, 133*(4), 682–689. doi:10.1542/peds.2013-2771

Berk, L. E. (2010). *Exploring lifespan development* (2nd ed.). Boston, MA: Allyn and Bacon.

Berman, M. G., Jonides, J., & Kaplan, S. (2008). The cognitive benefits of interacting with nature. *Psychological Science, 19*(12), 1207–1212.

Berto, R. (2005). Exposure to restorative environments helps restore attentional capacity. *Journal of Environmental Psychology, 25*, 249–259.

Bhargava, A. (2005). AIDS epidemic and the psychological well-being and school participation of Ethiopian orphans. *Psychology, Health & Medicine, 10*(3), 263–275.

Chamberlain, G. (1999). British maternal mortality in the 19th and early 20th centuries. *Journal of the Royal Society of Medicine, 11*, 559–563. doi:10.1258/jrsm.99.11.559

Cluver, L. D., Orkin, M., Boyes, M. E., Gardner, F., & Nikelo, J. (2012). AIDS-orphanhood and caregiver HIV/AIDS sickness status: Effects on psychological symptoms in South African youth. *Journal of Pediatric Psychology, 37*(8), 857–867.

DeSpelder, L. A., & Strickland, A. L. (2014). *The last dance: Encountering death and dying* (10th ed.). Boston, MA: McGraw Hill.

Dopp, A. R., & Cain, A. C. (2012). The role of peer relationships in parental bereavement during childhood and adolescence. *Death Studies, 36*(1), 41–60.

Ellis, J., Dowrick, C., & Lloyd-Williams, M. (2013). The long-term impact of early parental death: Lessons from a narrative study. *Journal of the Royal Society of Medicine, 106*(2), 57–67.

Fuller, R. A., & Irvine, K. N. (2010). Interactions between people and nature in urban environments. In K. J. Gaston (Ed.), *Urban ecology* (pp. 134–171). Cambridge, England: Cambridge University Press.

Garst, B., & Bruce, F. (2003). Identifying 4-H camping outcomes using a standardized evaluation process across multiple 4-H educational centers. *Journal of Extension, 41*(3), 1–7.

Henderson, K. A., Oakleaf, I., & Bialeschki, M. D. (2009). Questions raised in exploring spiritual growth and camp experiences. *Leisure/Loisir, 33*, 179–195.

Keniger, L. E., Gaston, K. J., Irvine, K. N., & Fuller, R. A. (2013). *International Journal of Environmental Research and Public Health, 10*, 913–935. doi:10.3390/ijerp10030913

Li, J., Vestergaard, J., Cnattingius, S., Gissler, M., Bech, B. H., Obel, C., & Olsen, J. (2014). Mortality after parental death in childhood: A nationwide cohort study from three Nordic countries. *PLOS Medicine, 11*(7), 1–13. doi:10.1371/journal.pmed.1001679

McClatchey, I. S., Vonk, M. E., & Palardy, G. (2009). Efficacy of a camp-based intervention for childhood traumatic grief. *Research on Social Work Practice, 19*(1), 19–30.

McClatchey, I. S., & Wimmer, J. S. (2012). Healing components of a bereavement camp: Children and adolescents give voice to their experiences. *Omega - Journal of Death and Dying, 65*(1), 11–32.

National Alliance for Grieving Children (NAGC). (2016). *About the NAGC.* Retrieved from https://childrengrieve.org/about-nagc

Readdick, C. A., & Schaller, G. R. (2005). Summer camp and self-esteem of school-age inner-city children. *Perceptual and Motor Skills, 101*, 121–130.

Social Security Administration (SSA). (n.d.). *Social security beneficiary statistics.* Retrieved from www.ssa.gov/oact/STATS/SRVbenies

Thurber, C. A., Scanlin, M. M., Scheuler, L., & Henderson, K. A. (2007). Youth development outcomes of the camp experience: Evidence for multidimensional growth. *Journal of Youth & Adolescence, 36*, 241–254.

U.S. Government. (2014). *Orphans and vulnerable children affected by HIV and AIDS.* Retrieved from www.usaid.gov/what-we-do/global-health/hiv-and-aids/technical-areas/orphans-and-vulnerable-children-affected-hiv

U.S. Government. (2016). *U.S. Government action plan on children in adversity—2016 report to congress*. Retrieved from www.usaid. gov/open/children—adversity/2016

U.S. Government. (n.d.). *Maternal mortality*. Retrieved from www.cia. gov./library/publications/resources/the.world.fact.book

2

Theories of Childhood and Adolescent Grief

Loss of a loved person is one of the most intensely painful experiences any human being can suffer. And not only is it painful to experience but it is also painful to witness, if only because we are so impotent to help. To the bereaved nothing but the return of the lost person can bring true comfort; should what we provide fall short of that it is felt almost as an insult.

—John Bowlby (1980)

The goal of this chapter is to describe theories of childhood grief, beginning with attachment theory and Bowlby's exploration of loss and moving into more current theories. Developmental understanding, trauma and grief, complicated and prolonged grief, persistent complex bereavement disorder, multidimensional grief theory, trauma-informed care, and posttraumatic growth are discussed. The chapter concludes with a brief summary of current neuropsychological findings related to childhood trauma.

Culture as the Milieu of Grief

Culture has a great impact on how individuals react to grief. Cultures, religions, and social identity frame how people grieve and how they look at death and loss. Awareness and knowledge of cultural influences are important, as is the realization that personal idiosyncratic strategies will influence a person's grieving style (Martin & Doka, 2000). Being from the same culture often still means different grieving patterns. To practice culturally competent grief interventions requires a personal understanding of death and grief. When working with a bereaved individual, the helper must be aware of that person's cultural and religious background while attending to any inherent biases the helper might hold. In the United States, grief is seen as a psychological process. This is not always true in other cultures, where the expression of grief may be seen primarily through physical ailments (Kleinman, 1986). There are some important assessment questions a clinician can use to demonstrate respect for clients' idiosyncratic and cultural viewpoints to assist in interventions with a bereaved person, including: 1) What are the family's beliefs about the afterlife? 2) What are the family's cultural rituals around death, burial, and memorializing? 3) How much of death and dying is shared with children? 4) How does the family look at suicide, homicide, HIV/AIDS, and other causes of death? 5) Are feelings expressed openly? and 6) How do the family's practices align with those within their culture?

With these thoughts in mind, the authors of this book review theories of childhood grief from a Western perspective. "Bereavement," "mourning," and "grief" are sometimes used interchangeably but mean different things and need to be reviewed. DeSpelder and Strickland (2011, pp. 268–269) have defined the concepts as follows:

- *Bereavement* is the state of being bereaved, the objective event of loss. The word actually means to be "shorn off" or "being robbed."
- *Mourning* is the way a person incorporates his or her loss into his life and this is determined by norms in the culture of the bereaved. Some objects become symbols of mourning specific to certain cultures. Examples of these may include memorial bands, flying flags at half-mast, and tearing clothing.
- *Grief* is the reaction to loss and includes cognitive (mental), emotional (affective), physical, behavioral, and spiritual reactions or responses. Cognitive or mental reactions include confusion, disbelief, anxiety, problems with concentration, intrusive thoughts, and sometimes paranormal experiences,

for example a sense of the deceased's presence. Emotional or affective reactions include sadness, longing, loneliness, guilt, hopelessness, frustration over not being able to control events, and anger at the injustice of the loss. Physical reactions may include sleep disturbances such as hypersomnia or insomnia, appetite changes, chills, fatigue, and headaches. Behavioral reactions include crying, incessant talk about the person lost and/or the circumstances of the death, or the opposite, avoiding talking about the deceased, restlessness, irritability, risk taking, and social withdrawal. Spiritual reactions may include questioning one's faith and the meaning of life. Nader and Salloum (2011) point out that all these reactions are natural when a loss occurs. Usually their intensity decreases after 6 to 12 months.

Grief theory for adults dates back to Sigmund Freud (1917), who established basic assumptions about grief and mourning: 1) mourning is a natural reaction to loss; 2) when grieving, a person confronts the reality of their loss; and 3) grief work is difficult and takes time. Freud believed that in normal mourning people let go of the attachment to the lost person. Grief then is a process of de-investing the psychological energy (libido) attached to that person. Melancholia is discussed as the maladaptive grief response. Bowlby (1980) first introduced four stages of grief: 1) shock/numbness, 2) searching and yearning for the deceased and reminders of him or her, 3) disorganization when prior coping mechanisms break down, and 4) reorganization when new coping skills are established.

Children and Grief

History of Theory

The exploration of childhood grief began in the mid-20th century with Anna Freud and Burlingham (1943, 1974), who studied children in orphanages established during World War II to remove children from the dangers of bombing in London. Spitz (1945), Bowlby (1980), Bowlby, Robertson, and Rosenbluth (1952), Robertson and Bowlby (1952), and Robertson's powerful film (1952) opened the door to the fact that children, even very young children, grieve the loss of a parent. Much of this research grew out of observations of children who were separated from their parents, often because of children's hospital procedures at that time. This work was strongly connected to the development of attachment theory.

Attachment theory speaks to the concept that infants and toddlers form a bond with their primary caregiver, usually their mother, that is significantly different from other relationships. This bond allows the child to safely explore the world around them, increasing individuation, self-confidence, an understanding of cause and effect, and emotional perception. As Bowlby and his colleagues developed their understanding of childhood grief, he wrote:

> Whether an author is discussing the effects of loss on an adult or a child, there is a tendency to underestimate how intensely distressing and disabling loss usually is and for how long the distress, and often the disablement, commonly lasts.
>
> (Bowlby, 1980, pp. 15–16)

Although Freud and Burlingham (1943) and earlier writers believed that childhood grief at the loss of a mother was short lived, limited to days or weeks, Bowlby (1960) believed that even very young children experienced grief and mourning, and that the loss of a mother could cause severe long-term psychological difficulties. Although therapists of this mid-20th-century period used lengthy psychoanalysis, often based in play therapy, Bowlby (1980) believed that there was little that therapists could do to mitigate childhood grief (p. 16).

Theorists who began work on children and grief in the 1980s and 1990s (Wolfelt, 1996; Worden, 1991, 1996; Worden, Davies, & McCown, 1999; Worden & Silverman, 1996) built on grief theory for adults. However, researchers noted that children grieve differently from adults (Christ, 2000; Willis, 2002). It is worthy of note that although grief is individual, children go through developmental stages that determine how much they can understand of the loss, influencing their reaction to the loss. Depending on developmental stage and other individual factors, their understanding of universality, irreversibility, nonfunctionality, causality, and their own mortality varies (Corr, 2010). Those who work with bereaved children and adolescents must be mindful that a child does not move from one stage to another seamlessly and does not go from mastering all tasks in one developmental stage one day and into the following stage the next. Instead, developmental tasks may overlap in individual children.

Developmental Understanding

Although developmental staging of children's understanding of death does not explain how individual children and adolescents experience death, the theory can be a helpful guideline. As noted, those working with bereaved children and adolescents must establish the individual and idiosyncratic understanding of death as understood by each child or adolescent. The child's previous experiences, environment, temperament, and emotional maturity all play a role in the understanding of grief. Table 2.1 summarizes child and adolescent developmental understanding of death.

Children at infancy through 2 years of age have no concept of death. This is the cognitive stage that Piaget and Inhelder (1969) call *sensorimotor*. Children during this stage have highly developed senses and can react to the separation from familiar touches, smells, taste, vision, and sound of a caregiver. When a death occurs in a family, children at this stage react to the emotions of adults around them and may regress. This is also the psycho-social stage that Erikson (1968) labels as *trust versus mistrust*. If needs are unmet or neglected during this stage, which may happen if a parent dies, the child may develop mistrust or the feelings that the world is an unpredictable place. This in turn may bring on feelings of frustration, suspicion, and low confidence (Erikson, 1968). Loss during this age, when children have developed mental representations of their caregivers, can result in abandonment anxiety (Di Ciacco, 2008).

The 2–4 age range is the beginning of the *pre-operational* stage (Piaget & Inhelder, 1969), also known as the *symbolic function* substage, and is characterized by egocentrism and pre-causal thinking. Egocentrism leads children to see the world from their own perspective, unaware that there may be other perspectives. Egocentrism is also expressed through concern for personal well-being. Pre-causal thinking prevents children from seeing the real relationship between cause and effect. Children at this stage enter the stage of *autonomy versus shame and doubt* (Erikson, 1968). If children in this stage are not allowed to master tasks they are capable of, such as feeding themselves, or are asked to do more than they are capable of, such as preparing food, they may develop doubts about their abilities and feel shame. When a parent dies, overprotection might lead to them not being able to master tasks. Parentification, that is taking on responsibilities that a parent would normally handle, might result in doubts about abilities.

TABLE 2.1
Child and Adolescent Understanding of Death

Piaget's cognitive stages	Approximate age range in years	Expressions	Erickson's psycho-social stages	Expressions	Reactions that may be displayed after death of a close person
Sensorimotor	0–2	Egocentrism, no to little concept of death. Does not understand cause and effect.	Trust vs. mistrust	Highly developed senses	Reacts to separation from familiar touches, smells, etc.; reacts to emotions of adults, may regress. Feels concern for own well-being. May develop mistrust if needs not met, feelings that the world is unpredictable, may feel frustrated, may develop low confidence, abandonment anxiety.
Pre-operational: Symbolic function substage	2–4	Egocentrism and pre-causal thinking; concern for own personal well-being.	Autonomy vs. shame and doubt	Likes to master tasks such as feeding self, washing hands, etc.	May feel overprotected, or feel pressure to perform above ability, which may lead to self-doubt and/or shame.
Pre-operational: Intuitive thought substage	4–5	Begin to see irreversibility and non-functionality but not universality; curiosity linked with primitive reasoning; magical thinking.	Initiative vs. guilt	Makes efforts towards independence and preparation towards leadership.	May assume blame for the death; unsupported efforts may lead to guilt about needs and desires.

Stage	Age	Cognitive development	Psychosocial stage	Social/moral development	Grief implications
Concrete operational stage	6–11	Understands irreversibility of death and to some degree universality; uses logic appropriately but lacks abstract hypothetical thinking. Understands cause and effect. Able to generalize but unable to use deductive reasoning.	Industry vs. inferiority	Reasonable at sharing and cooperation, moral values developing, can recognize individual and cultural differences.	Displays magical thinking; less egocentric; obsesses with surviving parent's health; may idolize person who died. Difficulty identifying feelings, which may lead to acting-out behavior. Lack of parental praise for efforts may lead to lethargy, lack of motivation, and low self-esteem.
Formal operational stage	12–17 Early and middle adolescence	Understands universality but may deny own mortality; understands abstract concepts, can do hypothetical and deductive reasoning.	Identity vs. role confusion	Working towards independence and differentiation. Experiments with various roles, activities, and behaviors. Wants to conform to peer norms, not be "different."	May exhibit risk-taking behavior. A loss makes them different, may lead to avoidance of peers or desperate attempts to belong. Parental death may either rush independence or put it on hold.
Formal operational stage	18–early 20s Late adolescence; emerging adulthood		Intimacy vs. isolation	Separation from parents and start of intimate relationships	May lead to fear of commitment or to becoming overly dependent in attempts to control things. Comparisons with a deceased idolized parent may lead to intimacy issues.

Sources: Balk (2014); Christ (2000); Di Ciacco (2008); Erikson (1968); Piaget and Inhelder (1969); Webb (2010).

Children aged 4–5 begin to see the irreversibility/non-functionality of death but are still unable to grasp the universality of death. This is another substage of the pre-operational stage, the *intuitive thought* substage. When in this stage, children are curious and want to know why things are a certain way. They use primitive reasoning. This in turn leads to "magical thinking" wherein children will see something they said or did as the cause of death of a loved one (Christ, 2000). This intuitive thought stage corresponds with Erikson's stage of *initiative versus guilt*. This is a stage where children like to do things, take initiative, and prepare to be leaders. In this stage, teachers and parents support the children's efforts and help them make appropriate choices in order to develop initiative and independence. If a parent dies, and the support of the child's efforts is absent or lost, the child may develop guilt about needs and desires.

Children aged 6–11 understand irreversibility of death and, to some degree, universality. Children in this age group may internalize and personify death, seeing death as a creature that comes to get people (Webb, 2010). They may exhibit magical thinking in regards to the death, obsess with a surviving parent's health, and idolize the person who died. Although magical thinking may impede the understanding of the cause of death, it may also have a restorative effect. Children at this age have difficulty identifying feelings, which may lead to acting-out behavior. This is the stage that Piaget and Inhelder (1969) call the *concrete operational* stage. At this stage children start using logic appropriately, but abstract hypothetical thinking is undeveloped. Children in this age group are able to generalize, but unable to use deductive reasoning, i.e., the ability to predict the outcome of an experience. They are able to use logic and to see points of views other than their own, thus they are not egocentric or are less egocentric. Erikson (1968) calls this stage of development *industry versus inferiority*. At this stage, children become more reasonable at sharing and willing to cooperate. They develop moral values, understand cause and effect, and recognize individual and cultural differences. As they work on more complex skills such as reading and writing, they depend on teachers and parents to provide praise, which then in turn leads to industry, defined by the desire to stay on task until a task is completed. If a parent is not available because of death to provide this feedback, the child may become lethargic, lack motivation, develop low self-esteem, and be labeled lazy.

Adolescents and Grief

Developmental Understanding

Adolescence spans several years, typically starting around the age of 12 and lasting throughout the teenage years and into the early 20s (Balk, 2014). As children grow into the adolescent years, they enter the *formal operational* stage (Piaget & Inhelder, 1969). The adolescent understands abstract concepts and is able to perform hypothetical and deductive reasoning. They are aware of universality but may deny their own mortality. Coupled with hormonal changes beginning in early adolescence and pressures to do well at school and be popular with peers, adolescence is a tumultuous time.

In early adolescence (approximate ages 12–14) peers become more important in the lives of teens as they start to gain more independence from their parents and separate from them emotionally (Balk, 2014). This separation continues in middle and late adolescence (approximate ages 15–17 and 18 through early 20s). In early and middle adolescence, adolescents move through the *identity versus role confusion* stage (Erikson, 1968), experiment with different activities and behaviors, and experience role confusion before their identity takes shape. A death during this stage, when adolescents are supposed to form their own identity, differentiate from others, and separate from home, may rush independence or put it on hold (Balk, 2014). Teens are also often concerned with their appearance and others' thoughts about them. They want to conform to peer norms, and losing a parent or significant other during this time makes them stand out in a way that is uncomfortable for them. Although peers start to become an important support during this time, adolescents may be uncomfortable sharing their loss and grief with peers for fear of being different from them. This may lead to an avoidance of peers or to desperate attempts to belong (Balk, 2014). Regretfully, peers will most likely not know how to support a friend who is grieving.

In late adolescence, from around 18 into the early 20s, also called *emerging adulthood*, adolescents enter the *intimacy versus isolation* stage (Erikson, 1968). Adolescents at this stage are expected to separate from their parents and start intimate relationships. Losing a parent or sibling at this stage may create fear of commitment. Adolescents may be afraid of losing another person, preventing them from fully committing. They may also compare a partner with a deceased idolized parent, leading to difficulties in an intimate relationship. However, instead of fear of commitment, an adolescent who loses a close loved one at this developmental stage may go to the other extreme and become overly dependent in order to try to control events (Balk, 2014).

For positive developmental outcomes, adolescents need to deal with five principal matters: predictability of events, development of self-image, sense of belonging, sense of fairness and justice, and increased mastery and control (Fleming & Adolph, 1986). The death of a parent during adolescence impacts all five of these matters. Predictability of events is shattered when a death occurs, and may create anxiety and fear of losing somebody else who is close to them (Worden, 2014). To handle the discovery of unpredictability, a bereaved teen may either engage in risk-taking behaviors or become behaviorally rigid in an attempt to ensure predictability (Balk, 2014). Self-image and sense of belonging are also impacted by loss in adolescence as the death may increase an adolescent's feelings of being different from peers (Worden, 2014). An adolescent may make desperate attempts at avoiding or seeking friends and this may lead to feelings of alienation when peers cannot relate to what the bereaved youth is experiencing. A bereaved youth may become clingy as a defense against feeling a lack of belonging. Fairness and justice will be questioned when an adolescent loses a parent or sibling to insidious diseases, suicide, or senseless crimes. Younger adolescents may react one of two opposite ways: either becoming overly cautious or self-destructive (Balk, 2014). Older adolescents may reach out to help the community. The sense of mastery and control is also affected by the loss of a loved one during adolescence. In an attempt to feel in charge, the bereaved teen may assume qualities of the person lost or the opposite, reject the deceased's significance (Balk, 2014).

It bears mentioning that children revisit grief as they transition from one developmental stage to another. Thus, children who lose a parent as 5-year-olds will grieve this parent in a different way when they are teenagers with different cognitive skills in their repertoire (Kaplow, Layne, Pynoos, Cohen, & Lieberman, 2012). It is important to take into account that children do not just develop cognitively as they grow; there is growth in social and spiritual areas. Fortunately, as they grow, children also learn to manage their emotions more effectively (Doka, 2000).

Other Influences

Factors other than the developmental stage can influence the child's grief, such as the relationship with the deceased. It can be assumed that a close relationship will put a greater stress on the loss experience than would an ambiguous relationship. However, teens in their quest for independence may have numerous fights with their parents. When that parent dies, the grief experienced by the adolescent can be magnified by feelings of guilt. Although it was formerly assumed that the mode of death, such as sudden, unanticipated death, and/or violent death such as homicide and suicide, would cause higher stress levels in the bereaved child, more recent research shows that this may not be the case (McClatchey, Vonk, & Palardy, 2009).

Research has shown countless short- and long-term effects of parental bereavement in children: difficulties in school; developmental delays; higher rates of substance abuse, depression, and deviance; increased risk of mortality into early adulthood; and other multiple physiological, health, social, and psychological issues (Dopp & Cain, 2012; Ellis, Dowrick, & Lloyd-Williams, 2013; Li et al., 2014; McClatchey, Vonk, & Palardy, 2009). Common reactions include posttraumatic stress, substance use, and separation anxiety (Goenjian et al., 2009; Kaplow, Saunders, Angold, & Costello, 2010). Yet most children navigate their grief without lasting pathology (Brown, Sandler, Tein, Liu, & Haine, 2007) and do not need interventions from professionals (Kaplow, Howell, & Layne, 2014).

Both risk and protective factors in the grief process of bereaved children and adolescents have been identified. These factors include individual (child intrinsic) variables, such as resilience, coping skills, sense of self-efficacy, positive self-image, and ethnicity; and environmental (child extrinsic) such as social supports, parenting style, and caregiver's emotional state (Brown et al., 2007; Worden & Silverman, 1996). A sense of self-efficacy, a good support system, a positive self-image, and child-centered parenting can serve as protective factors. By creating a warm and safe environment for children to grieve a loss, parents can help the child through the grieving process (Shapiro, Howell, & Kaplow, 2014).

Trauma and Grief

To further understand grief and children's reaction to grief, the trauma perspective slowly began to be used when studying bereaved children and adolescents. It was first applied to children and adolescents who had experienced a loss due to a violent death, with Pynoos and his colleagues forging the way (e.g., Pynoos & Eth, 1985; Pynoos, Nader, Frederick, Gonda, & Stuber, 1987; Pynoos & Nader,

1988; Pynoos et al., 1987). Through their work they found that children and adolescents who experience a violent loss oftentimes exhibit posttraumatic stress disorder (PTSD) symptoms. Trauma symptoms experienced by bereaved children often show up in their behaviors and in difficulties in learning.

The *Diagnostic Statistical Manual* 5th edition (DSM-5) describes the triggers of trauma and stressor-related disorders as the exposure to death or threatened death, serious injury, or sexual exploitation (American Psychological Association [APA], 2013). Exposure is defined as directly experiencing or witnessing a traumatic event, finding out about the traumatic event of a close family member or friend, or experiencing first-hand repeated or extreme exposure to adverse details of the trauma. Not everyone experiencing a trauma develops PTSD, but many may experience trauma symptoms, including intrusion, avoidance, negative alterations in cognitions and mood, and alterations in arousal and reactivity (APA, 2013).

Intrusive symptoms include painful memories, nightmares, flashbacks, prolonged distress, and obvious physiologic reactivity. Avoidance symptoms include avoidance of thoughts or feelings related to the trauma and/or external reminders of the trauma, such as people and places. Negative changes in cognitions and mood include an inability to remember important pieces of the trauma; constant negative beliefs and expectations of oneself or the world, such as "the world is dangerous," or "I am a bad person"; self-blame or blame of others for the trauma; enduring negative emotions related to the traumatic event such as anger, guilt, and shame; obvious lessened interest in important activities; experiencing detachment from others; and constricted affect and inability to feel positive emotions. Alterations in arousal and reactivity include aggressive, irritable, and self-destructive behavior; hypervigilance; exaggerated startle responses; loss of concentration; and sleep disturbances (APA, 2013).

PTSD symptoms manifest differently in different age groups. It is difficult to assess PTSD symptoms in very young children since they are not able to verbally express what they feel or think. They may show fear of strangers, engage in posttraumatic play repeating themes of the trauma, express separation anxiety, and show regression of developmental skills (Nader, 1997; Kaplow et al., 2012). Children of elementary school age may also partake in posttraumatic play, which includes habitual repetition of the trauma and also posttraumatic reenactment, i.e., where the children recreate the trauma or some aspect of it. One example would be a child who carries a gun after losing a parent to gun violence (Cohen, 1998). Teenagers may display PTSD symptoms by aggressive, impulsive, and risk-taking behaviors.

PTSD has been found among several populations of youth who have experienced a loss, such as children and adolescents who have lost a parent or other close person to homicide, community violence, sniper attacks, natural disaster, and suicide (Pynoos, 1992; Murphy, Pynoos, James, & Osofsky, 1997; Nader, Pynoos, Fairbanks, & Frederick, 1990; Pynoos et al., 1993; Pfeffer, Jiang, Kakuma, Hwang, & Metsch, 2002). Many researchers found that trauma symptoms often interfered with the processing of grief symptoms in surviving children—intrusive thoughts of how the person died interrupted or prevented the child from completing grief tasks and the child's grieving process would be delayed (Brosius, 2003; Eth & Pynoos, 1994).

More recent studies, however, have found that trauma symptoms can be present both among children who lost a parent or sibling to an unexpected/violent death or to an expected death (McClatchey, Vonk, & Palardy, 2009; Kaplow et al., 2012, 2014). In these studies, those children who had lost a parent or caregiver to a prolonged illness had the same or higher incidences of PTSD than those children who had experienced a sudden or violent death. Although a death from homicide and suicide may be looked upon objectively as traumatic, watching a parent die slowly from cancer may also create trauma symptoms. Seeing a parent's journey through treatments with severe side effects, emaciation, and fatigue, could be anxiety provoking for a child. It appears that the definition of trauma rests with the child, and traumatic is what the child subjectively sees as traumatic. McClatchey, Vonk, and Palardy (2009) hypothesized that losing a parent to a long, drawn-out process, such as cancer, can be described as a Type II trauma, a long-standing and expected blow (Terr, 1991). Experiencing a sudden loss could be seen as a Type 1 trauma, which Terr describes as a sudden, unexpected blow.

Some researchers looked at the relationship between PTSD symptoms and grief, and developed a construct called Childhood Traumatic Grief (CTG) (Cohen, Mannarino, Greenberg, Padlo, & Shipley, 2002; Mannarino & Cohen, 2011). In CTG, trauma symptoms interfere with the child's ability to complete the grief tasks. Other researchers see it as unnecessary to define one construct dependent on another and feel that grief and trauma symptoms should be assessed and conceptualized separately as two different constructs that may or may not coexist. When they do coexist due to the circumstances of the death, these researchers call it "traumatic bereavement" (Kaplow, Howell, & Layne, 2014). When grief exists together with trauma due to a separate event, these researchers call it "bereavement and trauma."

Prolonged and Complicated Grief

Other concepts discussed in the childhood bereavement field are prolonged grief, complicated grief, and persistent complex bereavement disorder (PCBD). Prolonged grief among adults involves symptoms such as separation distress, refusal to accept that the dead person is gone, and feelings of life being meaningless without the dead person. These symptoms remain intense for six months or longer (Prigerson et al., 2009). Prolonged grief is described as chronic and exacerbated mourning and is related to the loss of attachment. Length and intensity of the symptoms are the focus. Others call these symptoms "complicated grief" (Shear et al., 2011); Boelen and his colleagues (Boelen, de Keijser, van den Hout, & van den Bout, 2011) state that they are the one and same. Complicated grief among children and adolescents has been defined very similarly, with symptoms of yearning, struggles to accept the death, avoidance of reminders, and feelings of worthlessness (Spuij et al., 2012).

Complicated grief among children, according to a study by McClatchey and her colleagues (McClatchey, Vonk, Lee, & Bride, 2014), is a construct that indicates existential issues after the death of a parent or sibling such as *Life for me doesn't have much purpose since his/her death* and *I don't see myself having a good life without him/her* (Layne, Savjak, Saltzman, & Pynoos, 2001). In addition, complicated grief is grief that is unchanging or static, or continually disruptive (A. Dyregrov & Dyregrov, 2013). Layne et al. (2008) separates traumatic and complicated grief as two different constructs; traumatic grief represents reactions to the mode of death, whereas complicated grief is marked by prolonged and/or unproductive grieving (Layne et al., 2008). This separation of constructs has been borne out by McClatchey et al. (2014), who found the two constructs, complicated and traumatic grief, to be separate when conducting a confirmatory analysis of the Extended Grief Inventory (Layne et al., 2001). Nader and her colleague Solloum (2011) describe prolonged and traumatic grief as two constructs under the heading of complicated grief.

Adolescents who have experienced a violent loss have higher levels of prolonged grief than those who had experienced a non-violent loss (Dillen, Fontaine, & Verhofstadt-Deneve, 2009). However, there is no difference in PTSD or CTG symptoms in those children and adolescents who have experienced a sudden/violent death versus an expected death (McClatchey, Vonk, & Palardy, 2009); in some studies, those children who have experienced an expected loss have higher symptoms of posttraumatic stress (Kaplow et al., 2014). In summary, there are several constructs, with some terms used interchangeably, which may create confusion.

Persistent Complex Bereavement Disorder (PCBD)

PCBD is another construct. It is appended to the current DSM-5 for further consideration, and it is being assessed for its psychometric properties, developmental appropriateness, and cultural relevance (APA, 2013). Although the PCBD diagnosis relates to adult grief, the DSM-5 committee, based on suggestions by a child-adolescent grief workgroup, made revisions to the diagnosis based on theory, clinical experience, and research with children and adolescents. A PCBD checklist for youth assesses domains corresponding to the DSM-5 proposed PCBD symptom criteria, such as separation distress, reactive distress, existential/identity-related distress, and distress over circumstances of the death (Layne, Kaplow, & Pynoos, 2014).

Multidimensional Grief Theory

Researchers have discussed the need for a comprehensive developmental approach to childhood and adolescent grief (Kaplow, Layne, Saltzman, Cozza, & Pynoos, 2013). Kaplow and her colleagues discuss a theory that is based on the three core domains of separation distress, existential/identity-related distress, and distress over the circumstances of the death. Other factors intersect with these variables, including 1) causal precursors, e.g., "etiological risk factors" and "circumstances of death" (p. 325); 2) causal consequences, e.g., arrested development and limited functioning; and 3) moderators, e.g., developmental stage, available social support, and culture. The bereaved child can show manifestations of positive adjustment or maladjustment in each domain. Adaptive adjustment in separation distress includes missing the person who died, and longing to be with him or her again. Maladjustment may be expressed by wishes to be reunited with the deceased, including suicidal ideation; developmental regression to remain in the same developmental stage as when the person died, and thus stay connected to the dead; and assuming poor habits or behaviors of the deceased as a means to stay connected. Adaptive adjustment to existential/identity-related distress includes adjusting to difficulties created by role changes and finding meaning in life in spite of the loss. Maladjustment may include a post-loss identity crisis, hopelessness, a sense of meaningless existence, and survivor's guilt. Circumstance-related distress includes thoughts of how the person died, and adaptive adjustment includes both sadness and anger that will lessen with time, and the ability to incorporate positive memories of the person who died. Maladjustment is marked by unrelenting distress related to how the person died and can lead to functional impairment. This can manifest in ongoing feelings of anger, shame, guilt, and fantasies of retaliation. In maladjusted circumstance-related distress, PTSD symptoms may interfere with the execution of adaptive grieving tasks. Kaplow et al. (2013) state, "maladaptive *circumstance-related distress* is theorized to contain and subsume *classic PTSD symptoms encroaching upon adaptive grieving tasks*" (p. 326). The caregiving environment plays an important role in assisting children and teens through the grieving process. Thus, the clinician needs to take individual and socio-environmental factors into account when assessing for adjusted and maladjusted grief reactions (Kaplow et al., 2013, pp. 324–326).

Trauma-Informed Care

Trauma-informed care is a systemic approach that includes education, awareness, prevention, early identification, evidence-based trauma-specific assessment, and treatment. The Substance Abuse and Mental Health Services Administration (SAMHSA, 2014) created its own definition of trauma after soliciting input from experts in the field, such as researchers, practitioners, policy makers, and those who have experienced traumas and received trauma interventions in various settings:

> Individual trauma results from an event, series of events, or set of circumstances that is experienced by an individual as physically or emotionally harmful or life threatening and that has lasting

adverse effects on the individual's functioning and mental, physical, social emotional, or spiritual well-being.

(p. 7)

SAMHSA stresses three things: the event, experience, and
effects. The event element of trauma corresponds with the triggers
as described in DSM-5 in regards to "trauma and stressor-related
disorders" (APA, 2013, p. 265; pp. 271–274). Whether a youth experiences an event as traumatic or not depends on the meaning that
youth assigns to the event and is linked to cultural background,
accessible social supports, and developmental stage of the child or
adolescent (SAMHSA, 2014).

According to findings by SAMHSA, trauma interventions are
not enough to heal those affected by trauma. The organizational cli-
mate is also important. To that end, programs need to be "trauma-
informed" (SAMHSA, 2014). To be trauma-informed, the program
or system needs to 1) realize the impact of trauma and understand
the ways to recovery; 2) recognize signs and symptoms of trauma
with both clients and staff; 3) respond by using trauma knowledge in policies, procedures, and practices; and 4) work to avoid
re-traumatization (SAMHSA, 2014, p. 9). This approach can be used
in any setting or agency and is separate from interventions used to
promote healing from trauma.

A trauma-informed agency adheres to six principles: 1) safety;
2) trustworthiness; 3) peer support; 4) collaboration and mutuality;
5) empowerment, voice, and choice; and 6) sensitivity to cultural,
historical, and gender issues (SAMHSA, 2014, p. 10). The organization provides a physically, psychologically, and emotionally safe
setting for clients and staff. Decisions are made with transparency;
peers provide support and mutual self-help. For bereaved children
and adolescents, peers are those children and adolescents who have
also experienced a death, but family members may also be included.
Power differentials between staff and clients and among staff are
minimized and equalized. The organization, its staff, and its clients
use a strengths-based approach, believe recovery is possible, and
foster empowerment. Agencies and staff are culturally competent
and acknowledge historical trauma (SAMHSA, 2014).

A trauma-informed approach is different from specific trauma
interventions that address the trauma in order to promote healing. Programs that adhere to a trauma-informed approach use
interventions to deal with the trauma and recognize that trauma

survivors need "to be respected, informed, connected, and hopeful regarding their own recovery." Programs see "the interrelation between trauma and symptoms of trauma," and "the need to work in a collaborative way with survivors, family and friends of the survivor, and other human services agencies in a manner that will empower survivors and consumers" (SAMHSA, 2015, section 2).

Posttraumatic Growth

Although trauma can have serious effects on bereaved children, the trauma may also serve as a catalyst for growth. Posttraumatic growth (PTG) is a fairly new concept developed within the past 20 years. The concept was first discussed with adults (Tedeschi & Calhoun, 1996; Tedeschi, Park, & Calhoun, 1998). PTG differs from resilience in that those who experience PTG struggle with the trauma and this struggle leads to positive cognitive and emotional changes (Tedeschi et al., 1998) whereas those who are resilient adapt well in spite of the trauma (Levine, Laufer, Stein, Hamama-Raz, & Solomon, 2009). PTG has been defined as coming from "the *struggle* in the wake of trauma" (Tedeschi & Calhoun, 1995, p. 157) and can bring "a significant beneficial change in cognitive and emotional life that may have behavioral implications" (Tedeschi et al., 1998, p. 3). The struggle may consist of involuntary cognitive ruminations that may consequently stimulate coping efforts (Calhoun & Tedeschi, 2006). PTG has been established as a concept in its own right, different from natural maturation (Alisic, van der Schoot, van Ginkel, & Kleber, 2008; Taku, Kilmer, Cann, Tedeschi, & Calhoun, 2012). Markers of PTG include a stronger connection with others and/or a higher power, a change in life priorities, a new appreciation for life, an increase in personal strength, and the recognition of new possibilities.

PTSD symptoms have been linked repeatedly to PTG (Devine, Reed-Knight, Loiselle, Fenton, & Blount, 2010), and some suggest that PTSD symptoms serve as the catalyst for growth (Kilmer & Gil-Rivas, 2010). Other studies suggest that PTG is built upon the experiencing or re-experiencing of stress (Zebrack et al., 2015). However, some studies on PTG show no relationship with PTSD (McClatchey & Raven, 2017).

Studies involving children and adolescents and PTG exist, but there are few relating to youth and grief. Oltjenbruns (1991) studied older adolescents who had had a family member or friend die.

He found that these adolescents felt a stronger emotional bond with others and an increased emotional strength after their losses. After losing their parents, youth in the United Kingdom felt gratitude and appreciation of life, experienced a positive outlook and altruism, and wanted to live life to the fullest (Brewer & Sparkes, 2011).

Although studies show positive growth, not all researchers agree or consider cognitive growth enough to constitute personal growth. Hobfoll and his colleagues (Hobfoll et al., 2007) argue that real PTG needs to include proof of behavioral changes as well. Researchers also argue over whether PTG is a coping strategy or an outcome of coping, and question whether it has adaptive or maladaptive significance (Zoellner & Maercker, 2006). A two-sided model of PTG has been suggested: the Janus-Face model. This model supposes that PTG has an illusory self-deceptive side and a more realistic, beneficial, and self-transforming side. It is worth noting that the illusory component is not necessarily maladaptive and supposedly decreases over time, and the self-transforming side is associated with adaptive adjustment and increases over time.

Neuroscience

Expanding medical science related to mental health is opening a new way of looking at posttraumatic stress and a range of emotional difficulties. Although much of the research on the biological impact of childhood stress has focused on children who have been abused or neglected, parental death is equally stressful for children. Over the last 20 years the use of brain scans and other medical techniques have led to exploring the effects of childhood stress.

In a comprehensive review of studies from 1999 to 2010 of brain scans and the impact of abuse and neglect (primarily with children with PTSD), Hart and Rubia (2012) found significant brain changes reported among more than 500 subjects in 29 studies. Children with PTSD were found to have potential for difficulties with memory, planning, foresight, inhibition, attention control, social cognition, processing of emotions, and self-control. These were primarily reflected in the cerebellum, hippocampus, and amygdala regions of the brain (Hart and Rubia, 2012, p. 11).

Looking at the impact of stress from another medical perspective, Romens, McDonald, Svaren, and Pollak (2015) point out that associations between early adversity and the GR NR3C1 gene methylation have been discovered in five studies reviewed (p. 304). This finding was supported in their own study using blood samples of 56 children aged 11–14. They related these changes to the hippo-campus and to impaired regulation of stress response systems and behavior, concluding that "social experience can alter human phys-iology" (p. 308).

At present, no studies on the impact of complicated grief on the brains of children could be found, though there has been some research done with adults. O'Connor, Wellisch, Stanton, Olmstead, and Irwin (2012) studied differences in the cortisol levels of 24 adult women, 12 with complicated grief and 12 with non-complicated grief. They found a significant difference in the slope of cortisol levels between groups. The authors concluded that "the present findings serve both to identify a biological marker that appears to distinguish individuals with and without CG [complicated grief] and to suggest a mechanism through which bereavement, and CG spe-cifically, might confer risk for untoward health outcomes" (p. 727). Saavedra Pérez et al. (2015) used a large-population study to look at the impact of complicated grief on the brain. They identified 615 subjects with normal grief and 155 with complicated grief. They found that participants with complicated grief performed poorly in cognitive tests and had a smaller total "brain volume" (p. 1389) than other subjects.

Arizmendi, Kaszniak, and O'Connor (2016) studied "neural activity associated with grief severity" (p. 972) in 28 older adults: 8 with complicated grief, 9 with non-complicated grief, and 11 non-bereaved. Using functional magnetic resonance imaging (fMRI) they found significant differences in brain functioning between subjects with complicated grief and other study subjects. They concluded that difficulties with "avoidance and disruption of emotion regula-tion" (p. 975) in subjects with complicated grief were supported by their findings.

Overall, the importance of these studies is related to future understanding of the links between the physiological stress that chil-dren encounter and their ability to overcome resulting difficulties. O'Connor (2012) points out that "understanding the mechanisms of CG [complicated grief] may lead to improved treatment for this dis-order. Although pharmacological treatment seems the obvious way to use biomarkers, psychological treatment that takes advantage of biomarkers is also possible" (p. 146).

Physical and physiological knowledge is increasing each year. It is important that those who work to improve child mental health pay attention to new findings. Perhaps in the future the related techniques will help us understand the impact of programs, such as bereavement camps, and serve as guides in designing the most useful interventions for the children we aim to help.

In Summary

Theories about grief and trauma have developed considerably since Freud first explored these in the early 20th century. Evolving diagnoses such as PCBD and theories such as multidimensional grief theory are important considerations when working with bereaved children. The impact of trauma on the brain will continue to be an area in which researchers gain new knowledge. Theories underpin treatment and this will be discussed further in Chapter 3.

Recommended Reading

Balk, D. E. (2014). *Dealing with dying, death, and grief during adolescence*. New York, NY: Taylor & Francis.

Doka, K. J., & Tucci, A. S. (2008). *Living with grief: Children and adolescents*. Washington, DC: Hospice Foundation of America.

Doka, K. J., & Tucci, A. S. (2014). *Living with grief. Helping adolescents cope with loss*. Washington, DC: Hospice Foundation of America.

Worden, J. W. (2008). *Grief counseling and grief therapy: A handbook for the mental health professional* (4th ed.). New York, NY: Springer.

References

Alisic, E., van der Schoot, T. A. W., van Ginkel, J. R., & Kleber, R. J. (2008). Looking beyond posttraumatic stress disorder in children: Posttraumatic stress reactions, posttraumatic growth, and quality of life in a general population sample. *Journal of Clinical Psychiatry, 29*, 1455–1461.

American Psychological Association (APA). (2013). *Diagnostic and statistical manual for mental disorders (DSM-5)*. Arlington, VA: Author.

Arizmendi, B., Kaszniak, A. W., & O'Connor, M. F. (2016). Disrupted prefrontal activity during emotion processing in complicated grief: An fMRI investigation. *NeuroImage, 124*, 968–976.

Balk, D. E. (2014). *Dealing with dying, death, and grief during adolescence*. New York, NY: Taylor & Francis.

Boelen, P. A., de Keijser, J., van den Hout, M. A., & van den Bout, J. (2011). Factors associated with outcome of cognitive-behavioural therapy for complicated grief: A preliminary study. *Clinical Psychology and Psychotherapy, 18*, 284–291. doi:10.1002/cpp.720

Bowlby, J. (1960). Grief and mourning in infancy and early childhood. *Psychoanalytic Study of the Child, 15*, 9–52.

Bowlby, J. (1980). *Attachment and loss: Volume III: Loss, sadness and depression*. New York, NY: Basic Books.

Bowlby, J., Robertson, J., & Rosenbluth, D. (1952). A two-year-old goes to hospital. *Psychoanalytic Study of the Child, 7*, 82–94.

Brewer, J., & Sparkes, A. C. (2011). Parentally bereaved children and posttraumatic growth: Insights from an ethnographic study of a UK childhood bereavement service. *Mortality, 16*(3), 204–222.

Brosius, K. K. (2003). *Children who have lost their siblings due to homicide: A phenomenological study*. Doctoral dissertation. Retrieved from ProQuest Information and Learning Company (UMI No. 3100735).

Brown, A. C., Sandler, I., Tein, J., Liu, X., & Haine, R. (2007). Implications of parental suicide and violent death for promotion of resilience of parentally-bereaved children. *Death Studies, 31*(4), 301–335.

Calhoun, L. G., & Tedeschi, R. G. (2006). The foundations of posttraumatic growth: An expanded framework. In L. G. Calhoun & R. G. Tedeschi (Eds.), *Handbook of posttraumatic growth: Research and practice* (pp. 1–23). Nahwah, NJ: Erlbaum.

Christ, G. H. (2000). Impact of development on children's mourning. *Cancer Practice, 8*(2), 72–81.

Cohen, J. A. (1998). Practice parameters for the assessment and treatment of children and adolescents with posttraumatic stress disorder. *Journal of the American Academy of Child and Adolescent Psychiatry, 37*(10 supplement), 4S–26S.

Cohen, J. A., Mannarino, A. P., Greenberg, T., Padlo, S., & Shipley, C. (2002). Childhood traumatic grief: Concepts and controversies. *Trauma, Violence, & Abuse, 3*, 307–327.

Corr, C. A. (2010). Children's emerging awareness and understandings of loss and death. In D. Balk & C. A. Corr (Eds.), *Children's encounters with death, bereavement, and coping* (pp. 21–38). New York, NY: Springer.

DeSpelder, L. A., & Strickland, A. L. (2011). *The last dance: Encountering death and dying* (9th ed.). New York, NY: McGraw Hill.

Devine, K., Reed-Knight, B., Loiselle, K., Fenton, N., & Blount, R. (2010). Posttraumatic growth in young adults who experienced serious childhood illness: A mixed-methods approach. *Journal of Clinical Psychology in Medical Settings, 17*(4), 340–348.

Di Ciacco, J. A. (2008). *The colors of grief: Understanding a child's journey through loss from birth to adulthood*. London: Jessica Kingsley Publishers.

Dillen, L., Fontaine, J. R. J., & Verhofstadt-Deneve, L. (2009). Confirming the distinctiveness of complicated grief from depression and anxiety among adolescents. *Death Studies, 33*, 437–461.

Doka, K. J. (2000). Theoretical overview. In K. J. Doka (Ed.), *Living with grief: Children, adolescents, and loss* (pp. 1–3). Washington, DC: Hospice Foundation of America.

Dopp, A. R., & Cain, A. C. (2012). The role of peer relationships in parental bereavement during childhood and adolescence. *Death Studies, 36*(1), 41–60.

Dyregrov, A., & Dyregrov, K. (2013). Complicated grief in children— The perspectives of experienced professionals. *Omega - Journal of Death and Dying, 67*(3), 291–303.

Ellis, J., Dowrick, C., & Lloyd-Williams, M. (2013). The long-term impact of early parental death: Lessons from a narrative study. *Journal of the Royal Society of Medicine, 106*(2), 57–67.

Erikson, E. (1968). *Identity: Youth and crisis*. New York, NY: W. W. Norton & Co.

Eth, S., & Pynoos, R. S. (1994). Children who witness the homicide of a parent. *Psychiatry: Interpersonal & Biological Processes, 57*(4), 287–306.

Fleming, S. J., & Adolph, R. (1986). Helping bereaved adolescents: Needs and responses. In C. A. Corr & J. N. McNeil (Eds.), *Adolescence and death* (pp. 97–118). New York, NY: Springer Publishing.

Freud, A., & Burlingham, D. (1943). *War and children*. New York, NY: International Universities Press.

Freud, A., & Burlingham, D. (1974). *Infants without families and reports on the Hampstead nurseries 1939–1945*. London, England: Hogarth.

Freud, S. (1917). *Mourning and melancholia* (1925 translation). Vienna, Austria: Hugo Heller.

Goenjian, A. K., Walling, D., Steinberg, A. M., Roussos, A., Goenjian, H. A., & Pynoos, R. S. (2009). Depression and PTSD symptoms among bereaved adolescents 6 1/2 years after the 1988 Spitak earthquake. *Journal of Affective Disorders, 112*(1–3), 81–84.

Hart, H., & Rubia, K. (2012). Neuroimaging of child abuse: A critical review. *Frontiers in Human Neuroscience, 6*, Article 52, 1–24. doi:10.3389/fnhum.2012.00052

Hobfoll, S. E., Hall, B. J., Canetti-Nisim, D., Galea, S., Johnson, R. J., & Palmieri, P. A. (2007). Refining our understanding of traumatic growth in the face of terrorism: Moving from meaning cognitions to doing what is meaningful. *Applied Psychology: An International Review, 56*(3), 345–366. doi:10.1111/j.1464-0597.2007.00292.x

Kaplow, J. B., Howell, K. H., & Layne, C. M. (2014). Do circumstances of the death matter? Identifying socio-environmental risks for grief-related psychopathology in bereaved youth. *Journal of Traumatic Stress, 27*(1), 42–49.

Kaplow, J. B., Layne, C. M., Pynoos, R. S., Cohen, J. A., & Lieberman, A. (2012). DSM-V diagnostic criteria for bereavement-related disorders in children and adolescents: Developmental considerations. *Psychiatry: Interpersonal & Biological Processes, 75*(3), 243–266.

Kaplow, J. B., Layne, C. M., Saltzman, W. R., Cozza, S. J., & Pynoos, R. S. (2013). Using multidimensional grief theory to explore effects of deployment, reintegration, and death on military youth and families. *Clinical Child and Family Psychology Review, 16*, 322–340.

Kaplow, J. B., Saunders, J., Angold, A., & Costello, E. J. (2010). Psychiatric symptoms in bereaved versus nonbereaved youth and young adults: A longitudinal epidemiological study. *Journal of the American Academy of Child & Adolescent Psychiatry, 49*(11), 1145–1154.

Kilmer, R. P., & Gil-Rivas, V. (2010). Exploring posttraumatic growth in children impacted by Hurricane Katrina: Correlates of the phenomenon and developmental considerations. *Child Development, 81*(4), 1211–1227.

Kleinman, A. (1986). *Social origins of distress and disease: Depression, neurasthenia, and pain in modern China.* New Haven, CT: Yale University Press.

Layne, C. M., Kaplow, J. B., & Pynoos, R. S. (2014). *Persistent Complex Bereavement Disorder (PCBD) checklist—youth version 1.0.* Los Angeles, CA: University of California.

Layne, C. M., Saltzman, W. R., Poppleton, L., Burlingame, G. M., Pasalic, A., Durakovic, E., . . . Pynoos, R. S. (2008). Effectiveness of a school-based group psychotherapy program for war-exposed adolescents: A randomized controlled trial. *Journal of the American Academy of Child and Adolescent Psychiatry, 47*, 1048–1062. doi:10.1097/CHI.0b013e31817eecae

Layne, C. M., Savjak, N., Saltzman, W. R., & Pynoos, R. S. (2001). Extended grief inventory: University of California at Los Angeles and Brigham Young University.

Levine, S. Z., Laufer, A., Stein, E., Hamama-Raz, Y., & Solomon, Z. (2009). Examining the relationship between resilience and posttraumatic growth. *Journal of Traumatic Stress, 22*(4), 282–286.

Li, J., Vestergaard, J., Cnattingius, S., Gissler, M., Bech, B. H., Obel, C., & Olsen, J. (2014). Mortality after parental death in childhood: A nationwide cohort study from three Nordic countries. *PLOS Medicine, 11*(7), 1–13. doi:10.1371/journal.pmed.1001679

Mannarino, A. P., & Cohen, J. A. (2011). Traumatic loss in children and adolescents. *Journal of Child and Adolescent Trauma, 4*, 22–33.

Martin, T. L., & Doka, K. J. (2000). *Men don't cry . . . women do: Transcending gender stereotypes of grief.* Philadelphia, PA: Brunner Mazel.

McClatchey, I. S., & Raven, R. F. (2017). Adding trauma-informed care at a bereavement camp to facilitate posttraumatic growth: A controlled outcome study. *Advances in Social Work*, *18*(1). doi: 10.18060/21239.

McClatchey, I. S., Vonk, M. E., Lee, J., & Bride, B. (2014). Traumatic and complicated grief among children—one or two constructs? *Death Studies*, *38*(2), 69–78.

McClatchey, I. S., Vonk, M. E., & Palardy, G. (2009). The prevalence of childhood traumatic grief—a comparison of violent/sudden and expected loss. *Omega - Journal of Death and Dying*, *59*(4), 305–323.

Murphy, L., Pynoos, R. S., James, C. B., & Osofsky, J. D. (1997). The trauma/grief-focused group psychotherapy module of an elementary school-based violence prevention/-intervention program. In J. D. Osofsky (Ed.), *Children in a violent society* (pp. 223–255). New York, NY: Guilford Press.

Nader, K. O. (1997). Childhood traumatic loss: The intersection of trauma and grief. In C. R. Figley, B. E. Bride, & N. Mazza (Eds.), *Death and trauma: The traumatology of grieving* (pp. 17–42). Washington, DC: Taylor & Francis.

Nader, K. O., Pynoos, R. S., Fairbanks, L., & Frederick, C. (1990). Children's PTSD reactions one year after a sniper attack at their school. *American Journal of Psychiatry*, *147*(11), 1526–1530.

Nader, K. O., & Salloum, A. (2011). Complicated grief reactions in children and adolescents. *Journal of Child & Adolescent Trauma*, *4*(3), 233–257.

O'Connor, M. F. (2012). Immunological and neuroimaging biomarkers of complicated grief. *Dialogues in Clinical Neuroscience*, *14*(2), 141–148.

O'Connor, M. F., Wellisch, D. K., Stanton, A. L., Olmstead, R., & Irwin, M. R. (2012). Diurnal cortisol in complicated and non-complicated grief: Slope differences across the day. *Psychoneuroendocrinology*, *37*, 725–728.

Oltjenbruns, K. (1991). Positive outcomes of adolescents' experience with grief. *Journal of Adolescent Research*, *6*(1), 43–53.

Pfeffer, C. R., Jiang, H., Kakuma, T., Hwang, J., & Metsch, M. (2002). Group intervention for children bereaved by the suicide of a relative. *Journal of American Academy of Child and Adolescent Psychiatry*, *41*(5), 505–513.

Piaget, J., & Inhelder, B. (1969). *The psychology of the child*. New York, NY: Basic Books.

Prigerson, H. G., Horowitz, M. J., Jacobs, S. C., Parkes, C. M., Aslan, M., Goodkin, M., . . . Maciejewski, P. K. (2009). Prolonged grief disorder: Psychometric validation of criteria proposed for DSM-V and ICD-11. *PLOS Medicine*, *6*(8), e1000121. doi:10.1371/journal.pmed.1000121

Pynoos, R. S. (1992). Grief and trauma in children and adolescents. *Bereavement Care*, *11*(1), 2–10.

Pynoos, R. S., & Eth, S. (1985). Children traumatized by witnessing acts of personal violence. In S. Eth & R. S. Pynoos (Eds.), *Post-traumatic stress disorder in children* (pp. 17–44). Washington, DC: American Psychiatric Press.

Pynoos, R. S., Frederick, C., Nader, K., Arroyo, W., Steinberg, A., Eth, S., . . . Fairbanks, L. (1987). Life threat and posttraumatic stress in school-age children. *Archives of General Psychiatry*, *44*(12), 1057–1063.

Pynoos, R. S., Goenjian, A., Tashjian, M., Karakashian, M., Manjikian, R., Manoukian, G., . . . Fairbanks, L. A. (1993). Post-traumatic stress reactions in children after the 1988 Armenian earthquake. *British Journal of Psychiatry*, *163*(2), 239–247. doi:10.1192/bjp.163.2.239

Pynoos, R. S., & Nader, K. (1988). Psychological first aid and treatment approach for children exposed to community violence: Research implications. *Journal of Traumatic Stress*, *1*, 445–473.

Pynoos, R. S., Nader, K., Frederick, C., Gonda, L., & Stuber, M. (1987). Grief reactions in school age children following a snipe attack at school. *Israel Journal of Psychiatry and Related Sciences*, *24*(1–2), 53–63.

Robertson, J. (1952). *A two year old goes to hospital* (film). Retrieved from www.robertsonfilms.info/2_year_old.htm

Robertson, J., & Bowlby, J. (1952). Responses of young children to separation from their mothers II: Observations of the sequences of response of children aged 18 to 24 months during the course of separation. *Courrier du Centre International de l'Enfance*, *3*, 131–142.

Romens, S. E., McDonald, J., Svaren, J., & Pollak, S. D. (2015). Associations between early life stress and gene methylation in children. *Child Development*, *86*(1), 303–309.

Saavedra Pérez, H. C., Ikram, M. A., Direk, N., Prigerson, H. G., Freak-Poli, R., Verhaaren, B. F. J., . . . Tiemeier, H. (2015). Cognition, structural brain changes and complicated grief: A population-based study. *Psychological Medicine*, *45*, 1389–1399. doi:10.1017/S0033291714002499

Shapiro, D. N., Howell, K. H., & Kaplow, J. B. (2014). Associations among mother–child communication quality, childhood maladaptive grief, and depressive symptoms. *Death Studies*, *38*(3), 172–178.

Shear, M. K., Simon, N., Wall, M., Zisook, S., Neimeyer, R., Duan, N., . . . Keshaviah, A. (2011). Complicated grief and related bereavement issues for DSM-5. *Depression and Anxiety*, *28*, 103–117.

Spitz, R. A. (1945). Hospitalism—an inquiry into the genesis of psychiatric conditions in early childhood. *Psychoanalytic Study of the Child*, *1*, 53–74.

Spuij, M., Prinzie, P., Zijderlaan, J., Stikkelbroek, Y., Dillen, L., de Roos, C., & Boelen, P. A. (2012). Psychometric properties of the Dutch inventories of prolonged grief for children and adolescents. *Clinical Psychology and Psychotherapy*, *19*, 540–551. doi:10.1002.cpp.675

Substance Abuse and Mental Health Services Administration (SAMHSA). (2014). *SAMHSA's concept of trauma and guidance for a trauma-informed approach*. HHS Publication No. (SMA) 14-4884. Rockville, MD: Author.

Substance Abuse and Mental Health Services Administration (SAMHSA). (2015). *Trauma-informed care & alternatives to seclusion and restraints*. Retrieved from www.samhsa.gov/nctic/trauma-interventions

Taku, K., Kilmer, R. P., Cann, A., Tedeschi, R. G., & Calhoun, L. G. (2012). Exploring posttraumatic growth in Japanese youth. *Psychological Trauma: Theory, Research, Practice, and Policy*, *4*(4), 411–419.

Tedeschi, R. G., & Calhoun, L. G. (1995). *Trauma and transformation: Growing in the aftermath of suffering*. Thousand Oaks, CA: Sage.

Tedeschi, R. G., & Calhoun, L. G. (1996). The posttraumatic growth inventory: Measuring the positive legacy of trauma. *Journal of Traumatic Stress*, *9*(3), 455–471.

Tedeschi, R. G., Park, C. L., & Calhoun, L. G. (1998). Posttraumatic growth: Conceptual issues. In R. Tedeschi, C. Park, & L. Calhoun (Eds.), *Posttraumatic growth: Positive changes in the aftermath of crisis* (pp. 1–22). London: Erlbaum.

Terr, L. C. (1991). Childhood traumas: An outline and overview. *American Journal of Psychiatry*, *148*(1), 10–20.

Webb, N. B. (2010). The child and death. In N. B. Webb (Ed.), *Helping bereaved children: A handbook for practitioners* (3rd ed., pp. 3–21). New York, NY: The Guilford Press.

Willis, C. A. (2002). The grieving process in children: Strategies for understanding, educating, and reconciling children's perceptions of death. *Early Childhood Education Journal*, *29*(4), 221–226.

Wolfelt, A. D. (1996). *Healing the bereaved child: Grief gardening, growth through grief and other touchstones for caregivers*. Fort Collins, CO: Companion.

Worden, J. W. (1991). *Grief counseling and grief therapy: A handbook for the mental health professional*. New York, NY: Springer.

Worden, J. W. (1996). *Children and grief: When a parent dies*. New York, NY: The Guilford Press.

Worden, J. W. (2014). Adolescents coping with parental death. In K. J. Doka & A. S. Tucci (Eds.), *Living with grief: Helping adolescents cope with loss* (pp. 63–76). Washington, DC: Hospice Foundation of America.

Worden, J. W., Davies, B., & McCown, D. (1999). Comparing parent loss with sibling loss. *Death Studies, 23*, 1–15.

Worden, J. W., & Silverman, P. R. (1996). Parental death and the adjustment of school-age children. *Omega - Journal of Death and Dying, 33*(2), 91–102.

Zebrack, B., Kwak, M., Salsman, J., Cousino, M., Meeske, K., Aguilar, C., . . . Cole, S. (2015). The relationship between posttraumatic stress and posttraumatic growth among adolescent and young adult (AYA) cancer patients. *Psycho-Oncology, 2*, 162.

Zoellner, T., & Maercker, A. (2006). Posttraumatic growth in clinical psychology—a critical review and introduction of a two component model. *Clinical Psychology Review, 26*, 626–653. doi:10.1016/j.cpr.2006.01.008

3

Interventions for Bereaved Children and Adolescents

Så liten plats en människa tar på jorden
Mindre än ett träd i skogen
Så stort tomrum hon lämnar efter sig
En hel värld kan inte fylla det
A person takes such a small space on earth
Less than a tree in the forest
Yet such a big empty space she leaves behind
That a whole world cannot fill it

© Ingrid Arvidsson-licensed through ALIS, Sweden.
Translated from Swedish by Rene McClatchey

The goal of this chapter is to describe various interventions and settings for working with children after the death of a parent, sibling, or other close person. Interventions discussed include play therapy, art therapy, grief therapy, cognitive-behavioral therapy, and trauma-focused cognitive-behavioral therapy. Settings considered are individual therapy, family therapy, groups, and bereavement camps. In conclusion, special considerations for children with disabilities in the camp setting are addressed, and the use of technology in the grieving process is covered.

Types of Interventions

In recent years, ways of helping bereaved children have evolved with new understandings of the complexity of childhood grief. In the early and mid-20th century, long-term psychoanalysis was the preferred approach. Treatment has branched into interventions provided on a more short-term basis. A variety of modalities are now available to meet the needs of children and families.

Play Therapy

As professionals who counseled children reached out for ways to work with this special population, using play began to substitute for using the dreams of adults in the psychoanalytic approach. In Europe, Anna Freud (1926/1946), Karl Abraham and Melanie Klein were early proponents of play therapy. In Klein's introduction to the first edition of *The Psychoanalysis of Children* (1932/1960) she wrote, "At the first conference of German Psycho-Analysis in Wurzburg in 1924 . . . [Dr. Karl Abraham] declared in words that I shall never forget: 'The future of Psycho-analysis lies in Play Analysis'" (p. 9).

Today, play therapy, either as an adjunct to other interventions or standing alone, is used almost universally in work with children. As of this writing approximately 170 universities in the United States offer programs in play therapy (Association for Play Therapy, n.d.). Play therapy training in Europe, the Middle East, Asia, Australia, New Zealand, South Africa, and Canada can be accessed through Play Therapy International (2008). Webb (2011), who has written extensively on play therapy, said,

> Play therapy provides opportunities for children to play out their anxieties and to express their concerns, ultimately moving toward a calmer adjustment with a peaceful resolution. Whether play therapy takes the form of Hospice bereavement groups, conjoint parent-child play therapy, or individual therapy, a child-friendly treatment can bring about improved understanding, emotional healing, and adaptive coping.
>
> (p. 141)

Play has often been called the work of childhood, and it has a role in brain development and in social, emotional, and cognitive learning. Van der Kolk (2014) is a well-known author on the connection between trauma and the activity of the brain. He discusses reactions to trauma in the non-verbal part of the brain and conscious processing in the brain's frontal lobes, and he also identifies debilitating neuroendoctrine responses to trauma. His writing supports the idea that actions, rather than only words, promote healing of trauma. In regards to using play in the treatment of traumatized children, Homeyer and Morrison (2008) wrote, "Play provides physical activity, so that 'playing out' the event assists the brain in moving the memory from the nonverbal parts of the brain to the frontal lobes" (p. 211).

Specific play therapy activities are varied and related to the developmental stage of the child. Role playing can stretch from preschool-age children through teens involved with their parents or guardians. Role playing activities such as saying good-bye to a deceased parent can promote a more peaceful ending to that event than might have been experienced in the reality of a death. Puppets, stuffed animals, and dolls are used to act out difficult or sad experiences and allow children to gain some sense of mastery of their emotions around a loss. Often children will confide their thoughts to one of these rather than to people in the room. It can be surprising what a pre-teen or teen might say to a disconnected telephone or to an audio recorder more easily than to an adult therapist or guardian, even if the therapist is in the room, listening. Sand-tray play is a tool for expressing, through tactile stimulation, both real experiences and traumas as perceived from the child's perspective.

Art Therapy

As play therapy developed as a method of reaching children, art therapy was also seriously explored in the mid-20th century as a treatment method growing out of psychoanalytic theory. Edith Kramer (1972/1993) developed and wrote about art as therapy based on a psychoanalytic perspective in which the artistic process itself can be therapeutic. Margaret Naumburg (2015) developed a philosophy of art as symbolic speech, giving expression to feelings that could not be expressed in words. In the early to mid-20th century both women were central figures in the adoption of art therapy as a profession in the United States.

Although most mental health therapists do not hold their degrees or licensure in art therapy, most who work with children use some form of art work in therapeutically communicating with children. As early as 1989 Davis suggested the use of art therapy for grieving children and pointed out that "the objectives of art therapy are fourfold: awareness, expression of energy and feelings, working through a problem, and spontaneity, creativity, and joy. Art uses active methods to experience or to cathect feelings" (pp. 272–273). In writing about creative techniques for working with children who have experienced trauma, Desmond, Kindsvatter, Stahl, and Smith (2015) point out that

> talk therapy, because it is abstract and relies on higher-order thinking as a mechanism of change, can be difficult for some children. Children do not fully develop the higher-order cognitive skill of abstract thinking until adolescence, and if they are victims of trauma, it may be even later.
>
> (p. 441)

Art therapists are trained to integrate human development and psychological theory with expressive arts in order to help clients resolve difficulties. The approach has "the unique ability to unlock emotional expression by facilitating non-verbal communication" (American Art Therapy Association, 2016, para. 2). The American Art Therapy Association explains that art therapists "use art media, and often the verbal processing of produced imagery, to help people resolve conflicts and problems, develop interpersonal skills, manage behavior, reduce stress, increase self-esteem and self-awareness, and achieve insight" (2106, para. 1).

The use of non-verbal communication related to trauma, fears, and emotions is usually part of one-on-one, small groups, and camp modalities. Art tools most often used involve paper and markers, paints, or crayons. Clay and similar molding materials are also popular. Clinicians working with pre-teens and teenagers may introduce more complex tools such as plain masks that the pre-teens and teens can draw or write on, sometimes expressing the outside face that they show to the world and the inside feelings that they keep hidden. Bereaved children may construct art projects such as memory boxes or memory pillows with special messages to a deceased parent.

Creed, Ruffin, and Ward (2001) recommend "that strong consideration be given to using art activities, because they provide such a powerful, therapeutic, and nonthreatening means for children to deal with their grief" (p. 181). Resources for the use of art therapy with grieving children can be found on the websites of The Moyer Foundation, which makes available the art workbook *Draw It Out* and the National Alliance for Grieving Children, which produced *When Someone Dies: A Child-Caregiver Activity Book.*

Grief Therapy

Grief therapy involves addressing the four tasks of grief in children as described by Worden (1991, 1996, 2008). These tasks relate to his four stages of grief and include 1) accept that the death has happened, 2) express feelings around the loss, 3) adjust to an environment without the deceased, and 4) let go and invest in future relationships or things. Wolfelt (1996) later added two more children's tasks to this list: find meaning in the death and attach to another tending adult. Fox (1988), in a paradigm closely related to Worden's and Wolfelt's tasks, described the tasks of childhood/adolescent grief as: understanding, reacting, commemorating, and going on.

Very young children do not understand the finality of death and believe that death is reversible. Therefore, the first task of accepting that a death has happened (Worden, 1991, 2008), or understanding the loss (Fox, 1988), may be difficult. Play therapy may be a good choice for these children. However, grief therapists working with older bereaved children can help them accept the death by inviting them to tell their stories, including who they lost, how the death occurred, and when it happened. By telling their stories, children and adolescents progress from the shock and denial phase to a place of acceptance that the loss occurred. The cause of death may also be difficult for children who are still in the pre-causal thinking stage to grasp (Piaget & Inhelder, 1969). Clinicians working with this pre-causal group must be on the lookout for children experiencing magical thinking and assure them that the death is not their fault.

The second task is to express feelings, which may be awkward for young children, who often have difficulty identifying emotions (Salloum & Vincent, 1999). Bereaved children and adolescents may feel threatened by stating feelings because doing so may lead to the impression that things are out of control. They may also hesitate to state feelings if they are trying to protect loved ones who might be upset by the revelations (Christ, 2000). Grief therapists have devised creative ways to help young children express their feelings about their losses. One suggestion is the use of feeling charts where pictured faces depict multiple expressions, such as a sad, angry, scared, or happy face. Children then identify a picture that represents how they feel and begin to discuss it using words. Other ways used by clinicians to engage young children to express their feelings include card games, board games, grief walks, story books, grief-focused workbooks, ball games, and similar activities. Failure to address and identify feelings may lead bereaved children to express them in acting-out behavior, or the opposite, withdrawal, neither of which serves the child well.

To help bereaved children to adjust to an environment without the deceased, the clinician can encourage children to share memories verbally, to draw or write journal entries, or to perform ritual activities. It is also important for children to review changes that have occurred since the loss and how they have coped with those changes. The clinician may need to help the child clarify and accept the new family composition and roles. The counselor can help children see personal strengths by introducing positive self-talk.

The fourth task, letting go and investing in future relationships or things (Worden, 1991, 2008; Fox, 1988), harkens back to Sigmund Freud (1917), who saw the final stage of grief as detaching the libido from the lost object. Bowlby (1980) disagreed with this view and suggested that it was important to keep an ongoing relationship with the dead person, even if the relationship had to go through a transformation. In 19th-century Western European societies, love was considered superficial if the bereaved person "moved on." Indeed, studies have shown that children find comfort in keeping a relationship with their deceased parent (Ross, 1999). This can be accomplished in many ways that meet the needs of the child, such as keeping an ongoing journal or photo collection with thoughts and memories of the deceased and sharing new happenings with the deceased in writing. This combined—with investment of energy in friends, hobbies, and interests—can help the child cope in a healthy manner.

Grief-informed clinicians will assess bereaved children in regards to separation distress, existential distress, and circumstance-related distress (Kaplow, Layne, Saltzman, Cozza, & Pynoos, 2013). To assist with separation distress, the counselor encourages sharing of positive memories, participating in memorial rituals, and creating memory books or other items. For those children and teens who are experiencing existential distress, the counselor may identify the child's strengths and suggest engaging in new relationships. The clinician may also apply cognitive interventions. For those children and teens who experience circumstance-related distress, it would be appropriate for the clinician to encourage the child or teen to share the details of the death after learning certain coping skills, and then apply cognitive processing. These skills and processing are described in more detail in the next section.

Cognitive-Behavioral Therapy

Cognitive-behavioral therapy is based on behavior theory, which was first introduced by Pavlov, whose work in the 1890s underlies classical conditioning, and B. F. Skinner, who introduced positive and negative reinforcement in the 1940s. Behavioral therapy looks at changing or revising habitual responses to stimuli. Cognitive therapy is based on work by Ellis (1957) and Beck (1967). In cognitive-behavioral therapy, it is assumed that thoughts direct a person's emotional and behavioral state. If thoughts are maladaptive, experiences of emotional and behavioral disturbances emerge. Cognitive-behavioral therapy tries to change a thought and response pattern that creates stress and other unhealthy outcomes. This therapy looks at the feeling response to a thought and the behavior that this chain of thought and feelings might lead to. Ellis calls this the ABC model: A stands for antecedent or activating event, i.e., the actual event; B stands for beliefs about the antecedent/activating event; and C stands for consequences, such as feelings and behaviors. Beliefs about an event can be rational or irrational and are based on each individual's core beliefs and rules (Ellis, 1957).

An example of a core belief for many children is found in the belief they have powers to hurt people by their thoughts and words. This is referred to as magical thinking. An associated belief may be that it is bad to have hurtful thoughts. A child may have been mad at his mother and wished her dead. If the mother consequently dies in a car accident, the child may activate the core belief that he caused her death with his hurtful thoughts. For example, when the mother dies (activating event/antecedent), the child's thought is "I am bad because I caused this to happen" (the belief). The feelings of guilt and anxiety that the child experiences (consequences) lead to acting-out behavior. To summarize, according to cognitive-behavioral therapy, emotional and behavioral stress is caused by faulty core beliefs and rules that activate automatic maladaptive thoughts, leading to a maladaptive response when an activating event occurs.

Interventions used in cognitive-behavioral therapy include cognitive restructuring to revise faulty or illogical thinking, deep breathing, guided imagery, thought stopping, coping statements, and positive and negative reinforcement. Cognitive-behavioral therapy has been shown to be effective with grieving children (Saltzman, Pynoos, Layne, Steinberg, & Aisenberg, 2001), including those who have experienced prolonged grief (Spuij, Dekovic, & Boelen, 2015).

Trauma-Focused Cognitive-Behavioral Therapy

Trauma-focused cognitive-behavioral therapy (TF-CBT) uses cognitive-behavioral therapy with clients who have experienced trauma. A clinician applying this approach uses several components, preferably in a certain order. However, a skilled clinician will use an order that best fits the client. The components used with traumatized children are presented by Cohen, Mannarino, and Deblinger (2017). These components usually consist of the following: 1) psycho-education, 2) parenting skills, 3) relaxation, 4) affective expression and modulation, 5) cognitive coping and processing, 6) trauma narrative and processing of the trauma, 7) in vivo mastery of trauma reminders, 8) conjoint child-parent sessions, and 9) enhancement of personal safety and safety skills training. The following paragraphs present these components in further detail.

In the first component, psycho-education, the clinician gives children and families explanations of common reactions to trauma in order to normalize reactions they are experiencing. This can be done verbally or through the use of books or articles. Psycho-education also includes a description of interventions that are available to deal with the symptoms of trauma and a brief summary of the interventions used. It is beneficial for parents to hear that TF-CBT has been shown in research to be very effective for the treatment of trauma. Additionally, the psycho-education component includes some immediate ways to deal with upsetting symptoms, such as deep breathing, listening to soothing music, and talking about feelings with another person. Psycho-education is the first component but continues throughout the intervention period (Cohen et al., 2017, pp. 97–103).

The second component is the teaching of parenting skills. Many parents have difficulty parenting a child after the death of a spouse or sibling. One reason may be that parents feel guilty implementing discipline when the child is already having a difficult time. However, the child needs structure and discipline, which makes children feel safe in an otherwise unpredictable world. Helpful parenting skills include praising desirable behavior ("catching" the child doing something good), ignoring undesirable behavior that is not dangerous, using time-outs, and applying contingency reinforcement charts. Too often, parents ignore desirable behavior and give attention to undesirable behavior. Children crave attention, and if engaging in undesirable behavior is how they achieve it, this is what they will do, even if the attention is negative. Therefore, the counselor suggests that parents catch their children doing something desirable and communicate that the behavior is appreciated. The counselor encourages parents to ignore undesirable behavior if it is not dangerous to anyone. Ignored behavior will eventually cease.

The clinician teaches parents several methods of discipline. Time out is often used with young children, removing the child to a place without any means of stimulation such as toys and games. The child is asked to stay quietly until asked to come back. Cohen et al. (2017) suggest using one minute for each year of age, i.e., a 5-year-old would stay for five minutes. Using a reinforcement chart is another good parenting strategy—the child collects stars or some other token that is awarded each time a chore is performed or non-desirable behavior is absent. When the child has collected a certain number of these tokens, a reward is given. The child picks the reward, within reason (Cohen et al., 2017, pp. 107–119).

The third component in TF-CBT is relaxation. Relaxation techniques calm the body's tense muscles, rapid breathing, and other physiological responses to stress. Focused breathing entails breathing slowly in through the nose and out through the mouth for a few minutes using the stomach rather than the chest. In work with children, counting slowly to 5 during inhalation and backwards from 5 to 0 upon exhalation helps to deepen the breaths. Mindful breathing includes deep breathing, and as soon as the children's minds wander to thoughts outside of the breathing, the counselor asks them to make concerted efforts to bring their mind back to their breathing. Mindfulness or meditation simply means to stay in the present and think of nothing around you that has happened, what might happen in the future, or what tasks are needed. During deep breathing, if thoughts come into the mind, they are acknowledged but focus returns to staying in the present. Another part of relaxation is progressive muscle relaxation. Using this technique, children are lying or sitting comfortably and are asked to relax one muscle at a time, starting with toes and feet continuing with one muscle part at a time until reaching the head. Muscle relaxation will stop the hyperaroused physiological responses to stress, since one cannot be relaxed and aroused at the same time (Cohen et al., 2017, pp. 122–134).

The fourth component in TF-CBT is affective expression and modulation. During this component the clinician helps the child with identification and discussion of feelings experienced due to the trauma. Children learn about thought stopping and positive imagery, and creating a safe place to imagine when upset. Positive self-talk helps children develop an image of themselves as capable and courageous. Realistic safety statements are used to increase the child's feeling of being safe. Other techniques include increasing problem-solving and social skills (Cohen et al., 2017, pp. 138–154).

The fifth component includes cognitive coping and processing. In these sessions, children learn about the impact of thoughts on feelings and behaviors. First the clinician and child review various feelings. Next the clinician helps the child see the connection between feelings and thoughts using various activities. Together they review thoughts that are not useful and thoughts that are useful. Children practice replacing unhelpful thoughts with helpful thoughts (Cohen et al., 2017, pp. 138–141, pp. 159–164).

The sixth component has two parts, the trauma narrative and cognitive processing of the trauma. First the counselor asks the child to present the story from the beginning before the trauma event, then describe what happened during and after the event. This can be done either verbally or in writing. Prompts such as a time line; schemes for beginning, middle, and ending of the story; or other tools can be used to help. The child is asked to include as many thoughts and feelings as possible. The clinician asks the child to incorporate the "worst moment" of the trauma. In the second part of the sixth component, the counselor can use any unhelpful thoughts identified during the cognitive-processing component. The child and clinician look at the child's inaccurate thoughts and discuss ways to correct these. The clinician also helps the child see the difference between regret and guilt (Cohen et al., 2017, pp. 174–200).

The seventh component helps the child overcome innocuous trauma reminders that prevent the child from functioning fully. An example of an innocuous trauma reminder would be of a bedroom where a mother died. In the in vivo mastery of these harmless trauma reminders, the child and therapist first identify the feared situation. Parent, clinician, and all involved reassure the child that the fearful situation is safe. Through progressive exposure the child revisits the situation. The counselor reminds the child of coping mechanisms that he or she has learned in earlier components, such as deep breathing and coping statements. Tolerated exposure is rewarded with something desirable to the child as well as praise from adults involved (Cohen et al., 2017, pp. 205–211).

Conjoint child-parent sessions are the eighth component of TF-CBT. Parents have attended sessions with the therapist to learn parenting skills and have been educated about the various components the child has experienced. In some cases they are informed of what the child has shared in the sessions. The parents and children are brought together, usually after the children have finished the cognitive-processing components. During the conjoint session, the child reads his or her trauma narrative aloud to the parent. The parent has heard the narrative in an individual session with the therapist. This individual session helps the parent be adequately prepared to hear the narrative from the child in order to keep emotional composure. The parent is also prepared to make supportive responses when hearing the narrative (Cohen et al., 2017, pp. 213–219).

The ninth and final component addresses personal safety and safety skills training. For example, if a child lives in a dangerous neighborhood, the counselor helps the child identify places and times that are safer than others. Other skills include clear and open communication of feelings, trusting gut feelings, identifying people who can offer safety, and asking for help (Cohen et al., 2017, p. 227). Although it is paramount to ensure that the child is safe at the onset of therapy, safety skills training is addressed after the child has shared his or her narrative. If the clinician tries to teach these skills too soon, the child may not want to share the full narrative honestly, especially if the child did not exhibit safety skills during the trauma event (pp. 222–231).

The TF-CBT approach has been very successful with children who have experienced trauma, such as child sexual abuse (Cohen, Deblinger, Mannarino, & Steer, 2004), domestic violence (Cohen, Mannarino, & Iyengar, 2011), war (Cox et al., 2007), and death of a parent (McClatchey, Vonk, & Palardy, 2009).

Cohen et al.'s (2017) TF-CBT was originally intended for individual therapy with bereaved children with parallel sessions with the parent. In the new edition of their book, Cohen et al. (2017) have included a section on using TF-CBT with groups. They provide guidelines for using this intervention with groups: use two therapists, include members of similar ages in the group, and focus on a specific traumatic experience (Cohen et al., 2017, p. 235).

Settings for Delivering Grief Interventions

Individual Therapy

There are pros and cons to using individual interventions with bereaved children and adolescents. The question of individual therapy versus other formats depends on factors such as the age and developmental stage of the child, the functioning of the family unit, and the availability of group and camp options for the child. Individual sessions are preferred when children are so emotionally distraught that they would be disruptive to others if they participated in a group setting. An advantage of individual therapy is the attention that the clinician can give to the child in an individual setting—he or she is the only person that the clinician focuses on. For a child who is shy, or one who is overshadowed by others in the family, the individual setting may be preferred. Many children do better in an individual setting immediately following a loss before they are ready to listen to the pain of other children or family members. When they feel stronger, these children can transfer to a group, camp, or family setting once the shock and denial have subsided.

Individual bereavement therapy with children and adolescents can address a variety of issues. The positive and negative beliefs that have developed out of the trauma of parental death can be discussed and the facts of the death can be clarified. Younger children can be helped to understand and accept the finality of death. Adolescents can clarify their roles and individuation as they blend into the changed family constellation. Older children and adolescents can consider past and future choices and their consequences without the influence of other family members. Other losses—such as pets, grandparents, or friends—that might seem trivial to outsiders, but are important to the young person, called "disenfranchised grief" (Doka, 1989), can be acknowledged. It is not unusual for children and teens to feel guilt over misbehavior prior to a parent's death, and the misconceptions associated with this can be processed. Children and teens can safely vent and relieve anger at the deceased parent and at changes and losses associated with the parent's death. Rolls and Payne (2007) found that bereaved children "who attended individual sessions valued the ability to talk about things *they* were worried about, and to say what they wanted to someone whom they knew would not get upset" (p. 295). Overall the child or adolescent can gain insight into their own understanding of the death as well as the impact this has had on other family members and the family unit.

Several studies have examined the efficacy of individual therapy with bereaved children and adolescents using TF-CBT with positive results. Cohen and her colleagues found that this intervention significantly reduced PTSD and Childhood Traumatic Grief (CTG) symptoms in bereaved children (Cohen, Mannarino, & Knudsen, 2004).

Family Therapy

Family therapy has its roots in the 1950s. Some psychologists and psychiatrists deviated from the psychoanalytic trends of their times to engage the whole family in the treatment of the family member, often a youth, who was the "problem" identified by the family. Among those credited with early promotion of family therapy as a method of working with children's issues are Nathan Ackerman and Murray Bowen, who worked in child therapy; John Bell, a psychologist and professor; and Christian Midelfort, who made one of the first national presentations on family therapy. In the 1960s and 1970s the family therapy movement spread to therapists with varied backgrounds such as social work, counseling, and psychology. Virginia Satir, Murray Bowen, Jay Haley, Salvador Minuchin, and others trained and presented at conferences across the United States and in Europe. They developed individualized theories and techniques that added richness to family therapy methods.

Family therapy views the grieving child as a part of a system of interacting parts. In working with children who have had a parent die, the family equilibrium is seen as seriously disrupted and all parts of the system are seeking new homeostasis. As the counselor and family identify new ways to function and the family incorporates these, the family balance can be restored. Although one child might be the identified client whose problems brought the family into therapy, the family unit and the interactions both within the family and between the family and broader community networks are addressed. Issues include roles taken on by each family member, the hierarchy of power, both open and subtle communication, spoken and unspoken family rules, family secrets, expressed and unexpressed expectations, and inter-family and larger system conflicts. Often support of the child who appears to be most traumatized by the parent's death will uncover strengths and needs in other members of the family, further stabilizing or destabilizing the unit. Triangulation among family members in which some "side with" or more fully support part of the family unit also impacts the ability of the whole family to unite in successful coping. The family system interacts with outside systems such as extended family and schools. Family therapy strives to increase communication, cohesion, and mutual support that improve family connections to help all family members cope with their grief.

Family therapy is goal focused. In the case of grief-focused family therapy the goals include developing supportive communication, acknowledging and correcting unhealthy patterns of relating to each other, and clarifying roles and expectations of various members of the nuclear family. Beyond the nuclear family unit, improving roles and expectations with extended family is often a goal in the aftermath of parental death. Acknowledging the stresses, loss, possible sense of guilt, and sadness of all family members allows the nuclear family to build stronger support systems within the unit and with others. As a newly single parent or a new guardian takes on the responsibility for children, conflicts between the family unit and extended family members are common. Extended family members such as grandparents might be included in the therapy since their roles are often intertwined or enmeshed with others in the family. The support of these outside relatives might be crucial to successfully help children who are dependent on social supports as they deal with their own grief resolution. For troubled adolescents, therapy might be especially enlightening as they deal with needing both the support of their family and the individuation necessary for their developmental stage.

Family therapy is usually a short-term process and traditionally has been conducted by therapists in community clinics or office-based settings. An alternative approach, home-based family therapy, was developed in the 1980s as an option for some families. In this model the therapist works with the family in the home, placing the home environment within the therapeutic milieu. The choice between home-based therapy or more traditional office-based therapy is usually the result of several factors: the referral source for therapy, insurance coverage for therapy, the family's needs, and types of therapy available in the community. Home-based family therapy programs often developed out of the need to work with multi-problem situations such as when there was a possibility that a child might be removed from the family by the child welfare foster care system. Macchi and O'Conner (2010) state,

> Models informing HBFT [home-based family therapy] address five common components relevant to clinical practice in a

family's home. These components include the environment and context, the family's roles and expectations, the therapist's roles and expectations, the therapeutic relationship, and the focus of clinical work.

(p. 445)

Home-based family therapy is often time intensive, meeting more frequently and for longer sessions than office-based therapy. It has the advantage of being more accessible to the family. The therapist carries the burden of travel time and often works irregular hours to meet work and school obligations of family members.

Family therapy has evolved from a variety of theoretical frameworks. Central to these is systems theory. From an ecological point of view, the family, whatever its form, is a system that influences and is influenced by the social systems surrounding it. A change in one family member will result in a change in the family as a whole. These changes also impact the family system as well as the interactions between the family and its environment. When a parent dies, the family is forever changed and a new family emerges. Although differing treatment techniques such as role playing, reframing, and discussing hidden family rules are used based on theoretical training and beliefs of the therapist, the theory of interaction of shifting parts of systems remains. While families will never be the same after a death, families have innate strengths and resilience that provide healing and growth for all.

Groups

Group work with various populations is popular. The documented positive outcomes support the use of group work among people of various ages, educational backgrounds, and diagnoses (Wodarski & Feit, 2012). The group format is also cost effective, allows members to help and support each other, and has the potential to increase the group members' confidence and self-worth (Folgheraiter & Pasini, 2009). One strong reason to use the group format over individual therapy is the opportunity for the group members to learn universality and normalization, i.e., the realization that they are not the only ones experiencing the problem and that personal reactions and feelings are shared (Wodarski & Feit, 2012). Rolls and Payne (2007) reported that "being with other bereaved children was an important aspect for those children who attended a group activity, helping them feel less isolated" (p. 295).

Individual therapy takes into account the dynamics between the client and the clinician. A group format deals with many more dynamics—the dynamics of each individual member with the group leader, but also the dynamics between each group member and other members of the group. In a group, there will be greater cohesiveness between members who are more alike outside the group and who have joined the group for the same reason. This cohesiveness will create more acceptance among members.

Bereavement groups for children and adolescents may be supportive, psycho-educational, or counseling or therapy oriented in nature. A support group does not typically have a professional leader, but consists of people who share a common concern and provide each other with support and encouragement. Psycho-educational groups may or may not be led by a professional and have as goals to mediate educational deficits and provide factual information. They often include skill-building exercises (Corey & Corey, 2002). The counseling group is set apart by being led by a professional clinician who helps typically well-functioning group members grow in some area. For bereaved children and adolescents, using an experienced clinician, who can pick up on both verbal and non-verbal cues and negotiate dynamics between the group members, may be helpful to establish effective communication patterns between the group members.

When deciding to use a group format for work with bereaved children, there are several things to plan. The program needs to consider how long the sessions will be, the group size and format, who to include, how often to meet, when new group members can join, and what activities or interventions will be used. Most group sessions range between 60 and 90 minutes. It may be difficult to keep children's—especially young children's—attention much longer than that. Therefore, it is necessary to make sure that during this time all participants have an opportunity to share if they so desire. Regarding group size, three to four members work well for elementary school children; for middle school children, five to six participants; and for adolescents, six to eight members, which gives everyone a chance to share and to feel a sense of group belonging (Corey & Corey, 2002). It is always a good idea to have a co-facilitator in a children's counseling group. If a child becomes upset to a point of disrupting the other group members, the co-facilitator can temporarily remove that child until he or she is ready to return.

Consideration of group composition is important. With bereavement groups for children and adolescents, this consideration can include the type of death. Groups work best with a commonality among the members. Aside from everyone having lost somebody, there is the decision of whether to lead a group consisting of survivors of suicide, homicide, cancer, or to mix the causes of death. An option is to have a group where there are at least two members representing a cause of death; however, this consideration should not be a deciding factor in creating a group of bereaved children, since mixing losses also works. Another composition variable to consider is age and developmental stage of participants. Although mixing ages can work, developmental stages determine what is or is not meaningful to the group members. It is easiest to have the group members correspond in developmental stage. Mixing children with recent and less recent losses can be beneficial to both sets of children. Those with recent losses can learn from peers further out in the grieving process that life does go on after death and those further out in the grieving process can serve as mentors to those who are grieving more acutely (Lohnes & Kalter, 1994).

Another question arises: Should the group be open or closed? The open group format, which is usually ongoing over a longer period of time, allows a member who is ready to disengage from the group to do so, and another member can be admitted to the group. This format encourages "children and teens to determine their own timing and agenda for expressing their grief" (Schuurman, 2000, p. 171) since they leave a group when they feel ready. An advantage is that the group members get to interact with a larger variety of members. An added advantage is that an "old" member may help a new member, but the disadvantage is that the change in membership may create a lack of camaraderie. These ongoing types of groups may also be cost prohibitive. In the closed-group format, a specific time limit, such as six or eight weeks of weekly meetings, is given and no new members can join. The advantages include opportunities for strong friendships to develop and cost effectiveness. A disadvantage is the lack of change in membership, which can be problematic if members do not get along.

Another consideration for groups of any kind, and in this case bereavement groups for children and teens, is whether to follow a curriculum or simply let the participants guide the process depending on what is happening experientially. A time-limited closed group may be better suited for a curriculum to give the participants education in regard to their grief and tools to cope with it. However, when following a curriculum, it is important to ensure that the person who leads the group is thoroughly trained in the curriculum and is capable of addressing all concerns that may arise during the sessions. In other words, the person needs to be able to go off script and deal with important issues the child or teen may bring to the group on a particular day.

An issue relevant in the group format is confidentiality of all members. It is important to stress to members the importance of keeping confidential any information shared in the group sessions; it is a good idea for the group facilitator to remind group members of this at the end of each session. Of course, as in all cases of counseling, whether individual, family, or group, the members need to know the exceptions to confidentiality.

Most bereavement groups for children and adolescents aim to normalize the grieving process for its participants, provide support, and teach coping skills to aid the grieving process. One of the better-known centers for bereaved children and adolescents, The Dougy Center in Portland, Oregon, started grief groups for children and teens in 1982. The Dougy Center was established in memory of a young man by the name of Dougy Turno, who died as a teenager from a brain tumor (The Dougy Center, 2017). It operates on several guiding principles: grief is a natural reaction to loss, each child has an inner capacity to heal, each child's grief is unique and its duration and intensity is individual, and supportive caring and acceptance helps the child through the process (The Dougy Center, 2004). All bereavement groups for children and teens would do well to follow those principles.

Bereavement Camps

Bereavement camps have become a popular format for assisting bereaved youth through the grieving process. More than 350 such camps are currently operating across North America. They can be a cost-effective way to help a large number of children and adolescents process their grief. The formats of the camps vary, including weeklong and weekend overnight camps as well as weeklong day camps and one-day camps. Many of the camps are run by nonprofit organizations or sponsored by a local or national hospice organization. The majority of the camps are offered free to the children attending or have a cost that is lower than similar recreational camp programs. Most of these camps provide an opportunity for the campers to participate in traditional camp activities, such as canoeing, swimming, hiking, challenge courses, and arts projects. Most also have bereavement-focused activities such as a memorial service and balloon release. The most important opportunity provided by these camps is the ability for campers to meet other children and adolescents who have experienced similar losses and to share their feelings with these peers, who can relate, in a safe and supportive environment.

The overwhelming results of hundreds of post-camp surveys indicate that children and teens find these camps enjoyable and meaningful. In addition, there are benefits for the surviving parents or caregivers. Overnight camps may be more convenient for many caregivers who do not have the time and ability to transfer their children to and from weekly groups or individual therapy. Some camps even provide transportation to the campsite. The free or low-cost nature of bereavement camps opens the possibility of therapeutic intervention to all children, regardless of family financial and health insurance circumstances.

See Chapter 5 and Chapter 6 for a full discussion of bereavement camps.

Special Considerations for Children and Adolescents With Disabilities

Disabilities pose a special challenge to children facing the loss of a parent and those who are helping them deal with grief. Broadly differing abilities in children and adolescents can be placed in two categories: physical disabilities such as Muscular Dystrophy, Cerebral Palsy, Spina Bifida, and other specific limitations; and neurodevelopmental disabilities, such as Autism Spectrum Disorder, intellectual developmental disorders such as Down Syndrome, and learning disorders.

Children and adolescents who are coping with physical disabilities are living with differing abilities. Their abilities such as independent self-care skills need to be respected as camp staff recognize the unique limitations the camper might face. For example, paths to activities at a rustic camp setting might not be easily navigable by some wheelchairs. The camp may adapt activities that are beyond the physical abilities of the camper; for example, several scorekeepers might be used in some physically active games and several children, not only a child with disabilities, might be asked to be scorekeepers. If settings for therapeutic interventions to assist with grief are successfully adapted for the individual with physical challenges, there is no reason to hesitate to invite these youths to join in bereavement groups or camps. In light of the Americans with Disabilities Act, group and camp settings should already meet the accessibility needs of these participants. Activities such as art work or traditional camping activities such as canoeing might call for extra staff and specialized knowledge in order to be fully inclusive. For camps that use a one-on-one buddy program, having the buddy meet with the camper and parent before camp to discuss special needs and situations is recommended. It is important that all staff and volunteers attending the camp have a clear understanding of the camper's needed adaptations, that they are trained in respectful speech and behavior regarding limitations, and that they are aware of any special health and safety issues that pertain to the camper. Planning should include a pre-camp conference call with the parent, the camp medical personnel, the camper's cabin counselors, and the camp director. The camp needs to discuss its program and activities with the camper before camp begins in order to reduce anxiety about physical expectations. Sharing, normalization of grief, and the warmth of understanding peers and staff that are core parts of bereavement camps can benefit all children and adolescents, regardless of their physical limitations.

Providing bereavement services to children and adolescents with neurodevelopmental challenges and integrating them into group or camp settings can provide more of a challenge. Feelings of sadness, confusion, anger, and other normal reactions to the loss of a parent are not restricted to neurotypically functioning youth. Varying levels of cognitive functioning might impact a youth's ability to make sense of death, thus limiting the understanding of death. Working with limitations in receptive cognition and the need for concrete explanations can be difficult for families and therapists, especially considering the vague terms our culture tends to use about death, such as "gone to a better place" and "passed." Although limits of cognitive functioning can call for the use of techniques that might be used with children younger than the chronological age of the group member, it is important to use age-appropriate tools and examples. However, limits in expressive skills might make it difficult for those with neurodevelopmental challenges or other communication dysfunctions to express their grief. Adjustments such as using art for expression can sometimes help in this expression. Overall, it is important to think about activities often used in bereavement camps (e.g., balloon releases and memorial services) and explain their meanings on an individual basis as needed to be grasped by more concrete thinkers.

Special considerations need to be given to include children with mental and emotional differences in camp. Having a volunteer or staff member with training and experience dealing with the specific mental or emotional diagnosis of a camper can open a camp setting to these youth. A sense of personal space, such as receiving a hug, can differ widely for a child on the Autism Spectrum versus a child with Down Syndrome. Emotional or sensory overload might lead to the need for the child or teen to move to a quiet place under adult supervision to restore a sense of calmness and control. Young children under stress often experience regression in developmental skills, and such regression can also be evident in older children or teens who have mental and/or emotional challenges. Especially among adolescents, bedwetting, sleeping disturbances, eating difficulties, and digestive difficulties might be complicated for camp settings to address. Other campers might ostracize campers who express self-stimulation, anger, or emotional outbursts. Such expressions may also interfere with the healing experiences of other campers. One of the main benefits revealed in multiple camp evaluations is the campers' sense that they are not alone, that other children and teens feel the same way they do and can understand their stories. Integration of campers with unique mental processing is a challenge to be carefully considered and undertaken with full awareness of the supports needed to make the experience successful for those campers and for others who interact with them.

Overall, the key to success to provide a bereavement camp experience for a child or adolescent with disabilities is pre-planning. This takes place on several levels. The child and parent need to be involved in helping the camp understand the child's abilities and special needs. The child or adolescent needs to have a level of comfort with the expected experiences of camp and be enthusiastic about attendance. The staff and volunteers need to expect this specific camper and be fully prepared to interact respectfully and to meet any needs that arise. The director needs to review the camp schedule, physical structure, and diet with this camper in mind. Staff members need to pre-arrange any adaptations, even something as simple as a planned quiet space for downtime, and share these with all staff and volunteers. The goal is for each camper, regardless of limitations or special needs, to have a full and meaningful bereavement camp experience, difficult as that may be in practice.

Technology

Children and teens today are tech savvy. It should come as no surprise that many of them turn to technology to deal with their grief. Children and teenagers are ahead of most adults in the navigation of the Internet and social media, such as Facebook, Twitter, text messaging, blogs, Snapchat, and YouTube, although most of these require users to be at least 13 years old. In their book, *Dying, Death, and Grief in an Online Universe: For Counselors and Educators,* Sofka and her colleagues use the term "thanatechnology" to describe "all types of communication technology that can be used in the provision of death education, grief counseling, and thanatology research" (Sofka, Cupit, & Gilbert, 2012, p. 3). There are many ways to use technology and the ways change rapidly. Following are some that were used at the time of the writing of this book, but may be obsolete soon.

Using technology to reach out may be less threatening to some teenagers than reaching out in person. Teenagers may post thoughts on Facebook about a death they have experienced, although several young adults have expressed that Facebook is for "old people." Nevertheless, some teenagers still use Facebook. Facebook pages are usually accessible only to those whom the teenagers have chosen as their "friends." Teenagers will often comment not only on their own Facebook pages about their loss but often also on the deceased relatives' or friends' Facebook pages. Another way teens use technology is Twitter, where short messages can be shared with a more public audience. Many are more apt to use texting, or to send text messages to friends for a more immediate response to thoughts and expressions. Many teenagers state that it was through text messages that they were informed that a friend had died. Another popular way of sharing feelings surrounding the death of a parent or friend is blogging. The teenager can set up a blog account and write about what he or she is experiencing, and anybody who is interested can log in and read the posts.

As mentioned in Chapter 1, there are websites that provide resources for grieving children, teens, and their families, such as those of The Moyer Foundation, The National Alliance for Grieving Children, and Comfort Zone Camp. An additional website is The Dougy Center (2017). Children and teens can also access private email support at kidsaid.com, which is operated by Griefnet.

It is imperative that parents and grief counselors address the need for children and teens to use technology in a safe manner.

They need to understand that many things put on the Internet may be accessed by unintended recipients. There are ways to minimize backlash from postings using social media. The adults in the child's life should make a point to review and explain these with children and teens.

In Summary

A multitude of current practices can be beneficial in helping bereaved children and their families. An assessment of the family's strengths and challenges and the resources available in the community determine which modality and setting is ideal. Some tools, such as art projects, cross over most types of work with children. Often a combination of interventions will be most helpful for a bereaved child, such as family therapy in conjunction with a grief camp experience. Resources available and research into the ways to best help children are constantly being updated, and therapists and intervention programs need to stay current on the latest developments.

Recommended Reading

Cohen, J. A., Mannarino, A. P., & Deblinger, E. (2017). *Treating trauma and traumatic grief in children and adolescents* (2nd ed.). New York, NY: Guilford Press.

Doka, K. J., & Tucci, A. S. (2014). *Living with grief. Helping adolescents cope with loss*. Washington, DC: Hospice Foundation of America.

Richardson, C. (2016). Expressive arts therapy for traumatized children and adolescents: A four-phase model. New York, NY: Routledge.

Webb, N. B. (Ed.). (2010). *Helping bereaved children. A handbook for practitioners* (3rd ed.). New York, NY: Guilford Press.

Worden, J. W. (2008). *Grief counseling and grief therapy. A handbook for the mental health practitioner* (4th ed.). New York, NY: Springer.

References

American Art Therapy Association. (2016). *What is art therapy*. Retrieved from http://arttherapy.org/aata-aboutus/

Association for Play Therapy: United States. (n.d.). *Member search results*. Retrieved from www.a4pt.org/?page=PTUniversities

Beck, A. T. (1967). *Depression: Causes and treatment*. Philadelphia, PA: University of Pennsylvania Press.

Bowlby, J. (1980). *Attachment and loss: Volume III: Loss, sadness and depression*. New York, NY: Basic Books.

Christ, G. H. (2000). Impact of development on children's mourning. *Cancer Practice, 8*(2), 72–81.

Cohen, J. A., Deblinger, E., Mannarino, A. P., & Steer, R. (2004). A multisite, randomized controlled trial for children with abuse-related PTSD symptoms. *Journal of the American Academy of Child & Adolescent Psychiatry, 43*(4), 393–402. doi:10.1097/00004583-200404000-00005

Cohen, J. A., Mannarino, A. P., & Iyengar, S. (2011). Community treatment of posttraumatic stress disorder for children exposed to intimate partner violence. *Archives of Pediatrics & Adolescent Medicine, 165*(1), 16–21.

Cohen, J. A., Mannarino, A. P., & Deblinger, E. (2017). *Treating trauma and traumatic grief in children and adolescents* (2nd ed.). New York, NY: The Guilford Press.

Cohen, J. A., Mannarino, A. P., & Knudsen, K. (2004). Treating childhood traumatic grief: A pilot study. *Journal of the American Academy of Child and Adolescent Psychiatry, 43*, 1225–1233.

Corey, M. S., & Corey, G. (2002). *Groups: Process and practice* (6th ed.). Pacific Grove, CA: Brooks/Cole.

Cox, J., Burlingame, G. M., Katzenbach, R. J., Davies, D. R., Campbell, J. E., & Layne, C. M. (2007). Effectiveness of a trauma/grief-focused group intervention: A qualitative study with war-exposed Bosnian adolescents. *International Journal of Group Psychotherapy, 57*(3), 319–345. doi:10.1521/ijgp.2007.57.3.319

Creed, J., Ruffin, J. E., & Ward, M. (2001). A weekend camp for bereaved siblings. *Cancer Practice, 9*, 176–184.

Davis, C. B. (1989). The use of art therapy and group process with grieving children. *Issues in Comprehensive Pediatric Nursing, 12*(4), 269–280. doi:10.3109/01460868909026834

Desmond, K. J., Kindsvatter, A., Stahl, S., & Smith, H. (2015). Using creative techniques with children who have experienced trauma. *Journal of Creativity in Mental Health, 10*(4), 439–455. doi:10.1080/15401383.2015.1040938

Doka, K. J. (1989). *Disenfranchised grief: Recognizing hidden sorrow*. Lexington, MA: Lexington Books.

Ellis, A. (1957). Rational psychotherapy and individual psychology. *Journal of Individual Psychology, 13*, 38–44.

Folgheraiter, F., & Pasini, A. (2009). Self-help groups and social capital: New directions in welfare policies. *Social Work Education, 28*(3), 253–267. doi:10.1080/02615470802659415

Fox, S. (1988). *Good grief: Helping groups of children when a friend dies*. Boston, MA: The New England Association for the Education of Young Children.

Freud, A. (1926/1946). *The psychoanalytic treatment of children*. London, England: Imago Press.

Freud, S. (1917). *Mourning and melancholia* (1925 translation). Vienna, Austria: Hugo Heller.

Homeyer, L. E., & Morrison, M. O. (2008). Play therapy practice, issues, and trends. *American Journal of Play*, *1*(2), 210–228.

Kaplow, J. B., Layne, C. M., Saltzman, W. R., Cozza, S. J., & Pynoos, R.S. (2013). Using multidimensional grief theory to explore the effects of deployment, reintegration, and death on military youth and families. *Clinical Child and Family Psychology Review*, *16*, 322–340.

Klein, M. (1932/1960). *The psychoanalysis of children*. London, England: Hogarth Press.

Kramer, E. (1972/1993). *Art as therapy with children*. Chicago, IL: Magnolia Streets.

Lohnes, K. L., & Kalter, N. (1994). Preventive intervention groups for parentally bereaved children. *American Journal of Orthospychiatry*, *64*(4), 594–603.

Macchi, C. R., & O'Conner, N. (2010). Common components of home-based family therapy models: The HBFT partnership in Kansas. *Contemporary Family Therapy*, *32*, 444–458. doi:10.1007/s10591-010-9127-1

McClatchey, I. S., Vonk, M. E., & Palardy, G. (2009). Efficacy of a camp-based intervention for childhood traumatic grief. *Research on Social Work Practice*, *19*(1), 19–30.

Naumburg, M. (2015). *Margaret Naumburg papers*. Retrieved from http://dla.library.upenn.edu/dla/ead/ead.html?id=EAD_upenn_rbml_MsColl294

Piaget, J., & Inhelder, B. (1969). *The psychology of the child*. New York, NY: Basic Books.

Play Therapy International. (2008). *Training resources*. Retrieved from www.playtherapy.org/trainresources1.html

Rolls, L., & Payne, S. A. (2007). Children and young people's experience of UK childhood bereavement services. *Mortality*, *12*(3), 281–303.

Ross, N. A. (1999). *Children living with the death of a parent: An exploration of bereaved children's experiences and perception of support and connection*. Thesis/Dissertation, Institute of Transpersonal Psychology, Palo Alto, CA.

Salloum, A., & Vincent, N. J. (1999). Community-based groups for inner city adolescent survivors of homicide victims. *Journal of Child and Adolescent Group Therapy*, *9*(1), 27–45.

Saltzman, W. R., Pynoos, R. S., Layne, C. M., Steinberg, A. M., & Aisenberg, E. (2001). Trauma-and grief-focused intervention for adolescents exposed to community violence: Results of a school-based screening and group treatment protocol. *Group Dynamics: Theory, Research, and Practice*, 5(4), 291–303.

Schuurman, D. L. (2000). The use of groups with grieving children and adolescents. In K. J. Doka (Ed.), *Children, adolescents, and loss: Living with grief* (pp. 165–177). New York, NY: Taylor & Francis.

Sofka, C. J., Cupit, I. N., & Gilbert, K. R. (2012). Thanatechnology as a conduit for living, dying, and grieving in contemporary society. In C. J. Sofka, I. N. Cupit, & K. R. Gilbert (Eds.), *Dying, death, and grief in an online universe: For counselors and educators* (pp. 3–15). New York, NY: Springer.

Spuij, M., Dekovic, M., & Boelen, P. A. (2015). An open trial of 'grief-help': A cognitive-behavioural treatment for prolonged grief in children and adolescents. *Clinical Psychology and Psychotherapy*, 22, 185–192.

The Dougy Center. (2004). *Helping children cope with death*. Portland, OR: Author.

The Dougy Center. (2017). *Mission and history*. Retrieved from www.dougy.org/

van der Kolk, B. A. (2014). *The body keeps the score: Brain, mind and body in the healing of trauma*. New York, NY: Penguin Books.

Webb, N. B. (2011). Play therapy for bereaved children: Adapting strategies to community, school, and home settings. *School Psychology International*, 32(2), 132–143. doi:10.1177/0143034311400832

Wodarski, J. S., & Feit, M. D. (2012). Social group work practice: An evidence-based approach. *Journal of Evidence-Based Social Work*, 9, 414–420.

Wolfelt, A. D. (1996). *Healing the bereaved child: Grief gardening, growth through grief and other touchstones for caregivers*. Fort Collins, CO: Companion.

Worden, J. W. (1991). *Grief counseling and grief therapy: A handbook for the mental health professional*. New York, NY: Springer.

Worden, J. W. (1996). *Children and grief: When a parent dies*. New York, NY: The Guilford Press.

Worden, J. W. (2008). *Grief counseling and grief therapy: A handbook for the mental health professional* (4th ed.). New York, NY: Springer.

4

Nonprofit Organization and Administration

A nonprofit institution's "product is neither a pair of shoes nor an effective regulation. Its product is a changed human being."
—Peter Drucker (1990)

The goal of this chapter is to walk the reader through the development of a successful nonprofit organization with a focus on bereavement camps. The first steps in creating a freestanding camp involve developing a board of directors and establishing the mission of the program. Strategic planning is a form of management that keeps an organization on track. Funding—through grant writing, solicitation of individual donors, solicitation of businesses, and special events—is discussed.

Administrative Structure

Board Development

When forming any nonprofit organization, board development is paramount. Most people who launch nonprofit organizations realize the importance of having a diversified board and including a lawyer, accountant, and marketing professional. But who else? And how many members are needed? Stakeholders are central to the board. For a bereavement camp, this includes an adolescent or now adult who has attended camp, a past attendee of adult group at camp, or an adult who had a parent die when a child or adolescent. It also means having a referral source on the roster. Referral sources for this type of organization would include a school's counselor or a hospice social worker. A college professor also makes a good choice. There are many reasons for this choice. A college professor has access to college students, which is an excellent pool for volunteers. College professors also have access to listserves for grants and many have experience in grant writing. They can retrieve information from GALILEO, a compilation of databases with peer-reviewed journals and books, which is imperative in order to learn about evidence-based practices. Furthermore, college professors have training in research and program evaluation that can be extremely helpful in the program evaluation process.

The Camp MAGIK director is often asked about the importance of affluent board members/donors rather than those with a passion for the cause. Both are important. A primary donor on the roster is vital. Loss and grief are not partial to any age or income bracket. Even wealthy people may have experienced the death of a loved one, such as a parent or sibling, at a young age. These people will most likely have a passion for the cause. However, do not exclude those with passion who do not have financial resources to give to the program. One suggestion for a board composition is to divide members into three categories: *Doers, Diplomats,* and *Donors*. All of these members should have a strong interest in the program. *Doers* are members who have some type of talent useful in running the program. They have passion for the cause but may not have affluence. It could be that they can keep social media active because they are skilled in that area. Others might be adept at logistics and helping organize and structure activities. *Diplomats* are those who are capable of spreading the word about camp, people with connections and influence who can talk about camp at any social event they attend. *Donors'* tasks are self-explanatory, but bear in mind that they may not only donate money but also may make in-kind contributions such as office space, event sites, or meals. Each of the categories has a job description so that the board members know what is expected of them. This model works well not only for bereavement camp organizations but also for other nonprofit organizations.

The other question is how many members are needed on the board. Some states regulate the minimum size of a board of directors, and the IRS may reject nonprofit status to organizations with only one board member. At a minimum a chairman, a secretary, and a treasurer are needed on the board. There are no laws regulating the maximum number of directors. However, a high number, over 12, will mean more input but possibly more dissention. A lower number of directors may mean less input but possibly more efficient decisions. Often an odd number is helpful in order to avoid a tie when members vote on various issues. By-laws need to state what constitutes a quorum for board meetings and what issues need unanimous approval and what issues do not. Finally, the organization needs to make sure board members have diverse backgrounds, including ethnicity.

Mission Statement

A mission statement includes three components: the organization's purpose, its values, and the population served. In the process of writing the mission statement it is helpful to review mission statements of other organizations. The mission statement should be clear, memorable, and concise. Staff should be able to recite it at any time. Some of the best mission statements include no more than 10 to 20 words. Comfort Zone Camp's mission statement is, "Comfort Zone provides grieving children with a voice, a place and a community in which to heal, grow and lead more fulfilling lives" (Comfort Zone Camp, 2016, p. 1). In 23 words, it provides the purpose ("to provide a voice, a place and a community to heal"), its value ("fulfilling lives"), and the population it serves ("grieving children"). Camp MAGIK's mission statement is expressed in 15 words: "Where bereaved children and their caregivers begin to heal in a safe and nurturing environment" (Camp MAGIK, n.d., para. 2). The purpose is "to heal," the value lies in being "safe and nurturing," and the population served is "bereaved children and their caregivers." These two camps concentrate on grieving children. Camp Erin's mission is based on The Moyer Foundation's mission statement and is composed of 14 words: "To provide comfort, hope and healing to children affected by loss and family addiction" (Moyer Foundation, n.d., p. 1). Here the purpose is clear (providing "comfort, hope, and healing") and the values are the same (comfort and hope). However, the population is broader: children who have been "affected by loss," which could include any type of loss, as well as "family addiction." If this organization wants to expand to serving children who have had a loss other than death, such as an incarcerated parent, it can do so without changing its mission statement.

The organization needs to set measurable, time-limited goals that flow from the mission statement and compel actions that will drive the evaluation of the camp. Some camps list their goals on their website, others do not. Camp MAGIK has the following goals: "Participants will feel supported, will be able to normalize feelings surrounding their loss, will have healthy coping skills, and will experience less distress surrounding the death" (Camp MAGIK, para. 3). So, when evaluating this camp, these are the factors that need to be held to account. For a proper evaluation, these variables need to be operationalized into measurable terms. For example, an instrument can be used to gauge perceived support at camp. Another instrument can be developed to measure knowledge about certain feelings that are part of the natural grieving process, while another can be devised to ascertain the coping skills that campers learned to use when experiencing certain feelings, and another for changes in various stress levels after camp. Chapter 7 explains evaluation of camp in more detail.

Strategic Planning

Planning strategically is important for the early development of a small nonprofit organization such as a grief camp program. A formal or informal needs assessment leads prospective founders to believe that a program is needed, to evaluate the possibilities of securing ongoing funding, to create a board, and to write a mission statement. Beyond the beginning stages of development, many for-profit and nonprofit organizations use strategic planning to maintain the organization's focus, direct changes in activities or mission, and plan for needed funding. The SWOT (Strengths, Weakness, Opportunities, and Threats) model of organizational review has been used for many years by a variety of organizations. However, most bereavement camps and other small nonprofits would probably also benefit from a more individualized approach, looking at the needs of their campers, the demographics of their community, and the resources that might become available to provide for camps.

Once a camp organization has been established, the board holds strategic planning meetings annually and invites key staff, intensively involved volunteers if available, reliable established funders if these exist, and all board members. The board may also invite past program participants as these become available. This is a time to examine what the program has accomplished in the past year and over a longer span of its history as the agency ages. With this information, participants can evaluate possible change and growth. Although large corporations and organizations might need strategic planning meetings annually, small bereavement camps are not likely to experience change or growth at a rapid rate. A small program that runs one or two camps a year might address planning and changes through board and director input and hold formal strategic planning bi-annually.

Funding

There are two central elements in funding a program such as a children's bereavement camp. First is a succinct and passionate description of the program and needs. Second is a dynamic marketing plan that can meet financial needs while responding to the changing environment of possible funders. An Internet presence, written materials such as brochures or business cards, and prepared verbal information all need to reflect the program's mission, uniqueness, and location.

The Elevator Speech

Be prepared to share both written information, such as brochures and business cards, and verbal information about camp. An "elevator speech" is the briefest of prepared verbal presentations. This often-used term indicates the length of time that the presentation should last: approximately the 30 seconds that one might have if faced with a curious potential donor on an elevator ride. Although an elevator speech is specially prepared to represent a specific organization, the central elements are usually the same. These include the organization's mission and that the camp is free for all children. Include why the community needs the program. For example, mention local rates of parental death and how the children who attend camp benefit. Bereavement camps have an advantage over many programs. In a brief sentence or two, a camp representative can present an example, in a memorable way, of a child who could benefit from the program, using an anonymous composite story such as "Children who come to camp might be like the 8-year-old whose mother and grandmother were killed in an automobile accident, or the teenager who cared for her mother as she died of breast cancer. These children find a way to express their grief to others who really understand. It helps them move on to re-focus on succeeding in life. Our camp is free of charge and relies on community donations." Followed with a brochure and business card, the elevator speech gives potential donors enough to remember and to reach back later for information on how they can help. Finally, in thinking about an elevator speech, practice out loud with sympathetic but honest friends and board members. This cements the details of what needs to be said in a way that will make the speech possible and natural.

Marketing Materials and Public Relations

Telling the program's story is an important part of fundraising. Marketing materials such as a camp logo, brochures, business cards, and a website are classic aspects of organizational identity. The camp website identifies the mission and can convey the emotions that surround parental death, plus the impact that camp has.

A marketing plan is a combination of a clear set of goals and a flexible plan that can respond to opportunities when they arise. Often the skills and availability of staff and board members will circumscribe the extent of a marketing plan. The plan might include both advertising and fundraising ideas for the coming year and indications of who will be responsible, what the goals are, and when they will be met. The audience and purpose of the plan should be considered, since grieving families, camper referral sources, and funders are recipients of marketing efforts. Marketing plans set goals that can be reviewed at board meetings. Having a plan helps guide and motivate an organization to strive towards the goals it sets.

Local newspapers, television, radio, and magazines can carry local interest and feature stories. Often by identifying television or radio talk shows that feature local organizations, the program director can make successful approaches to have the camp presented. Civic organizations need speakers every week and often welcome representatives from local organizations. Letters to the Editor and community announcement columns are free publicity as well. Board members and staff often have original ideas of how to get information about the program into the local community.

Grant Writing

When applying for grants, consider joining forces with another regional organization that also works with bereaved children. Grantors love collaboration among organizations because this often helps reach and impact more bereaved children.

There are several different types of grants, which can be put into two categories: private foundations and government grants. Private foundation grants are the ones that small organizations will most likely pursue unless a large federal or state grant is of interest. Private foundation grants are divided into four types: 1) national general-purpose foundations, 2) special-purpose foundations, 3) community foundations, and 4) family foundations. The first two are national. National general-purpose foundations look for models and innovations; examples of these are The Rockefeller Foundation and the Ford Foundation (Bauer, 2011, pp. 236–240). These usually have a broad range of projects they fund, and they give away millions of dollars each year. Special-purpose foundations have a limited focus and the organizational interests must match grantor interests; examples of these are the New York Life Foundation and the Annie E. Casey Foundation. Community foundations serve the community where they are located. They provide funds for operations, buildings, equipment, and board development, as well as actual program funding. Family foundations are usually local. Look at their mission statement to become familiar with their interests. In some cases a family foundation has been set up only to fund one or two pre-identified programs.

In addition to government and private foundation grants, local service clubs, such as Kiwanis and Rotary, make grants for projects that align with their missions. Grants from community foundations, family foundations, and service organizations are usually small, in the range of $1,000 to $10,000. When applying for a small grant, the application needs to assure the grantor that the organization will have adequate resources to make the program successful.

When searching for a grant opportunity, first ensure that the mission of the granting organization matches the program. Once a match is found, research the foundation. Discover who the board members are. Often grants from a foundation will go to the board members' favorite nonprofit organizations, which are usually led by people they know and reflect foundation board members' passions. If a board member is known, contact him or her to discover the board's agenda and needs—then discuss the program's needs and abilities to help them with that agenda. Ask about the likelihood of the proposal being accepted. There is no need to submit a proposal if a board member says it is of no interest. If board members are not known, find someone who can make contact with a board member. It is imperative to contact the funding agency in some way to determine its agenda and interests.

Learn how to locate grants. If you are looking for a federal grant, search Grants.gov (at www.grants.gov) using key words. Key words for a bereavement camp might be "bereavement," "education," or "youth services." Applying for federal grants is a long and tedious process. A good federal grant proposal cannot be written in a few weeks. Creating a federal proposal often takes two months or more and a team of three or four people. If a good project matches a current federal funding area, and if the organization's project needs that level of funding, find the manpower and time to submit an application. It is imperative to contact the listed contact person for the grant to discuss the proposal before deciding to apply. Often federal grant administrators will have a pre-submission meeting by teleconference of all applicants wanting to submit; this meeting will clarify many areas of the grant and application process. Also, federal grant proposals usually require collaboration and regional planning, necessitating an investment of time and energy to create this collaboration. One point to consider when discovering an area of interest covered by a federal grant: Themes often repeat themselves for several years in a funding stream. If the nonprofit program is unable to meet the time line for a grant, it is usually worth exploring when the next grant funding cycle will be and working with cooperating agencies to submit a collaborative proposal.

When looking for a private foundation grant, use a Foundation Center office if available. Foundation Center offices are located in New York City; Washington, DC; Atlanta, Georgia; San Francisco, California; and Cleveland, Ohio (Foundation Center, 2017). Foundation Center offices allow for research of grant opportunities through the Foundation Directory Online free for a limited period of time. In the Directory, data indicate granting foundations, board members, fields of interest, geographical limitations, contact information, names of decision makers, previous grantees, size of grants, and sample grants. The Directory also provides the foundation's financial data. These data disclose amounts of yearly endowments. According to the Internal Revenue Service's tax laws for foundations, foundations must distribute 5% of their investment returns per year for designated recipients (IRS Part 7, Chapter 27, Section 16).

Most universities subscribe to the Foundation Directory Online, and professors should be able to access it as a resource for the organization. Some university librarians will assist with this search based on your residency in the university's area. Another source of grant information is the individual foundation's website; however, note that most small local foundations do not maintain a website or office. It may be worthwhile for the program director to contact programs in the organization's geographic area that have been funded in the past to discuss their insights into their funders. Make sure to support the worthwhile services in your area, and not to steal reliable funding from another program by competing for grants from the same foundations. Many foundations limit the number of consecutive years that they will support a program, so there is room for a newcomer to enter the funding stream at some point.

Read and follow carefully all of the information in the grant application. This is especially important in a large grant application, such as for as a federal grant. Critical information is likely to be missed if you do not read every word of the "Request for Proposals" or other documents. If the funding organization has a format for applying for grants, follow all instructions carefully. Funding organizations have established the format for a reason and do not want variations.

Letter of Proposal

If the grantor is simply asking for a proposal of four to five pages or a Letter of Interest of one to two pages, there is a formula that will provide an application edge. Five components are needed for the proposal (Bauer, 2011): assessment of the community need for the program, specific unique solution to the problem, unique qualifications as the best organization to solve the problem, budget for carrying out the solution, and planned evaluation to show accomplishments. (See Appendix A for a sample Letter of Proposal.)

1. An assessment of the community need for the program informs the funding agency of the service needs of the population. Why are you doing the work? What is the problem to be addressed? This assessment has six points that need addressing (Bauer, 2011):
    a. Describe the problem or need that the agency addresses. This often includes statistics and concrete data. For bereavement camps, this includes the number of children

and adolescents who lose a family member to death nationally in a year, followed by local numbers. If the number is higher locally than the national statistic, highlight that statistic.

b. Describe how this loss affects children and teens. There is good research on the detrimental effects of losing a parent. Cite the sources.

c. Tell the funding source what is available in the area—presumably there is very little available for bereaved children, which makes the program stand out.

d. Present the difference between the need and current resources. For example, if all children need support services to help with their grief, that is what is needed, but if there are not enough resources available to support grieving children, that is what is lacking in current resources. It is helpful to have a key informant (somebody who works with bereaved children and teens, or some other kind of expert, including someone who lost a parent during childhood) to provide a quote that can be used to describe this gap.

e. Describe the impact of lack of immediate attention to the problem. What is the urgency? Will children and teens in the area suffer needlessly? Will they experience depression, low self-esteem, school failure, or other problems because there are too few resources (use the effects you found when researching 1b)?

f. Conclude the needs assessment with the proposed change in the situation that has just been described.

2. Your unique solution to the problem needs to include objectives and outcomes. Before formulating these, consider the area of improvement to be addressed, the indicator of this problem, the expected level of change, the time frame, and the cost. For example, an objective/outcome could be: To improve participating children's mental health (problem needing improvement) by reducing PTSD symptoms (indicator) by 50% (level of change) in two months (time frame) at a cost of approximately $250 per child (cost). Then describe who will do what, when, and where.

3. The program's unique nature will explain to the funding source why their help is needed. It is not enough just to say that "we are the only organization in the area to help bereaved children." Instead, include how the organization's

qualifications are ideal to provide these services. Speak to the education and experience of the staff and how the board and staff are composed. The funder will require that the board and staff be diverse.

4. When creating a budget, check and double-check your numbers to ensure accuracy. If there are any errors, the grantor is unlikely to trust that the program can handle its money correctly. The listed projected expenses need to match exactly the listed projected income. A nonprofit's projected income should not be higher than projected expenses.

    If the grantor is asking for matching funds, i.e., that the program provide funds to help cover the proposed budget, these may include things already paid for, such as salaries and other overhead. When calculating in-kind resources, remember volunteers. Translate what volunteers do into money amounts. Track actual matching money or in-kind values carefully. Be prepared to show how the program spent the matching dollars. Failing to do this opens the possibility of reimbursing the grantor the unmatched amount, guaranteeing that the grantor will not work with the program again.

5. The grantor may want to see evaluation tools and to be assured that the end assessment will actually happen. There are several ways to evaluate objectives. For more information on this topic, see Chapter 7.

Logic Model

Many grantors today ask for a logic model, which is a free-standing document that concisely describes the proposal in a flow chart format. The logic model includes the problem, goals, input, throughput, output, outcome, and impact. Input includes everything that goes into the program, such as a campsite, volunteers, food, and money. Throughput denotes activities such as counseling, ropes course, balloon release, etc. Output denotes a number, e.g., how many campers will go through the program in a year (or other time frame), or how many hours the campers spend in the program per year. Outcome is the desired effect of or change due to camp, and how many campers will reach this outcome, e.g., 25 campers will have PTSD symptoms reduced by 50%. While the outcome reflects the effect the camp will have on its participants, impact speaks to the effect that the outcome will have not only on participants but also the community at large. (See Appendix B for a sample logic model.)

Important Considerations

There are several critical points to consider when applying for a grant. Attention to detail is necessary for success. Most importantly, submit by the deadline. Use shipping service with a tracking system if the grant is not submitted online. If the application is completed online, do a trial submission to yourself beforehand to make sure it appears as it should when it arrives in the grantor's inbox. Follow the guidelines exactly. Fill in all the blanks even if the question was previously answered. Be sure spelling and calculations are correct. Ensure that all the information the grantor requests is provided. Taking care of these details demonstrates responsibility and encourages trust with any funds the grantor might be willing to give. As much as possible, make the proposal visually attractive. A cluttered page with several different fonts is annoying. The grantor may ask you to use a specific font; if so, follow instructions (Bauer, 2011).

The four most important factors in submitting a grant proposal are: a match of the applicant's mission with that of the funding agency, a persuasive needs assessment, programmatic uniqueness in accomplishing the project, and personal contact with those responsible for awarding the funds. When applying for a grant, ensure several things. Look for the funding agency's agenda. The program director may need to communicate with somebody from the grantor's staff or board to find out. Then tailor the request to the grantor's agenda. Frame the application for each grantor; do not copy an application to one agency to send to another. Do not apply for a grant at the last minute—it will most likely be sloppily done and give the grantor the impression that you are irresponsible. Remember that almost all grants are offered for more than one year. Although a grantor's focus might change, the organization is better off looking for a grant in the next grant cycle or future deadline than rushing to meet a last-minute deadline and creating a poor impression with the grantor. Use a person who is not familiar with the program to review the application for meaning and clarity and to search for careless mistakes. Bauer (2011) has one more suggestion: Instead of asking the granting agency to "give" you money, ask them to "invest" in the population you serve, e.g., "We ask you to invest in bereaved children's healthy future."

If the organization follows these suggestions, and the proposal is still rejected, thank the grantor for reviewing the proposal, then ask for suggestions to improve on the application next time. Often grantors will be looking for applications from programs that were not funded in the past year in order to share their influence with many different programs in the community. In conclusion, grant writing has been referred to as an art, but success comes from per- severance and careful planning and writing.

Soliciting Individual Donors and Businesses

Many individuals who run wonderful nonprofit organizations have difficulty with "the ask"—actually asking an individual donor to support that program. People may say "no" to a request for fund- ing, but without asking, the camp representative will never know if a prospective donor will say "yes." Keep a positive attitude and remember that the children and families that the camp serves are worth every effort. There are several key points in asking for money or in-kind donations for the program. First, be enthusiastic about the benefits of camp for the children and adolescents served; clearly express these benefits. Second, and equally important, in both indi- vidual giving and when approaching businesses or grant makers, know the audience. People, businesses, and foundations all give to programs that align with their interests. Be clear about the pro- gram's needs. If the organization is asking for a small donation in a large budget, it needs to be prepared to explain how it will raise funds for the rest of the money needed so that the donor knows the money will be spent on a quality camp. Share all successes. Donors give to organizations that have a track record and have shown the potential to accomplish what they propose. Like the benefit of prac- ticing the elevator speech described earlier in this chapter, practic- ing the "ask" can help with a sense of being in control and focused when approaching donors.

Partners in funding can be found in all types of organizations. For example, many banks, utility companies, pharmacies, national and local retailers, and even hospitals have foundations or giving programs that support local organizations. Sometimes these favor organizations where their own staff can volunteer. Friends and board members often work at businesses sponsoring charitable groups, and these people can open the door to explain the program. Major partnership funders such as hospices and hospitals have become primary sources covering the cost of some bereavement camp pro- grams. Such organizations might also provide assistance in apply- ing for grants in the local community. If the camp is not a hospice program and has never approached the local hospice organizations, this is a valuable resource to explore. When partnering for funding, be aware that major funders will expect to be recognized on the grantee's website and in other ways. Be careful that the partnering funders reflect the program's values and those of the families served.

Special Events and Other Forms of Fundraising

Although fundraising is crucial to the success of any program, care needs to be taken in thinking about raising money in the community. Solicitations, asking for donations, and special events can be either created by the organization or created on its behalf. Although the same activities might fall into both categories, they are presented here separately.

Organizations need to evaluate several considerations before they create fundraising events. These are discussed here with thoughts on the impact on program, community perception, replication, and sustainability. Fundraising events require the work of a committed team to invest appropriate time and energy without distracting from the mission of the organization. In a small organization with a part-time or volunteer staff, the director should be focused on the value of the program to the children and families in the community. Board members or other volunteers need to take on the primary roles in organizing fundraising events. Although funders will want to meet the head of an organization, it is important that the community view the director as interested in more than fundraising. In addition, organizations must carefully consider the finances of a fundraising event. Standard bearers in community funding, such as the United Way, have strict guidelines for the percentage of an organization's budget that can be used for fundraising. An exposé on funds raised going to purposes other than the organization's mission can be devastating.

In the context of the commitment of both staff time and funding described, create fundraising efforts that can be duplicated year after year. Organizations can considerably reduce the time and effort needed to create an idea, make the connections, and address the logistics of a fundraising event by successfully replicating an event or funding campaign. In addition, the organization gains name recognition by repeated exposure. Members of the community come to expect to support an event that returns on an annual basis. Well-known examples of this are the annual Girl Scout cookie sale and the sale of holiday gift wrapping paper at local elementary schools.

A golf tournament, a reception at a local historical home, or a holiday dinner and auction might become an event identified with your bereavement camp.

The setting, partnerships, sponsorships, and type of fundraising event need to reflect the character of the organization as well as the pool of potential donors. Since these might differ, the directors of programs and the board need to use their judgment in decision making so that sponsors reflect the values of a family and child-focused organization.

Programs may solicit organizational fundraisers in their community or fundraising events may spontaneously arise outside of the organization. Past clients, board members, volunteers, friends of campers, friends of their families, and community members who know about the program only from a local newspaper or magazine may unexpectedly come forward with a fund-raising event or community-raised donation. Some homeowners' organizations, women's clubs, and similar community groups take an interest in their community and seek to support worthwhile programs. In one example of unexpected community support, a fourth-grade teacher whose class had held an entrepreneur day, where students made things to sell to parents and friends, approached a camp. An aspect of the lesson was to donate part of the proceeds to a charity. The students searched online and found a local bereavement camp that one of the students had attended. The donation of more than $1,500 from this school's fourth-grade class has become an annual event. Bereavement camps can easily be perceived as warmhearted and worthy of support. New relationships can grow into annual and regular sources of income. If the community organizations surrounding the program do not know of the need for ongoing funding, or do not know details of the services provided, the board has the opportunity to reach out with this information.

Community Involvement and Partnerships

It is imperative to create community partnerships for camp to be sustained over the years. This is accomplished in the areas of fundraising, camp participation, volunteer recruitment, art supplies, food, and recreational activities. There are many ways to partner with community organizations to raise money for camp. Restaurants and vendors may be happy to donate gift cards or in-kind products to be used as silent auction or raffle prizes at fundraising events. Tax laws vary from state to state, but many allow a double deduction of in-kind donations. Some restaurants will dedicate certain days to a charity by donating a proportion of their proceeds for the day to this charity. Other organizations will donate items such as T-shirts or bags in exchange for having their organization's name printed on the merchandise.

There are several reasons for partnering with a university. These include access to GALILEO, a research database, access to experienced grant writers and program evaluators, access to student volunteers, and access to listserves of available grants.

Camper recruitment is another area requiring community partnerships. Schools are obviously the place where children spend most of their time, and school social workers and school counselors are invaluable resources in identifying prospective campers. In most cases they would know what student has lost a parent or sibling, and they are able to assess children who may need intervention. One way to build relationships with school social workers and counselors is to attend their annual conferences and to offer to speak at these. Thanks to the Internet and email, it is easy to communicate with local schools. Most schools have their own websites that list the staff, including the school's counselor or social worker.

At some camps participants create memory pillows and/or other artwork in remembrance of their lost ones. A church sewing group, which might donate not only their time sewing the pillow cases, but also the material (cloth, yarn, etc.), is an excellent and important partner. Local arts and crafts shops can often donate art materials, such as fabric markers, stencils, and stamps. If the campsite allows purchased food to be brought in, other partnerships may include restaurants in the area that are willing to donate or sell food at cost.

A unique partnership can be created with a local Kaiser Permanente Educational Theatre Group (KPETG). KPETG is a nonprofit entity of Kaiser Permanente and is strongly committed to good health. KPETG has several shows in its repertoire that professional actors perform in an effort to support physical health, after-school safety, coping skills, and similar issues. When Camp MAGIK began, it needed a puppet show for the younger campers. The local KPETG artistic director, Bett Potazek, was intrigued by the request and the Camp MAGIK program, but KPETG did not have educational puppet shows related to grief. It did have one related to healthy eating, however, so Mr. Body Wise came to visit Camp MAGIK in the fall of 1996. He was a great success, but did not address grief. Together Ms. Potazek of KPETG and the Camp MAGIK director decided to create a puppet show geared towards bereaved children. The camp director provided Ms. Potazek with the content needed in the show, and Ms. Potazek created "Uncle Gherkin's Magical Show," which follows Pickle and Relish after Uncle Gherkin dies. After camp organizers introduced Uncle Gherkin's Magical Show to its participants, it became clear that the older campers needed a similar show. Ms. Potazek received materials on the struggles that teenagers often experience when grieving, and subsequently created "Fragments of Grief," which follows two teenagers, Heather and Andrew. Heather lost her mother to a car accident, and Andrew his brother to murder. Both shows serve to identify and normalize feelings for the two groups of campers in a non-threatening, sad, and uplifting way. KPETG provides professional actors for both shows as well as all the props. Camps in other areas can create similar partnerships with theatre groups.

To relate to the community, the camp program must have a well-designed website. It should present the history of the organization and list the members of the board of directors. Critical components of a website include the email and telephone contact options. With an awareness that websites are viewed from all over the world, it is imperative that the location is clearly displayed on the home page. It is of interest to note that many programs described on the Internet fail to make clear the geographic service area for their program. Some do not provide an email contact person. Programs need to include information about costs and the application process, plus provide a description of camp activities. The organization needs to make access to services easy, such as providing application forms that can be submitted through the site. Websites sometimes include endorsements of former campers or summaries of program evaluations. If the organization uses quotations and client pictures, proper permission must be obtained. It is helpful to have an unfamiliar viewer periodically review the site to ensure it is well done and clear.

In Summary

The successful management of a nonprofit organization takes planning, collaboration, and ongoing fundraising. A program is defined by its mission statement, and all activities should grow out of this statement. In a bereavement camp program, board members, funders, and other community stakeholders need to share a passion for helping youth who have suffered from the death of a loved one.

Leadership must aim for quality in all aspects of the work, from the impression that the organization presents to the community to the ability to provide quality services to those they seek to help.

Recommended Reading

Bauer, D. G. (2011). *The "how to" grant manual. Successful grantseeking techniques for obtaining public and private grants* (8th ed.). Westport, CT: Praeger.

Worth, M. J. (2017). *Nonprofit management: Principles and practice* (4th ed.). Thousand Oaks, CA: Sage.

References

Bauer, D. G. (2011). *The "how to" grant manual. Successful grantseeking techniques for obtaining public and private grants* (8th ed.). Westport, CT: Praeger.

Camp MAGIK. (n.d.). *About camp MAGIK*. Retrieved from camp-magik.org/overview.html

Comfort Zone Camps. (2016). Retrieved from www.comfortzonecamp.org/

Drucker, P. F. (1990). *Managing the non-profit organization: Principles and practice*. New York, NY: Harper Collins.

Foundation Center. (2017). Retrieved from http://foundationcenter.org/

Moyer Foundation. (n.d.). Retrieved from https://moyerfoundation.org

5

Critical Components of Camp

When we send the message to children that they should not talk about their grief, we are really saying, "don't make me think about it." When children talk about their grief, it makes us feel uncomfortable, sad, and, most of all, helpless. Keeping our children from talking about their losses saves us from our own pain and discomfort. The implicit message children receive is that no one cares about their loss and that they are utterly alone in their grief.
—Fiorini and Mullen (2006)

The goal of this chapter is to walk the reader through important steps to take when conducting a camp. First, the camp organization needs to decide what camp modality and model to base its program on. Next, the organization needs to decide upon a series of critical components of camp, including site selection; insurance coverage; volunteer recruitment, selection, screening, and training; medical staff; and transportation. The chapter discusses ways to recruit campers, and work needed before, during, and after camp. Each section is followed by a discussion of the Camp MAGIK process of the various tasks of developing and running a camp.

Choice of Camp Modality and Model

There are several different formats for healing camps that serve bereaved children, including day camps of different length, weekend camps, and weeklong camps. The most common appears to be the three-day/two-night weekend camp. Children arrive on a Friday afternoon and stay through Sunday afternoon. There are advantages and disadvantages to all of the structures. Weeklong camps may serve to create stronger bonds among the campers but are expensive to put on. Another concern with weeklong camps is the location. Weeklong camps would have to occur in the summer or during various breaks when children and adolescents are off from school. However, campsites often have their own programs during the summer, and this may present a challenge in finding a location. Also, it may be difficult to find volunteers that are available for a weeklong overnight camp. To create continuity, a camp would want the same staff and volunteers through the week. Day camps miss the opportunity for bonding among campers that occurs by spending the night away from home with only new friends for support. However, using the day camp modality may make it easier to find staff and volunteers. Weekend camps may not create as much bonding as weeklong camps but do offer more bonding opportunities than the day camps.

Camps follow various models—there are recreational bereavement camps, psycho-educational camps, and therapy camps, and those that are a mix of these. Recreational camps have a play agenda where campers bond and support each other through the different activities. Psycho-educational camps have volunteers or professionals who help educate the campers on natural grief reactions and teach coping skills. At therapy camps, professional grief counselors lead small groups of campers who discuss their grief and other emotional issues with each other. Recreational and psycho-educational camps may use only one professional grief counselor for emotional issues that may arise. Small group sessions may be led by trained volunteers. Therapy camps usually divide their campers into smaller counseling groups of 6–8 campers by age, with one professional grief counselor per group leading the groups together with co-counselors. Is the goal to provide support? Education? Or is the aim to assist children and adolescents to sort out deeper feelings of trauma that need professional assistance? The mission of your work would be the guide and the choice of model is partly based on your resources. Can the program hire professionals? If the program needs to depend on volunteers, are there enough professionals who will give their time?

Is the program goal to get bereaved youth together to have fun, participate in grief activities, and learn coping skills, or is there more? Additionally, considering staffing of any camp, therapeutic and medical professionals need to be available if children react to activities with unexpected emotional or physical responses.

Camp MAGIK decided from the start to provide a therapy-oriented camp for its campers. There was very little research on or evaluations of bereavement camps, so the camp director began evaluating Camp MAGIK's therapy-related activities in order to adapt them as needed. Professionals lead groups of 6–8 campers. The camp agenda originally consisted of grief activities such as sharing the story, identifying feelings, writing letters to the deceased, a memorial service, and a balloon release. A discussion with a children's organization in Virginia working with children who had experienced the 9/11 attack at the Pentagon led the camp director to wonder if campers in her state might have PTSD symptoms. If so, was camp reducing PTSD symptoms among campers? Using the Revised Impact of Events Scale by Horowitz and his colleagues (Children and War Foundation, 1998) counselors pre- and post-tested campers on PTSD symptoms. To the dismay of the camp director, the posttests showed an increase in PTSD symptoms. The change was not at a statistically significant level, but this was still an alarming discovery (Searles, 2004). The camp director speculated that providing grief interventions to children who may have PTSD symptoms could increase PTSD symptoms by stirring trauma without addressing it. Furthermore, research indicated that trauma symptoms prevented bereaved children from processing their grief (Cohen & Mannarino, 2004). Subsequent research on Camp MAGIK focusing on the subject of PTSD validated this (McClatchey, Vonk, & Palardy, 2009). Because of the findings, the camp director decided to implement trauma interventions. This was not difficult to do with some rearranging of the schedule. Further research led to a camp model based on the work of Pynoos, Steinberg, and Wraith (1995), Wolfelt (1996), and Worden (1991), and some years later Cohen, Mannarino, & Deblinger (2006).

Camp MAGIK has been evaluated in regards to PTSD and Childhood Traumatic Grief (CTG) symptoms (McClatchey et al., 2009), acting-out behavior (McClatchey & Peters, 2015), and posttraumatic growth (PTG) (McClatchey, in press; McClatchey & Raven, 2017) in quantitative studies. This camp model has also been evaluated in qualitative studies (McClatchey & Wimmer, 2012, 2014; McClatchey, 2017). The results have all been positive.

It is important to note that to proceed with a therapy camp such as Camp MAGIK, professional grief counselors trained in grief-informed and trauma-informed work must be employed. Although there is a script for the various sessions, inevitably something will be said by campers that needs immediate and professional attention. It is crucial that campers are protected by counselors' knowledge and training.

Camp Components

Although camps follow various curricula, there are similarities in various components of preparing for camp and various components of executing any camp. Several policies are needed for all camps. These include staff respect for confidentiality and a non-discrimination statement that will apply to campers, their families, staff, and volunteers. There are several categories to include: gender, cultural or ethnic background, spiritual or religious beliefs, sexual orientation, and national origin. In addition, policies are needed for emergency situations and for critical incidents. For example, at Camp MAGIK, if a child has suicidal thoughts but is not actively suicidal and has no means, the director will contact the camper's family to ask if they would like to pick the child up or if they would like for the child to stay at camp until its conclusion. If the child is staying, he or she is watched under 24-hour supervision by camp counselors. With such campers intensive follow-up including the provision of low-cost referrals occurs first thing on Monday morning after camp ends. Another emergency situation would be if signs of abuse or neglect are detected. In this case Camp MAGIK policy directs volunteers and counselors to report the observations to the camp director. The camp director then reports the suspicions to the appropriate state authorities immediately upon opening time on Monday morning and informs the family of the suspicions and of the obligation to share the information with authorities.

Campsite Selection

A campsite that suits the program's needs has to be secured well in advance of the program execution. Often the availability of a site determines the dates of the camp session. Bereavement camp staff needs to visit prospective sites before making a decision. Not only must the site satisfy program needs physically, but also the camp program needs to develop a good working relationship with site management. Camp MAGIK requires comfortable sleeping cabins for campers, staff, and volunteers; a place for a clinic for the medical staff (some campsites have those, while others need a bit of improvisation); a lodge for meals and meetings for the whole group (e.g., for opening and closing ceremonies); canoeing; and a ropes course. Camp MAGIK insists that the camp facility provide the staff everything that is necessary to use standard services such as the ropes course, in addition to a lifeguard for water activities and an instructor for archery. All instructors, whether from the campsite or hired independently, must have proper training and verified credentials. The site must also have a kitchen facility with staff that can provide nutritious and desirable meals for everyone, or at least have a kitchen that can be used by a catering business. Two of Camp MAGIK's current campsites cook the food for us; at other sites we bring in a caterer. Meal preparation must take special needs and allergies into consideration, and Camp MAGIK adheres to the practice that if a camper is allergic to peanuts or seafood none of these are served or prepared in the kitchen during the visit.

Bereavement camp staff need to evaluate the safety of the site before campers arrive. Areas of concern are functioning smoke detectors, entrance to the site by unauthorized intruders, wild animals, natural hazards such as streams and lakes, adequacy of safety items such as fire extinguishers and life jackets, and local car or boat traffic. Emergency procedures for the campsite, such as fire evacuation, should be written and clearly posted. Program staff must also consider appropriate access for campers or staff with disabilities. Membership in the American Camp Association, or similar accreditation, reflects a level of confidence in the facility itself.

Include in the decision-making process access to the nearest emergency room. In case of an emergency involving transportation of a camper for medical attention, all staff and volunteers will want to know the emergency room location and its contact information.

Camp directors must read contracts carefully. Camp MAGIK was surprised at one camp during its first visit to find that bereavement camp staff were asked to sweep the floor in the dining hall after each meal. However, when the camp director looked at the contract, this was stated in the fine print. It was a valuable lesson. In addition, ensure knowledge of the site's cancellation policy. Camp MAGIK has never had to cancel a camp session, but it is important to be prepared if the need arises.

Insurance

Liability insurance is a must for all bereavement camp programs, since the risk of finding the organization in litigation cannot be ignored. Once camp staff has selected a site, the site may need to be named as a co-insurer on your insurance policy. If the camp program is providing a therapy camp, or is using professional therapists in any capacity, it is strongly suggested that in addition to general liability insurance, professional liability insurance be offered to these mental health professionals. It is a programmatic decision whether to ask these professionals to volunteer their time, or if they will be reimbursed for conducting group counseling sessions. If they are paid, it is highly recommended to provide insurance.

Volunteer Recruitment, Screening, Training, Ratio, and Supervision

Volunteer Recruitment

Volunteers come at all levels of professionalism and can fulfill all roles in a camp setting. Retired or semi-retired professionals such as nurses and counselors often have the time and credentials to help. Teachers who have seen the benefit of camp to students they have referred might also be able to volunteer themselves or advocate for volunteer professionals in their spheres of contact. People volunteer for various reasons: Some are motivated by a desire to help others or by a love for children. Others have more self-centered motives such as educational credits, resume credits, socialization, a chance to use skills and talents, and increased feelings of self-worth. If volunteers bring their own background of grief and loss, it will be important to ascertain that they are ready to come to camp, have support throughout camp, and are well informed beforehand of the emotional nature of the camp experience.

If the ethnicities of camp professionals and volunteers do not match those of the campers, the program must make every effort to increase diverse representation. Often when professionals or volunteers from an underrepresented community become volunteers, they become the conduit for recruiting others if an effort is made to engage their community in this way. It cannot be stressed strongly enough that backgrounds of campers and staff need to correspond as much as possible.

There are more than a million nonprofits in the United States who compete for volunteers. Because of this, bereavement camps must think outside the box when trying to recruit. Universities, local health organizations, and schools are excellent sources of volunteers. Consider partnering with local universities for students who might serve as buddies or co-counselors. Graduate students in mental health areas such as social work, psychology, human services, and counseling make excellent volunteers. Many colleges and universities require their students to provide a certain number of volunteer hours, so participating in the camp organization is a win-win situation. Social work schools require their students to complete internships, another reason that students might be a good fit for a camp. Recent graduates who are searching for employment find volunteering at camp a worthwhile use of their time and an addition to their resume. Camp MAGIK typically has seven or eight graduate students supporting the lead counselors at each camp.

Camp MAGIK's lead counselors are professionals who guide the counseling groups. Professional mental health providers can be found at hospices, hospitals, and the school system, as well as in community agencies and private practices. Camp MAGIK's counseling professionals are part volunteers, part staff. They are paid for conducting the counseling sessions together with their co-counselors, but as volunteers they accompany and supervise the campers throughout the weekend (except for designated downtime). These lead counselors—who typically hold a master's degree in social work or counseling but occasionally hold doctoral degrees in their fields—are recruited from hospices, schools, hospitals, and through word of mouth. One incentive for these professionals is the chance to practice their skills and to network for future job opportunities. A second incentive is the pay for leading the counseling sessions. Of course, paying the professionals for their group time adds to the cost of running camp, and it is Camp MAGIK's biggest expense other than the money paid to the campsite for lodging, food, and camp activities. This means that we have to minimize expenses in other places. Fortunately, most of Camp MAGIK's overhead is donated, so camp is able to afford professionals for ten counseling groups plus two counselors for the adult group. However, without pay there are other ways to reward these counselors. If the camp operates out of a hospice, for example, the administration may allow a social worker a few days off in exchange for serving as a counselor at camp. Hospitals and school systems that would benefit from supporting camp may allow the same arrangement for their social workers and counselors.

There is one other type of volunteer needed. We strongly suggest what Camp MAGIK has come to call "shopping volunteers." Campers have been provided a list of what they need to bring. Yet, there will be campers who come without a sleeping bag, toiletries, or a change of clothing. Camp MAGIK has found that some of the campers are very poor, which explains the lack of a fully stocked bag for the weekend. Other campers have a parent who is not yet used to tending to details as newly single caregivers. It is also possible that in spite of every effort, the camp staff left something behind, be it marshmallows, stuffed give-away animals, or downtime toys such as soccer balls. Camp MAGIK always has volunteers with a car who are ready to make a needed shopping trip.

Volunteer Screening

At a minimum, every prospective volunteer should complete a volunteer application and be screened by the agency using both references and criminal background checks. These should be done yearly once a volunteer has joined the organization. Camp MAGIK recommends that all volunteers be interviewed by those with knowledge of the emotional stresses of the camp program. The volunteer needs to come prepared to cope with the discomfort of the tragedies that campers have endured and be aware of their own personal losses that might be uncomfortably triggered by camp. It is vital that one person be available at all times to assist or counsel volunteers, should the need arise.

References and the results from the background check will serve as guides for decision making to accept the volunteer or not. Some items on the criminal background check may not be enough by themselves to deny the volunteer acceptance to the program. As an agency, executive decisions can be made for what is acceptable and what is not. Obviously, any crimes involving children would be an automatic denial, but a "Driving Under the Influence" violation 15 years ago may not be, provided the volunteer is not expected to transport any of the campers. The program committee will set the threshold of what is and is not acceptable on the background checks. Some states have laws regarding what crimes exclude work with children. Before you set the thresholds, verify your state's guidelines.

Volunteer Training

All volunteers should be trained in the agency's policies, procedures, volunteer position job descriptions, and administrative structure, in addition to childhood bereavement, trauma, child/adolescent development theory, cultural humility, potential emergency situations and procedures, confidentiality, and exceptions to confidentiality. In addition, all volunteers need to be trained to detect suicidal ideations as well as signs of abuse and neglect. They also need training to respond to these situations if they occur. Any indications or signs of abuse or neglect, and suicidal ideations, at Camp MAGIK must be reported to the camp director, who will then continue with her own assessment.

Volunteers need training in avoiding high-risk situations including one-to-one camper/volunteer interactions or one-to-one camper/camper interactions, such as inappropriate touching. Avoiding high-risk situations protects campers from the risk of being abused, physically or emotionally, and the volunteers and staff from false accusations. Camp MAGIK's policy clearly states that volunteers cannot be alone with a camper. They may, however, interact with a camper one-on-one in plain view of another volunteer or staff member. Camp MAGIK has been fortunate that no allegations of staff misconduct have been brought over the years. However, the risk is always there. There was an incident where a teenage girl had to be chased down in the night when she ran away to join her boyfriend, who had driven to the camp to pick her up. Fortunately, the incident ended calmly, but the angry teenager could have thrown unfair accusations at the staff members and volunteers involved.

Bereavement camp volunteers are usually at camp because they love working with children and teens, which is often combined with a personal history of loss. However, they are not present to make friends with the campers. Volunteers need training to maintain good boundaries with their charges. This does not imply a cold and distant stance with the campers—on the contrary—but this is not a friendship relationship with the campers. There is a delicate balance, and volunteers must be trained to understand the difference. Obviously, the same applies to all staff members. At Camp MAGIK volunteers do not give out email addresses or phone numbers to campers. Volunteers work with campers over a short, limited, time period, and campers are a vulnerable population. It is possible that some volunteers could develop a healthy friendship relationship with a camper, but some will not be able to do this. Therefore, the Camp MAGIK policy states that all volunteers will refrain from giving out contact information to our campers. If a camper wants to speak with his or her counselor or buddy after camp, the camp director facilitates that contact by asking the counselor or buddy to contact the family.

Volunteer–Camper Ratio

The camp program should establish a volunteer/staff to camper ratio. The American Camp Association has recommendations that should at a minimum be followed. They recommend that young children aged 6–8 have one adult per six campers, while children aged 9–14 have one adult per eight campers. Teenagers aged 15–18 may have one adult per ten campers. However, these are recommendations for minimum staffing, and often bereavement camps have a higher ratio. Some, using the buddy system, have a one-to-one ratio. Volunteers might be drawn from community groups such as retirees or church organizations, and are matched with the campers. However, keep in mind that combinations of older, less-agile adults with active adolescents or including church members who want to spread their religion's point of view might not be successful in supporting the atmosphere needed at camp.

For younger campers, aged 6–11, Camp MAGIK has one lead counselor (professional) and two co-counselors for each group of six to eight campers. For older campers, aged 12–18, we staff the groups of eight campers with one lead counselor and one co-counselor. All counselors, lead and co-counselors, stay with their group of campers at all times during the weekend, including all recreational activities. This model ensures that the mental health professional is available to the campers at any time during the weekend, since some issues do not surface in the group sessions but at some other time, particularly bedtime. The only absence exception is one hour on Saturday afternoon when the lead and co-counselors take turns to break away from the campers somewhere on campus.

Volunteer Supervision

Since volunteers play a key role in working with campers, they need to have clear job descriptions and to be given clear expectations. Every camp needs a policy on the volunteer-supervision ratio and the relationship between volunteers and supervisory staff. The ratio varies depending on the volunteers' tasks. If the volunteers are involved directly with the campers, a ratio of one supervisor per 15 volunteers is appropriate. At Camp MAGIK, two staff members supervise 15 volunteers (five lead counselors and ten co-counselors) each. We call these staff members who report to the camp director "unit leaders." These unit leaders, together with all other volunteers, are supported by a professional who is on hand specifically for their support throughout the camp weekend. Each volunteer should have a clear understanding of the supervisory structure.

Medical Staff and Medications

A bereavement camp must have at least one registered nurse or physician on-site at all times. The medical staff needs to have current licenses and professional insurance in the state where the camp is held. If the camp numbers exceed 50, it is highly recommended that two medical professionals attend. At Camp MAGIK, one registered nurse and one doctor are in attendance at all times (our number of campers typically run between 75 and 80). The duties of the medical staff include collecting medications for all campers, asking questions upon arrival about health conditions (e.g., fever, diarrhea, rashes, etc.) in the days prior to camp, distributing medications, and attending to any minor medical situations or emergencies during the camp weekend. All medications that are brought to camp—whether prescription or over the counter—must be in their original containers and supervised by professionals at all times. All medications are to be stored in a safe place where no one other than the medical staff on-site has access to them. A locked storage location is ideal. Some camps require the families to get a "bubble pack" from their pharmacies, containing the exact number of medications for as many days as the camper specifies to the pharmacist. This involves a bit of extra effort on the family's part, but it is more convenient for the medical staff. Furthermore, the "bubble pack" ensures there will be no medications left behind. The medical staff must keep records of all dispensations of a medication. The camp nurse must record any medical incidents, such as a sore throat, fever, or nausea. A clear medication management policy must be established. Camp MAGIK's application forms include a statement allowing the medical staff to administer prescriptions and first aid to the camper, and gives permission to the camp director together with the medical staff to secure proper treatment for the camper in case of an emergency. Legally, such a statement is to be signed by the camper's guardian.

Medical staff must thoroughly document injuries or emergency treatments and report all illnesses and injuries to the camper's family. In addition, the medical policy needs to state the procedure to follow if a child develops a fever or any acute illness. At Camp MAGIK, counselors will bring the camper to the medical staff and notify the camp director of examination by and treatment from the medical staff. The camp director notifies the camper's family of the situation. If a minor injury can be treated by the medical staff, the family has the option to leave the child at camp or pick the child up. If a child develops a fever or nausea, he or she receives treatment from the medical staff and is isolated from other campers. The family is notified. If the family opts to keep the child at camp for observation, and the child agrees, camp can keep the child in isolation for up to four hours to see if medication clears the condition. If this is successful, the child will stay in isolation for another four hours, and if no symptoms present, can then assume activities with other campers. If medication does not clear the condition after four hours, the parent is asked to pick the child up. Other families are notified of incidents when they retrieve their children at the closing of camp.

Transportation

Each camp handles transportation differently. Some will not provide any extra transportation and rely on parents to get their campers to the site. Many of Camp MAGIK's campers live at a distance from the campsites and the family car may not be reliable enough to take for such a drive. Many have a single parent who cannot take off from work to bring the camper to camp. Others approve of their child going to camp, but do not care enough about the experience to take them. To address these situations, some camps will rent vans and have volunteers or staff members pick up campers and transport them to camp. Others will hire transportation companies with their own liability to do the driving of the campers. Finally, some camp organizations are able to work out transportation with the local school system to use its school buses and drivers. However it is accomplished, follow liability insurance requirements. Staff or volunteer drivers must have clean driving records. If a bus or van is used, a staff member must be on board to greet campers at pick up/drop off points and to keep campers supervised to and from camp, no matter who drives. A transportation company should provide a copy of their vehicle and liability insurance before employment.

Campers' guardians should sign a transportation waiver form reviewed and approved by an attorney in the camp's state. Camp MAGIK has chosen to use a transportation company since the cost of insurance to provide our own transportation is prohibitive. Most of Camp MAGIK's campers are transported by their own families, though for a significant number that is not an option; approximately a quarter of the campers use the transportation company service.

Camper Recruitment

To recruit campers, contact school counselors, and school, hospital, and hospice social workers. It is an easy task to find email addresses on the Internet, since most organizations have their own websites. A dedicated volunteer can easily compile a list of email addresses to use to send out the announcement for the camp. It is tedious work, but it pays off—sometimes too well, as there may be more appropriate applications than the camp can handle. Prepare an easy-to-read announcement of the camp session that can be attached to the email messages. Also, attach the application form to the announcement. Both the announcement and the application form should be available on the camp's website.

To make Camp MAGIK known, we contact schools and ask to conduct an in-service on grief among children and adolescents. Often school counselors attend monthly continuing education sessions, which could provide opportunities to promote camp. We also contact local civic associations and offer to speak at their regular meetings. Our camp director was fortunate enough to speak at a Kiwanis meeting in the early 2000s where a member, who is passionate about childhood grief after the loss of his guardian grandmother at age 14, heard her presentation. He has contributed tens of thousands of dollars each year to the mission. He was invited to become a board member some years later. Write a letter to the editor of your local newspaper whenever a connection can be made to children and grief. Mass shootings that have occurred in our society can be addressed in a letter to the editor about the impact of violence on children and teens and how it can be attended to. Inviting news media to the camp is obviously a great way to get the word out. However, the camp director must take particular care to protect anonymity. Parents and guardians must sign media releases before any pictures are taken. If any campers are wards of the state, ensure that the state's public child welfare system rules are followed.

Pre-Camp Preparations

Whatever means are used to send notices of camp, it is paramount that camps ensure applicant assessment once they have applications in hand. Most of the data can be collected on the application form; other information can be obtained through a face-to-face or phone interview. At a minimum, camps need the following information on prospective campers: name; age; gender; grade; who died; how the person died; when the person died; length and quality of the relationship with the person; other losses to death or otherwise (such as a move or a parental incarceration); emotional, behavioral, and social issues; bedtime or sleep routines; family composition; medical and allergy information; and emergency contact while camp is in session. During conversations with the families, gather information on the children and their family situation. Provide information to the families about how camp is organized and what to expect from camp. Allow time for questions and answers.

A readiness evaluation of campers should be made: Are they ready to be separated from their family for the weekend? Campers have experienced a traumatic event, and the remaining caregiving family serves as main support. Separating campers from their families may add to the trauma if the children are not ready for this. As a trauma-informed camp, Camp MAGIK seeks to avoid re-traumatization at all costs. When planning the assessment of the camper's appropriateness, decide who does the evaluations. This person should have some type of mental health training to be able to accurately assess the camper's fit for the camp experience. The initial contact, usually made by telephone, is a chance to establish rapport with the family and establish the organization as a professional agency that the family can trust. In addition to training staff on rapport building, create a list of questions with possible follow-up questions to ask during the first contact. The list depends on what questions have already been posed on the application form. Camp MAGIK uses a short application form that is easy for families to use and that ascertains the basic requirements for attendance at camp, demographics, and medical information. The follow-up assessment information form includes several more details and is used to assess the camper's readiness. A sample of a follow-up assessment form is in Appendix C. It is a good idea to review the answers on the application form during this call. Remember to verify the street address and email address since it is easy to misread these if the application is handwritten.

In addition to talking to the child's parent, talk with the child if at all possible. Such a conversation gives an opportunity for the camper to ask questions and to avoid situations where the camper is unaware of the focus of the camp. Both conversations, with the parent and the child, can be by telephone. A conversation in person is always better, but for many families it is a hardship to get a camper transported to and from camp; to meet in person before the camp may be impossible unless staff makes home visits. If possible, a pre-camp party or gathering is a great way to help campers with nervousness, but arranging time and transportation for such an event is often difficult with the families that Camp MAGIK serves.

Once the appropriateness of the campers has been established and they have been accepted to camp, provide them with an acceptance package that describes the camp and the experience. Inform families of what will be needed, directions to camp, ways to contact camp during session, and drop-off and pick-up times. Include a list of what they may not bring, such as valuable or sentimental items (they are too easily lost), electronics (this is a time for reflection that is easily distracted by video games and cell phones), or things easily broken such as items made of glass. Include a schedule of the camp session with this acceptance package. Camp MAGIK's acceptance package also includes a "Camper's Pledge" that the camper is asked to sign. It has two components, the first of which states, "I want to come to camp to learn more about my grief and to get support for my grief." This statement is added to the form to avoid campers coming without their parents telling them the focus of camp. The second component states, "I promise to obey camp rules and to respect other campers." It is imperative to include camp rules with the package, so that the campers know these before coming to camp and before signing a pledge to obey them. Make the rules as few as possible, including rules of confidentiality with exceptions, rules of staying with their adult counselors, rules of showing respect for other campers and adults, and the property of the camp and campsite. Camp MAGIK's final rule is to "have fun." By having the campers sign this pledge there is better buy-in to attend camp and to comply with directions.

Camp Segments

Check-In

Check-in is an important event. This is when campers decide whether they really want to stay or not. The campers make this decision quickly. All hands must be on deck. Instruct staff and volunteers to "sell" camp to the campers immediately upon arrival. This includes observing the campers as they arrive and making quick decisions about who needs extra attention. Camp MAGIK partners with local nonprofit therapy dog organizations who have dogs on hand at check-in. These dogs are very popular. It is vital to make check-in a pleasant and welcoming time for all families with enough staff and volunteers available so that no one falls through the cracks. At check-in, collect paperwork that has not already been gathered, such as release forms. Medical staff needs to collect medications. Medical staff handles all medications except medications such as inhalers for asthma or insulin pumps for diabetes that campers use to care for themselves independently.

Camp organizers need to develop a system for campers to easily identify peers from their own cabin. Name tags work well for this. Campers at Camp MAGIK receive name tags at check-in with colored dots—everyone with a red dot belongs to the same counseling group, everyone with a green dot belongs together, and so on. The dining tables in the dining hall are similarly color coded. Some camps use color-coded T-shirts for their campers. To assist with any anxiety of parents dropping their children off, make sure they leave with information and with a number to reach camp while in session. Again, include the pick-up time. It is a good idea to confirm the family's emergency number at check-in.

Expect difficulties for campers and their guardians in saying good-bye. To help, ask guardians to walk with their campers to their cabins and help their children make their beds. To assist with the good-bye and to help campers' comfort levels with camp, Camp MAGIK distributes small stuffed animals to all bunk beds in the cabins prior to the campers' arrival. When the campers reach their assigned sleeping space there is a "friend" waiting. Camp MAGIK also stations additional therapy dogs at the cabins, and volunteers engage the newly arrived campers in some type of activity as soon as the guardians have helped make the camper's bunk bed. Activities include ball games, a hula-hoop and jump roping tournament, a game of tag, etc. Volunteers also hand out personalized, refillable water bottles to each camper at this time so that they may stay well hydrated for the duration of camp.

Camp Time

An opening ceremony includes an overview of what to expect at camp and the camp director reminds everyone why they are there. This helps with initial camp nerves. Camp MAGIK's opening ceremony starts immediately after dinner when everyone has arrived and everyone is fed. Others may want to have this ceremony before dinner. Camp MAGIK campers cannot miss school without penalty; therefore, some campers may arrive late. During the opening ceremony, campers learn "this is a safe place for you to share your experiences if you choose to do so." The camp director introduces volunteers and staff, reviews rules, posts schedules, and the program starts. For a more detailed description of camp models and schedules, see Chapter 6. Just a word about food at camp: All campers should have been assessed for food allergies, so the campsite kitchen staff and the camper's counselors should be aware of special needs.

Leaving Camp

At the conclusion of camp, to mark the campers' accomplishment of participating in the weekend camp, a closing ceremony is held. Some camps hold a drumming circle; others have an art show and/or put pictures taken during the weekend into a slide show that rolls as parents arrive. Camp MAGIK holds a closing assembly where each camper is recognized and receives a backpack with a yo-yo, jump rope, and other little trinkets inside. Each camper also gets a certificate of completion. Parents receive an information packet that includes information about children/adolescents and grief; developmental expectations; suggestions for approaching the child's grief; suggestions for discipline; suggestions for self-care; a list of readings for children, adolescents, and adults; and a list of community and Internet resources. If parents are not present, camp staff mail the handout after camp. Counselors also explain the campers' journals to the parents and encourage them to ask their children about them without pressuring them to share. At Camp MAGIK we have found no need to encourage campers to stay in touch with each other and us, but we still suggest staying in touch through social media. The camp director lets the campers and families know about the Camp MAGIK Facebook page and encourages parents and teens to join.

After Camp

It is crucial to stay in contact with campers after camp, such as with regular phone calls and mailings to check in. During these contacts, camp staff must help those families whose campers need extra follow-up to contact referral sources in their community. Camp MAGIK routinely asks families about negative changes in their campers, such as cutting, nightmares, or talk of suicide. If these have been noticed, therapeutic issues can be addressed. In addition, campers greatly appreciate receiving mailings of group pictures from camp. Camp MAGIK uploads camp pictures onto a password-protected section of its website and gives families the password so that they may log in to view them.

Some camps hold a reunion party for campers. There is no ideal time for this event, but summertime seems to work. Though some campers are traveling, for those who are in town, the schedules are more flexible as the school calendar does not have to be taken into account. It is also important to stay in touch with the volunteers. After a Camp MAGIK session, the volunteers are invited to a debriefing a week or two later. They are, of course, also invited to the camp reunion.

In Summary

Although each bereavement camp responds to the unique nature of its community, camps can learn from one another to improve their programs. Using Camp MAGIK as an example, this chapter gives ideas and illustrations of various components of camp. The Moyer Foundation, together with camp and childhood grief specialists, has created an excellent document titled "Bereavement Camp Standards of Practice" that can be found in Appendix D. Chapter 6 provides more details on Camp MAGIK and other bereavement camp models.

Recommended Reading

Ruffin, P. A., & Zimmerman, S. A. (2010). Bereavement groups and camps for children. In N. B. Webb (Ed.), *Helping bereaved children: A handbook for practitioners* (pp. 304–314). New York, NY: Guilford Press.

Schreiber, J. K., & Spear, C. (2014). The magic of grief camps: The impact on teens. In K. J. Doka & A. S. Tucci (Eds.), *Helping adolescents cope with loss* (pp. 309–320). Washington, DC: Hospice Foundation of America.

References

Children and War Foundation. (1998). *The Children's Revised Impact of Event Scale (CRIES-13)*. Retrieved from www.child

renandwar.org/measures/children%e2%80%99s-revised-impact-of-event-scale-8-%e2%80%93-cries-8/ies13/

Cohen, J. A., & Mannarino, A. P. (2004). Treatment of childhood traumatic grief. *Journal of Clinical Child & Adolescent Psychology*, *33*, 819–831.

Cohen, J. A., Mannarino, A. P., & Deblinger, E. (2006). *Treating trauma and traumatic grief in children and adolescents*. New York, NY: The Guilford Press.

Fiorini, J. J., & Mullen, J. A. (2006): *Counseling children and adolescents through grief and loss*. Champaign, IL: Research Press.

McClatchey, I. S. (in press). Trauma-informed care and posttraumatic growth among youth: A pilot study. *Omega - Journal of Death & Dying*.

McClatchey, I. S. (2017). Fathers raising motherless children: Widowed men give voice to their lived experiences. *Omega - Journal of Death and Dying*, *76*(4). Advance online publication. doi:10.1177/0030222817693141

McClatchey, I. S., & Peters, A. (2015). Can trauma focused grief education improve acting-out behavior among bereaved youth? A pilot study. *Journal of Human Services*, *35*(1), 14–27.

McClatchey, I. S., & Raven, R. F. (2017). Adding trauma-informed care at a bereavement camp to facilitate posttraumatic growth: A controlled outcome study. *Advances in Social Work*, *18*(1). doi: 10.18060/21239

McClatchey, I. S., Vonk, M. E., & Palardy, G. (2009). Efficacy of a campbased intervention for childhood traumatic grief. *Research on Social Work Practice*, *19*(1), 19–30.

McClatchey, I. S., & Wimmer, J. (2012). Healing components of a bereavement camp: Children and adolescents give voice to their experiences. *Omega - Journal of Death and Dying*, *65*(1), 11–32.

McClatchey, I. S., & Wimmer, J. (2014). Coping with parental death as seen from the perspective of children who attended a grief camp. *Qualitative Social Work*, *13*(2), 221–236. doi:10.1177/1473325012465104

Pynoos, R. S., Steinberg, A. M., & Wraith, R. (1995). A developmental model of childhood traumatic stress. In D. Cicchetti & D. Cohen (Eds.), *Developmental psychopathology: Vol. 2, Risk, disorder, and adaptation* (pp. 72–95). Oxford, England: John Wiley.

Searles, R. (2004). *Camp MAGIK—program evaluation*. Atlanta, GA: Camp MAGIK.

Wolfelt, A. D. (1996). *Healing the bereaved child: Grief gardening, growth through grief and other touchstones for caregivers*. Fort Collins, CO: Companion.

Worden, J. W. (1991). *Grief counseling and grief therapy: A handbook for the mental health professional*. New York, NY: Springer.

6

Camp MAGIK
and Other Models

I lost my mummy when I was very young too. I was 15 and my brother was 12. So we lost our mummy when we were young as well. Do you speak about your daddy? It's very important to talk about it, very, very important.

—Prince William, talking to a 9-year-old girl when
visiting Child Bereavement UK (Perry, 2017)

The goal of this chapter is to describe various grief camp models that can be used as a basis of implementing new camps or revising existing camps. An in-depth description of Camp MAGIK follows, which is an evidence-based model in existence for over 20 years. Then shorter descriptions of camp models are described, generously shared by camp directors across the country. This chapter also describes the buddy system, an approach used by many camps.

Camp MAGIK Model and Curriculum

This section describes Camp MAGIK, which the first author of this book founded in 1995. Camp MAGIK provides three to four camp sessions a year in the Atlanta area. One or two of these sessions are funded by The Moyer Foundation through its Camp Erin network. Camp MAGIK's approach is developmentally informed and grief-informed and is based on the trauma-informed approach outlined by SAMHSA (2014). Although all counselors follow a scripted curriculum, it is important to note that one intervention does not fit all children. To ensure that each camper gets what he or she needs from camp, Camp MAGIK uses professional grief counselors who are trained to assess the needs of the campers and can stress various parts of the curriculum with each camper appropriately.

Trauma-Informed

Camp MAGIK adheres to the four assumptions of trauma-informed care: 1) realization about trauma and how trauma affects people, 2) recognition of the signs of trauma, 3) response to trauma, and 4) resistance to re-traumatization. It also applies the six principles of the trauma-informed approach: 1) safety; 2) trustworthiness and transparency; 3) peer support; 4) collaboration and mutuality; 5) empowerment, voice, and choice; and 6) sensitivity to cultural, historical, and gender issues (SAMHSA, 2014, p. 10). Camp MAGIK trains its staff and volunteers on the impact of trauma, teaching the latest research for dealing with and treating trauma. Staff and volunteers also receive training in recognizing the signs and symptoms of trauma among campers, their families, referring professionals, and among themselves. Policies address situations that cause trauma and are formulated with the input from staff and volunteers with a goal of minimizing re-traumatization. Campers' readiness for camp is evaluated to avoid re-traumatization by separating prospective campers from their families, who are usually their main support during a time of high stress.

The first principle of trauma-informed approach, *safety*, is primary at Camp MAGIK. To protect staff and volunteers, Camp MAGIK clearly informs everyone of policies as these relate to their work with campers and their families. Staff and volunteers are trained to handle and report emergency situations. They also know that if their own personal traumas are triggered, they are allowed to step away from their camp responsibilities for a while without repercussion.

Camp MAGIK stresses safety with families and campers. Camp informs families of all safety precautions, such as criminal background checks for our staff and volunteers, licenses of all medical staff and professional volunteers, certifications of life guards and canoe instructors, training and education of the grief counselors, storage of medications, policies on camper/staff ratio, and privacy rules. Camp requires all families to sign an informed consent form for each of their campers. Families and campers alike are apprised of confidentiality. Lead counselors who speak with parents and guardians after the camp are trained in the delicate balance of answering parents' questions without divulging confidential information shared by campers in group sessions and other times during the camp weekend. Camp does not ask campers to share any stories or information until they feel safe. For some this means they share during the first counseling session, for others it means the last counseling session—and for some, not at all.

Children and adolescents feel safe when they know what is expected of them and how their environment is structured. Camp rules are sent to families before camp and are reviewed in detail during the welcome to camp. Camp staff posts daily schedules in each cabin. Camp MAGIK seeks to instill feelings of safety among the campers by maintaining continuity of counselors and volunteers. Lead and co-counselors all commit to remaining the full weekend with an assigned group of campers whom they stay with 24 hours a day. Camp MAGIK does not allow any visitors to join the counseling groups for observation or any other reason.

The camp facility is checked prior to the arrival of youth and families, paying attention to physical safety and risk areas. Camp MAGIK is careful to inform staff and volunteers of any observed concerns. Camp ascertains the location of community emergency assistance, and alerts the local police and fire departments of the camp, including the numbers of campers and volunteers attending.

The second principle of the trauma-informed approach, *trustworthiness*, is shown by keeping promises to staff, volunteers, campers, and their families in all areas. Camp MAGIK ensures a level of staff expertise that is promised to parents and referral sources. Counselors adhere to confidentiality and other policy rules. Campers know that if camp promises to do something, it will. This is noteworthy for post-camp actions. If camp has promised a camper or family to follow up on a personal concern, camp does. If staff are unable to help with something as they had hoped, they inform the camper of this. Similarly, if a camper has specifically asked camp staff not to share something with the outside world, such as a parent or teacher, staff keeps this promise as long as the camper's safety is not at risk. In the name of *transparency*, camp informs families during the application process what they and their campers can expect. This includes what recreational activities will be used and what the counseling sessions address. The staff and volunteers know that they can trust the organization to support their work with campers and their families. Policies and policy changes are created with staff and volunteer input, often based on camper or camper family suggestions.

Peer support, the third principle, is the basis for the bereavement camp concept. Simply by bringing the campers together and giving them the opportunity to share their stories with each other, campers receive peer support. This peer support, provided through the group sessions and other activities, helps normalize trauma and grief reactions experienced by the participants. The peers in the group can also help correct each other's faulty cognitions revealed in group sessions. Camp MAGIK counselors are careful to avoid re-traumatization of campers when campers share their stories. Campers are offered the opportunity to continue peer support after camp through a private Facebook page established by Camp MAGIK. Camp also arranges a reunion, usually held at a professional baseball game.

Parents are offered peer support in weekend camps for adult family members that are held during the same time and at the same place as the camp sessions for children and youth. The adult camps thus run parallel to, but are separate from, the youth camp sessions. Camp also offers peer support to the parents after camp through the private Facebook page and the reunion.

Peer support is provided to the staff and volunteers before, during, and after camp. All volunteers meet for training before camp sessions and are encouraged to discuss camp situations with each other between group sessions when campers are involved with other activities. Counselors are invited to volunteer appreciation events, though these are typically not well attended.

Following the fourth principle of the trauma-informed approach, camp staff and volunteers *collaborate* intensively with the campers' families and the community. Several contacts are made between camp and families prior to camp to assess need, attain narratives, and establish readiness of the campers for a weekend-long camp experience. There is extensive collaboration with other stakeholders, including referral sources of school counselors and school, hospital, and hospice social workers. School staff often assist with camp paperwork reaching families and arranging transportation for the youth to and from camp. In addition, Camp MAGIK regularly has co-counselors from graduate social work departments of universities in the area. Graduate students receive experience in working with bereaved children in a group setting, and in addition, they receive credit for hours towards their internship or volunteer requirements. *Mutuality* is shown in Camp MAGIK's approach to decision making. Staff is included in policy decisions, which are often based upon input from campers and their families. Campers are always given a choice of how much, or how little, they want to share or participate at camp.

Empowerment, including *voice* and *choice*, the fifth principle, applies to campers, families, staff, and volunteers. Campers are empowered and given voice in their choices at camp. In addition, counselors encourage them to share in the counseling sessions; whether to do so or not is their choice. Campers are empowered by learning about grief, trauma, and various coping skills. They have a voice in whether to participate in recreational activities. Campers, families, staff, and volunteers have shared their voices in the creation of the curriculum and constantly bring suggestions for improvements. Camp MAGIK uses a strengths-based approach. Staff and volunteers actively assess for and express strengths identified to campers, their families, and each other.

To follow the sixth and final principle of the trauma-informed approach, staff and volunteers receive training in *cultural* competence and cultural humility. Training includes education on and consideration of *historical* traumas. Every effort is made to recruit staff and volunteers who are representative of the camper population. Staff and volunteers respect all ethnicities. Grief activities are designed to fit the ethnicities in the community. If a camper is uncomfortable, the camper can refrain from any activity without question or consequence. Camp MAGIK trains staff and volunteers in intersectionality—that is, how culture, demographic, social, educational, and economic variables intersect and compound discrimination. Respect for and acceptance of *gender* identification and sexual orientation of campers and staff is included in Camp MAGIK's philosophy. Camp encourages volunteers to reflect on their own inherent biases, how these influence their work, and how to prevent these biases from interfering with their work.

In keeping with the trauma-informed approach, the Camp MAGIK model includes six counseling sessions led by grief professionals. The counseling sessions are based on evidence-based research on children, trauma, and grief. Many of our campers have experienced violent or sudden deaths of important people in their lives, which may have caused PTSD symptoms. However, emerging research shows that expected deaths create PTSD symptoms to the same degree as a violent and/or unexpected death (McClatchey,

Vonk, & Palardy, 2009). Because of this, Camp MAGIK has decided to include trauma-focused grief interventions for all campers. In addition, many children and adolescents experience magical thinking and some experience existential distress (Kaplow, Layne, Saltzman, Cozza, & Pynoos, 2013), which are important reasons for including cognitive restructuring during camp. The Camp MAGIK model incorporates Cohen, Mannarino, and Deblinger's (2006, 2017) trauma-focused cognitive-behavioral model as well as work by Pynoos, Steinberg, and Wraith (1995). Trauma-focused activities at camp include review and teaching of positive coping skills, relaxation, imagery, deep breathing, coping statements, thought stopping, retelling narratives, and cognitive restructuring.

Grief-Informed

Camp MAGIK includes grief-informed work based on Worden's four tasks of mourning (1996, 2008), Kaplow and her colleagues' theory of multidimensional grief (Kaplow, Layne, Saltzman, Cozza, & Pynoos, 2013), and Normand, Silverman, and Nickman's (1996) findings on maintaining relationships with a deceased parent. Grief-informed activities include sharing the story of the loss, identifying and expressing emotions around the loss, sharing memories, identifying traits (both positive and negative) in the person lost, memorializing the person who died by making memory pillows, holding a memorial service, journal writing, identifying strengths in themselves, identifying strengths in new peers, and letter writing to and from the person who died. Camp MAGIK includes these activities to assist campers who experience separation distress, existential distress, and/or circumstance-related distress (Kaplow, Layne, Saltzman, Cozza, & Pynoos, 2013).

Developmentally Informed

Although the counseling sessions for each age group have the same focus, they are implemented based on the developmental stage of the campers. Campers are divided into counseling groups of six to eight, depending on their developmental age. When interviewing families and talking with campers before camp, the counselor gains a general idea of what group the camper belongs in. The activities for the counseling groups are geared towards the developmental stage of the campers to help them complete tasks and grasp concepts appropriate to their stage of life.

Camp Structure

Camp MAGIK is overseen by the camp director, who has two unit leaders to help run camp. One unit leader supervises the volunteers for the younger campers (aged 7 to 11); the other unit leader supervises the volunteers for the older campers (aged 12 and up). The professional lead counselors under the unit leaders are the main resource for handling emotional issues among campers in their groups, with backup from the camp director. Two co-counselors serve under each lead counselor for every six to eight campers in the younger age group, and one co-counselor per counseling group for the older campers. Another volunteer is present to serve as a resource for any emotional issues that arise among volunteers. The camp director serves as the spokesperson for the camp and is the primary contact for parents and for dealing with emergencies that arise among the campers or within the setting. In addition, there is a volunteer on hand for errands, and the two medical staff members.

To streamline the six counseling group sessions and to ensure that the counselors follow a similar outline, Camp MAGIK created a curriculum with a script for each session. Counselors do not read the script verbatim when meeting with campers; instead, they use it as a basis for the focus of each session. Trained professionals serve as lead counselors. Their knowledge and seasoning are imperative in using this model. Camp MAGIK depends on these professionals to know when to depart from the set curriculum and focus time in a session to address a particular issue with a camper. The outline of the curriculum will be presented here in the order of occurrence at camp. The outline is interwoven with the camp schedule.

It is also worthy of mention that it is vital to mix counseling sessions with fun recreational activities. Camp MAGIK, like most other bereavement camps, provides physical activities typical of any type of camp, such as a ropes course, canoeing, swimming, hiking, treasure hunts, and a talent show. In addition, many bereavement camps have a memorial service and a balloon release. Although it is essential to give campers an opportunity to verbally share their experiences and feelings, Doka (2000) mentions that it is a myth that talk is the most effective way to deal with loss. Instead, other creative opportunities to express grief are also important, such as art, music, play, and rituals. In addition, play is a child's "job" developmentally, and it is how children make sense of their feelings and experiences (Schuurman, 2000).

Camp MAGIK's official goals are for each camper to feel supported during and after camp, normalize feelings around their loss, have healthy coping skills, and experience less distress surrounding their loss. Camp strives to meet these goals in and outside of the counseling sessions.

Camp MAGIK starts the camp counseling program by focusing on the trauma experience, followed by grief activities on Saturday night and Sunday. The first session occurs before bedtime on Friday night. Before this session there has been a welcome, introductions, get-acquainted games, and a campfire. At the welcome, each counseling group receives a backpack with rocks that have feeling words written on them. The campers are not allowed to look in the backpack, but can feel it and make guesses about its contents. They take turns during the evening's and next morning's activities carrying it. At this time, each camper also gets a journal with activities that correspond with the various group sessions.

Group Session 1 Focus: *Learn about camp and common reactions to grief/trauma, introduce coping skills, and tell a bit about your story*

Goals

- Campers will know purpose and expectations of camp.
- Campers will become aware of some common reactions to grief and trauma.
- Campers will become familiar with methods to reduce arousal, avoidance, negative cognitions, and re-experiencing symptoms.
- Campers will feel safe and in control.

Process Objectives

- Review together with campers the reason for being at camp.
- Review possible reactions to grief and trauma, and educate about stress inoculation (feeling identification, relaxation, thought stopping, cognitive coping, and safety statements).

The first counseling session occurs after the campfire on Friday night when the camp schedule nears bedtime. Campers go to their groups with their lead counselors and co-counselors to review camp expectations, discuss common reactions to grief and trauma (e.g., sadness, anger, guilt, mixed up, confused, like hitting, relieved, nervous, like screaming, having flashbacks, having nightmares, worrying, agitation, loneliness, irritation, regrets, not talking or thinking about it) and to learn about coping skills (e.g., a short description of thought stopping, a demonstration of deep breathing, mindful breathing, and muscle relaxation). Counselors stress safety at camp, review confidentiality, and inform campers they are allowed to choose whether to share their narratives or not. Counselors tell them that, in their experience, it is helpful to share even if at first it may hurt to do so. At the end of this first session, counselors encourage campers to share with the group pictures of the person they have lost, briefly explain the relationship (e.g., mother, father, sibling), and how and when they died. Counselors keep campers' sharing of the death event to a minimum this first evening. Too much sharing, too soon, may make campers feel they have opened themselves up to too much vulnerability. Campers have journals with activities that correspond with each group session. During and after each session campers get an opportunity to work with their journals.

After this session, campers settle into bed, and one of the counselors reads a relaxation and guided imagery script. Relaxation is an integral part of stress inoculation and has been shown to decrease arousal symptoms (Srilekha, Soumendra, & Chattopadhyay, 2013). Camp MAGIK has two different versions of the relaxation and guided imagery script—one for the younger group of campers and one for those aged 12 and up. The readings are modified from *Hypnotic Suggestions and Metaphors* edited by D. Corydon Hammond (1990).

On Saturday morning, campers are reminded to bring their backpacks to breakfast. After breakfast, campers return to counseling groups for the second session. In this session, counselors address how to cope with feelings surrounding the death. This, and each session from now on, begins and ends with a few minutes of mindful breathing and relaxation. Deep breathing is another stress inoculation technique that helps campers, including those who have stress symptoms, to slow down and center. Some groups, on the counselor's or the campers' suggestion, create positive statements about each other. Before the mindful breathing of each session (or at the end of each session after the mindful breathing), the counselor suggests that the group members share those positive statements about each other out loud.

Group Session 2 Focus: *Feelings and coping*

Goals

- Campers will identify and experience normalization of feelings and of reactions around grief, separation, existential distress, and circumstance-related stress.
- Campers will know safe ways of expressing and coping with feelings.
- Campers will be able to identify personal support systems.

Process Objectives

- Identify and review common grief feelings and trauma reactions such as mental, emotional, behavioral, physical, physiological, and spiritual reactions to grief and trauma.
- Identify children's own support systems.

In the second session, campers open the backpack to see what it contains. Counselors ask everyone: "What was it like carrying it around at all times? What would it be like to carry this when you eat breakfast at home, when you shower, or when you watch TV?" Campers have usually guessed that there are rocks in the backpack, but have not guessed that the rocks have feelings written and drawn on them. The rocks are used to help campers identify their own feelings surrounding their losses and to help normalize those feelings. This is also the session where campers learn coping skills.

Counselors tell campers that the feelings and reactions experienced when someone dies are called "grief." They also explain that there are no right or wrong feelings; there are simply feelings that people experience in response to the loss. Counselors ask campers to pick up rocks marked with feelings or reactions they have experienced. For younger campers, it is helpful to have a chart of feeling faces. Fox and Lentini (2006) provide some interesting ideas of how to present and use feeling faces. After counselors remind campers that "this is a safe place to share" by stressing confidentiality, they ask campers to share when they have had the feelings and how they coped with them. There are feelings on the rocks that campers are often hesitant to bring up. One such feeling is "relieved." If no camper is ready to share this, the counselor mentions and normalizes it by saying something like: "Many children feel relieved when their person dies. Maybe they feel relieved because that person does not have to suffer anymore, or maybe this was a person who was not so nice to them all the time, maybe drinking too much and hurting them. It is perfectly natural when somebody is suffering, or when somebody has been difficult to live with, to feel relieved when they die. This does not mean we do not love the person. Has anybody here experienced this feeling?" Another feeling often overlooked is "guilty." For children who have magical thinking and the belief that something they said or did caused or partially caused the death, it is difficult to admit to the guilt because by doing so they have, in their minds, admitted to fault. Again, the counselor normalizes the feeling by explaining how common it is among campers to think they are at fault, and therefore, to feel guilty. The conversation continues with "But you really are not at fault, since the death was caused by illness, a murderer, depression, etc." The counselor then asks if anybody has experienced this feeling of guilt.

After campers have reviewed the various feelings they have experienced, and discussed how they dealt with them, counselors and campers review a list of acceptable ways to deal with emotions. Campers have a list of alternatives available in their journals, and together the group members add more as they create ideas. Counselors ask group members to express their feelings in ways that do not hurt themselves, others, or property. As campers review the list of various coping skills in their journals, the group takes time to act out some of these skills together, such as screaming in the woods, wringing towels, and punching pillows. By 10 o'clock on Saturday morning, the woods are full of screaming kids! Other coping strategies include journaling, listening to music, exercising, talking to a trusted friend or family member, practicing yoga, positive self-talking, and composing coping statements, to name a few.

This session ends with campers identifying adults in their lives whom they can turn to when they need support in their grief journey. Counselors ask the campers to identify adults both at home and in the community. If a counselor identifies a camper with limited support, the counselor makes a note to bring this up with the camper's parent.

After this session, campers and counselors participate in a ropes course for team building. The ropes course takes two hours. Fortunately, Camp MAGIK is able to use campsites with both low and high ropes courses. Younger campers complete the low ropes course and older campers the high ropes course. Camp MAGIK gets highly positive feedback from campers on this activity. Therapeutically, it builds trust among campers and counselors. The ropes course exercises also strengthen feelings of teamwork and feelings of safety.

Group Session 3 Focus: *Trauma experience—a movie of your story*

Goals

- Campers will learn coping skills.
- Campers will experience less maladaptive circumstance-related stress.
- Campers will experience less severe emotional distress and lowered behavioral and physiological reactions.

Process Objectives

- Explain purpose of narrative/exposure.
- Teach coping skills and strategies.
- Allow children to tell their narratives.

This session, the third, is held immediately after lunch. Counselors again review common feelings campers may experience when somebody close to them has died, and campers learn more in detail about muscle relaxation, deep and mindful breathing, corrective action, thought stopping, and creating their "perfect moment"—a place or situation they can go to in their minds in order to calm themselves when they feel upset. This moment does not have to be real; it can be pure fantasy. Counselors ask that this "perfect moment" not include the person who died, since for many of the campers, including this person may create an upset or induce stress feelings. Campers get time to draw and/or share their perfect moments with the other group members.

After spending time learning these coping skills, campers tell their stories. Younger campers tell their stories by pretending they are watching a movie, with themselves as the lead actor, and describe what happened to them. The movie format makes it less threatening to tell what happened. Older campers are OK telling their stories without using this technique. Counselors remind everyone of confidentiality and stress that this is a safe place for them to share. Counselors ask campers to tell the story, including: How they heard about or found out about what happened (*the beginning*), what happened next (*the middle*), and then finish the story a few days after the funeral, memorial service, or after going back to school, depending on cultural customs and rituals (*the end*). By putting the story into a context of a beginning, middle, and end, campers understand that although the pain is there, the event is over. They rely on their workbooks to help share their stories. Campers include thoughts and feelings while telling the different stages of the story. Counselors remind the campers of the newly learned coping skills that they may employ if upset during the telling of the narratives. A counselor who notices an upset child reminds the child during the narrative that it is all right to stop, use a coping skill, and then proceed, or stop completely if need be. Counselors let campers share without interruptions, waiting until after the story is complete to ask to amplify feelings at different points if they were not included. If a child becomes unduly distressed, according to camp policy one of the co-counselors removes the child from the group and brings the child to the camp director.

This session in particular needs to be led by a trauma- and grief-informed professional counselor. By the time this session begins, counselors have had an opportunity to assess campers for various types of distress, such as separation, existential, and circumstance related. Depending on the professional assessment of the counselor, the counselor can gauge the emphasis that is placed on various parts of the camper's narrative.

This session precedes canoeing and a puppet show ("Uncle Gherkin's Magical Show") for the younger group of campers and a play ("Fragments of Grief") for adolescents. Both shows were created in collaboration with KPETG following the camp director's contact of Kaiser Permanente in 1996 to inquire about a possible project for camp. KPETG provides professional actors to present the shows. The shows serve to normalize feelings for campers in a non-threatening way. In "Uncle Gherkin's Magical Show" Pickle, Relish, and Rob have lost Uncle Gherkin to a heart attack. The characters go through many different feelings, among them magical thinking and guilt. In "Fragments of Grief" Heather has lost her mother to a car accident and Andrew has lost his brother to murder. Heather and Andrew meet people who do not understand their grief and who respond in well meaning, but insensitive ways. Both the puppet show and play serve as reminders that everyone grieves differently, allowing for humor to help campers know that it is all right to laugh and have fun, too, even in grief.

Both age groups process what they saw, heard, and learned from the shows in the last counseling group of the day. The adult parent group joins the viewing of the play. Both shows are now also used by other camp organizations inside and outside of Georgia. It is understood that most camps do not have this relationship with Kaiser Permanente, though it is a national organization invested in prevention; KPETG invites contact with the artistic director of the

Atlanta office for assistance. She is the copyright holder of the script and is willing to discuss and share her work.

Group Session 4 Focus: *Trauma and loss experience; reminders, thoughts, feelings, behaviors, and changes*

Goals

- Campers will be able to express feelings surrounding loss.
- Campers will feel less maladaptive circumstance-related distress.
- Campers will cope with loss and change reminders.
- Campers will be free of feelings of guilt, hopelessness, and distorted perceptions.

Process Objectives

- Identify and review trauma, loss, and change reminders.
- Teach the difference between trauma reminders and actual trauma.
- Teach cognitive processing and positive coping statements.

The last session of the day involves cognitive therapy. As this session begins, counselors review the puppet show or play with campers to hear the messages they received about neutralizing magical thinking, normalizing feelings, and realizing how all people are individuals with their own individualized way of grieving. After again stressing that the camp group is a safe place to share and reminding the campers about confidentiality, the counselors shift the group focus into trauma and loss reminders—the puppet show and the play often remind campers of situations in their own grief journeys. The counselors ask, "How can you deal with reminders?" taking examples from the campers' own stories. If, for example, a mother was taken to the hospital in an ambulance with the siren on, how does the camper deal with hearing ambulance sirens? What are some ways campers have learned at camp?

The session on cognitive therapy ties campers' thoughts, feelings, and behaviors together. For younger campers, counselors may want to use the "Cognitive Triangle" (Cohen, Mannarino, & Deblinger, 2017, pp. 315–316). In addition, Shelby (2010) has described the use of CBT and play therapy to address trauma stress. Counselors review samples of how thoughts influence feelings, and how feelings may influence behavior. The counselor may give an example such as, "Your best friend did not say 'hi' to you when you walked by her in the hallway in school this morning. What does your brain tell you? Maybe your brain says you must have done something and that she is mad at you. So, because you think she is mad at you, how do you feel? Maybe you feel upset and hurt. Your feelings of hurt make you act mean in class towards your other friends, which in turn gets them angry at you. Instead, if, when your friend walks right by you without saying 'hi,' what else can your brain tell you? Maybe to think, 'oh, she is absent minded today.' You may instead feel a bit amused, or maybe not feel anything in particular. Because you are not upset or hurt, you act naturally with your other friends and the morning progresses nicely for you."

The group meeting proceeds into feelings children and adolescents experience when they are grieving. Most of these feelings are natural, but there are some that bereaved people do not need to have. One of those is guilt for having caused the death. If possible, counselors use incidents from the campers' real life with examples of distortions they have heard during their stories or at any other time during the previous sessions. If a child has a difficult time "correcting" his or her thoughts—e.g., if a boy feels guilty for not saving his father from suicide—the counselor may ask the camper, "If your best friend felt like he should have saved his father, what would you say to him?" At Camp MAGIK, peers in the group are very sensitive in helping other campers "correct" their thinking. In this session, campers also review changes in their lives and how these can be good, bad, or neutral. In their journals, campers can mark on the provided list changes they have experienced and they may add others if not listed.

After this session, campers enjoy some free time spent on practice for the talent show, or free play, supervised by their counselors. After dinner, the talent show takes place. This is a highlight of the weekend. Talents vary from the ability to burp on command to elaborate dance and musical performances. There are a few rules for the talent show: One is that everyone participates, either as a performer on the stage, or as an attentive audience member who claps after a performance. The other, more important, rule is to respect those who are courageous enough to stand and perform. No one is allowed to make fun of campers' performances on the stage.

After the talent show, there is a complete change of focus as campers prepare for the memorial service. Camp shifts into grief activities. The memorial relates to Worden's (2008) task of letting go and investing in future relationships or things, as well as addressing separation distress as outlined in multi-dimensional grief theory (Kaplow et al., 2013). Each group of campers works together to prepare a poem for their group, picking an existing poem (campers have a collection of poems included in their activity boxes) or writing one themselves. The campers have been asked to bring poems or lyrics that give them comfort—teenagers often bring lyrics of popular music. These can serve as a basis for writing their own group poem. Sometimes the campers write poems by contributing one or two lines each so that in a group of six campers they create a 6- to 12-line poem. Once the groups have selected or created their poems (this usually takes about 30 to 45 minutes) the campers gather. As one large group, campers and counselors walk quietly down to the lake. Groups take turns reading their poems, starting with the youngest campers. Once campers in this group have read their poems, each camper lights a candle (a "trick" candle that does not extinguish until burned down, glued to a magnolia leaf). These are launched onto the lake water. This youngest group is then followed by the next youngest group, and so on. After all groups have read their poems and lit their candles, they listen to Eric Clapton's "No Tears in Heaven" while the candles burn down as they float on the lake. Campers then return to their cabins in silence and are allowed to process in any way they need to—they may cry while being comforted by counselors or each other, they may need to run around, or they may choose to go straight to bed. Campers are offered hot chocolate at their cabins. Their choice is paramount at this point. There is no attempt at "fun" after the memorial service. However, if campers want to start playing ball, the counselors play ball with those who want to. If campers want to sit in a group and talk, counselors let them. This is one way they can start to learn to regulate their emotions on their own, though counselors are there to offer comfort to those who want it. There is no harm in doing "fun" activities if they take place after campers have had sufficient time to process the memorial service. After campers are tucked into bed, a counselor reads the relaxation and guided imagery script again.

Group Session 5 Focus: *Interaction of trauma and grief; memories*

Goals

- Campers will no longer have arousal, avoidance, and re-experiencing symptoms that interfere with grief work.
- Campers will be able to reconstitute a non-traumatic mental image of the person who died.

Process Objective

* Allow campers to create/share memories of the person who died.

Sunday morning begins with the fifth counseling session after breakfast. Like the memorial service, this counseling session is a transition from trauma-focused work to grief-related work. In this session, campers share their memories of the person who died. Counselors briefly remind them of ways they have learned to deal with trauma and loss reminders, such as thought stopping, deep breathing, and relaxation exercises. Counselors normalize for campers that many people, children, adolescents, and adults alike, seem to think that if they stop actively grieving and thinking about their lost loved one, or if they have fun, they will forget them. Counselors remind campers that talking about and sharing memories about their loved ones are good ways not to forget, and writing or drawing memories allows them to have the memory at hand so there is no risk of forgetting. Counselors encourage campers to share both what made their person special and things they did not care for that much. Many campers are somewhat unwilling to admit to things they did not like about the dead person, but counselors normalize that "nobody is perfect," and this does not imply a lack of love for that person. Although counselors do not tell campers this, if a child or teen idolizes a parent who died, there will be difficult issues to deal with, particularly if a surviving parent decides to date.

After campers have shared their memories, they receive premade pillowcases, created by volunteers, that they decorate using textile markers, stencils, stamps and stamp pads, etc. Camp MAGIK used glue and glitter in past years, but that created messy situations so it was stopped. There are several feeling words available on small slips of paper that counselors offer the campers to put into their pillowcases, or blank slips that campers can use to write their own feeling words, together with the stuffing materials for the pillows. Words that campers may decide to use include "happy memories," "love you," "sadness," "guilt," "sorry," "miss you," "wish you were here," etc. When it comes to the youngest campers, counselors suggest that they work on decorating the pillowcases while sharing their memories. This may help them to share in a more non-threatening manner.

After recreational archery for older campers and a scavenger hunt for younger ones, the final group session occurs.

Group Session 6: *Adjustment and maintaining contact; letter writing*

Goals

- Campers will be able to maintain bonds with the person who died.
- Campers will experience less maladaptive separation distress.

Process Objective

- Assist children in writing letters to and from the deceased persons to communicate symbolically with them.

This sixth and final group session allows campers to write a letter to their loved ones and consider what their loved ones may want to communicate back to them. Counselors discuss with campers the importance of living and being interested in new things and people. Before bereaved youth can adjust, counselors suggest it helps to tell the person who died everything that needs to be said. Campers are encouraged to write in their journal a letter to the person that has died, to include content such as how they are doing, how they miss the person, how they love the person, to apologize for anything they are feeling bad about, and to write what they hope to do with their future. Counselors explain that they do not have to say a final good-bye to the person that died—instead, letter writing or journaling is one way to communicate with them. Counselors tell campers that after this session they will get an opportunity to send their messages in a balloon to the one who died. After they have written their letter, counselors ask them to write another letter, as if that person has written back to them.

Counselors encourage campers to read their letters aloud to the others in the group. Some are willing; others are not. Counselors coax some to encourage sharing, since it is therapeutic to read the messages aloud, but without undue pressure. Occasionally, campers who do not want to read their letters aloud will allow new group friends to read them to the group.

Before this session ends, counselors tell campers that they will be talking to their parents. Counselors let campers know that they will keep what has been shared in the group confidential, but if there is specific information they would like the counselor to share they will. In keeping with camp policy, expressed intentions or thoughts of self-harm, or harm to others, have already been shared with parents.

After the final group session, campers walk together to a field where each is given a helium-filled balloon. When possible, Camp MAGIK uses environmentally friendly balloons. On the field, one group at a time comes forward—starting with the youngest and ending with the oldest. The group gathers in a circle, each camper with a balloon. Holding the balloons close to their hearts, they transfer into the balloon what they want to say to their loved ones, guided by the content they wrote in their letters. After reflection, the group releases the balloons at the same time. In the past, counselors have tried to use paper that is light enough to be sent with the balloons. However, this type of paper is fragile and challenging to write on, though it is a possibility for those who do to send the actual letter with the balloon. At Camp MAGIK the letters remain on pages in the campers' journals.

After the balloon release each group gathers for a counseling group picture. Then comes the cookout. Since grief affects the whole family, Camp MAGIK invites parents of campers and other close relatives of the deceased to participate in our adult retreat, which is held parallel with each camp session but separate from the campers. During the weekend, adults receive professional and peer support during counseling sessions, participate in expressive arts sessions, and participate in several recreational activities (hiking, canoeing, archery, etc.). Parents and campers meet on Sunday for the lunch cookout. This is a time when the parents have a chance to meet with their campers and campers' counselors. Not all parents participate in the adult retreat due to time and other constraints. Camp invites those who cannot stay for the weekend to a psycho-educational workshop that begins early on Sunday morning and finishes when the campers' closing ceremony begins. These parents are included in the cookout, as are parents who attended neither the retreat nor the workshop but can come for lunch. At this time, as campers, counselors, and parents share a meal together spread out over the camp, lead counselors seek out their campers' parents to give a "report" on how each camper did in group. Counselors are careful to keep confidentiality, but will let parents know if the camper does or does not need further assistance in the grieving process, including steps the parent can take to help the camper along.

Campers leave the cookout together with co-counselors when everyone has finished eating. Parents and lead counselors usually stay for another hour so everyone has a chance to talk. During this hour, campers have a chance to play with their new friends, picking activities they enjoy. Half an hour before the closing ceremony, co-counselors usher campers to their cabins for packing and final cleanup.

A photographer takes pictures of the whole group of campers and counselors/volunteers immediately prior to the closing ceremony. At the closing ceremony, each camper is asked to come forward for a certificate of completion, a T-shirt, a backpack, and other donated knick-knacks, such as yo-yos, jump ropes, etc. Campers also collect their decorated pillows, which volunteers have finished by sewing up the seam left open for easy stuffing. Parents receive an informational hand-out on grief and resources.

Camp MAGIK has a full schedule, yet campers continually give feedback that most of all, camp is fun. The schedule alternates between group counseling sessions and fun activities as outlined in the curriculum. The fun activities include physical activities such as get-acquainted games, a campfire, a ropes course, canoeing, practice for the talent show, a talent show, archery, a scavenger hunt, etc. The program also includes various expressive arts activities such as journaling, writing poetry, writing letters to and from the deceased, decorating pillow cases, drawing, and music. All of these activities serve to assist the campers in expressing their grief.

Other Curricula and/or Formats

Buddy System

Many camps use some type of formal format or curriculum to conduct their camps, whereas others are more flexible and use different activities each camp session. Before describing other camp models, just a few words on the buddy system, a format used by many camps. When using the buddy system, the camp staff matches each camper with an adult buddy. Buddies usually spend their time with their assigned campers throughout the camp session, go with them to all activities, and spend the night together. Buddies are volunteers from the community who are trained by the camp in working with bereaved children and teens. Campers are then matched with "their" buddy. At Camp Chimaqua in Pennsylvania, a program of Hospice & Community Care's Pathways Center for Grief & Loss, for example, staff members interview each prospective camper in a face-to-face assessment. They determine how the child is impacted by the death, how they are grieving, what their bedtime routine is, whether they have been away from home overnight before, and try to get a sense of their overall personality. Staff also meet with all prospective buddy volunteers in person to get a sense of their personalities as well as whether they have a preference in terms of the gender of the camper they might be paired with. Each camper's and each buddy's information is written on index cards that are then posted on a board. Matching begins based on each camper's and buddy's information (P. Anewalt, personal communication, December 19, 2016). Volunteers serve as small-group leaders, which enables each buddy to completely focus on his or her camper while the group leader introduces the activities, keeps the group on schedule, and coordinates anything needed for each activity. Camp Evergreen in Indiana, a program of Center for Hospice Care, uses a slightly different ratio for the buddy system. At this camp, the small processing groups are led by professional grief counselors and each young camper has a buddy. Two or three teens share a buddy. Buddies spend all weekend with their campers, including during mealtimes, free time, and bedtime, when they share large bunk rooms at night (N. Patterson, personal communication, December 16, 2016). Buddies are hospice volunteers or other volunteers recruited from the community and trained by camp staff. Using the written applications for camp, the camp staff matches buddies with campers based on type of loss, gender, and what is known of each personality.

Camp Courage, Iowa

Communications with various camps across the country show that outlines of camps differ in some aspects but not in others. Most camps interweave physical, fun activities with grief activities. Some use a set curriculum, while others do not. Many camps that use a set curriculum base their outlines on Worden's four tasks of mourning (2008). One such camp is Camp Courage in Iowa, a program of Hospice of Siouxland (J. Giorgio, personal communication, December 19, 2016). During the camp weekend, campers are divided into groups of six to eight campers based on age. On Friday night campers briefly share their stories, who died, when, and what the relationship was, to help them accept the reality of the loss (Worden, 2008). On Saturday, three stations are set, each addressing one of Worden's three remaining tasks. There is a Pain/Emotions station with two substations. At one substation, campers participate in a scavenger hike to find bags with questions in them. An example of a question may be, "What did it feel like to hear that your mother had died?" At the second substation, there are coping/walking sticks. Each camper carves a stick with names of people to reach out to for support and ways to cope. These two substations help campers work through the pain of grief (Worden, 2008). The second station, Create a Memory Box, is arranged to help campers adjust to an environment where the dead person is no longer present (Worden, 2008). Campers decorate and compile memories for a memory box. The third and last station, The Time Line, assists campers in continuing their connection with the dead person while moving forward (Worden, 2008). Campers create a time line of their relationship with the person who died from as far back as they remember. Thus, campers move through one grief activity on Friday and four on Saturday. The rest of Saturday is spent in non-grief activities. A memorial service, held with the campers' families, and balloon release on Sunday morning conclude the camp (J. Giorgio, personal communication, December 19, 2016). Camp Courage uses three counselors for each small group. One of these is a professional counselor such as a school counselor or social worker. The other two counselors are community members who volunteer because of their interest in and love for children. Other volunteers are trained in organizing activities but do not facilitate discussions. This camp model does not use the buddy system, so the counselors who facilitate the discussions may or may not spend the night with the campers—other volunteers are recruited to do that.

Camp Evergreen, Indiana

Camp Evergreen in Indiana strives to meet the following goals: to decrease isolation and normalize the grief process, provide education on the grief process and typical grief reactions, use the camp participants to teach and practice coping skills, provide opportunities for campers to tell their stories and express their thoughts and feelings, provide opportunities to participate in rituals of remembrance, and provide opportunities for fun and friendship. Camp starts with volunteers participating in a high ropes course before the teen campers arrive in order to increase their understanding of the teens' high ropes experience. As mentioned previously, two or three teens share a buddy, and buddies meet with the camp director before camp begins to gather information on their campers (who died, demographics, allergies, narrative from parents, etc.). One of the first activities after campers arrive is designed as a creative way for campers and buddies to bond and get the lay of the land—a challenge and scavenger hunt combination. Campers and their buddies receive a map of the camp grounds with various stops where they have to perform or tackle a challenge together. Another creative activity occurs after dinner, when teens use numbers listed on a wall or on the floor to represent answers on a Likert scale to questions such as, "I wanted to come to camp today," or "My family talks about the person who died." As counselors and buddies observe their campers' responses, they gain further information on their campers that will be helpful in small group discussions (N. Patterson, personal communication, December 16, 2016).

One large group activity includes a wristband ceremony where campers are offered a memory wristband of a certain color depending on their relationship with the dead person, such as a navy-blue wristband to represent parent loss or a green wristband a grandparent loss. Wearing these helps to decrease the campers' sense of isolation. Other large group activities include a teen peer mentor panel where former campers sit on a panel and answer questions about their grief and coping, a campfire, and two memorial service ceremonies. One is a lantern luminary ceremony on a dock. The dock is covered with memory lanterns decorated by the campers while in small groups. The lanterns serve as a visual reminder of campers' memories. Counselors hold up lit candles to ask a group of campers and buddies "What would be helpful in your life right now?" or "What would your loved one want for you right now?" After the camper answers the questions, counselors make a wish for what the camper hopes to be helpful, or what the camper thinks their loved one would want for them. The camper receives a lit candle from the counselor and puts it on a disk with other campers' candles. The disk is launched onto the water when all campers have received a candle. The second memorial service takes place in the large group on Sunday morning as the campers write wishes or thoughts on notepaper. These are placed on an evergreen tree planted by campers. The camp director reads the names of the camper and the deceased as the campers place their notes. In addition, counselors and buddies write personal wishes on rocks for their campers as a final wish or blessing.

This camp model also includes several small group activities. The first small group activity takes place on Friday night. Campers take part in icebreakers and answer questions about themselves. Counselors talk about loss in general and ask the campers to talk a little about who died and how they died. During the second small group activity on Saturday, campers provide more details about their losses. In addition to sharing who died, how, and when, camp-ers also tell about how they learned of the death, describing their reactions then and what their feelings are now. They also create a memory lantern in memory of the person who died (this is used during the lantern luminary service later that night that is described earlier). Other small group activities on Saturday include the high and low ropes course. Processing questions used for the high ropes course include what item, activity, or person helped the teenagers feel most safe and how they faced the challenges of the ropes course: Did they feel stuck? Scared? Confident? What helped them through rough spots, etc.? How did this activity relate to their grief? How are they coping with their grief, especially in relation to their family and friends? Another topic during small group activities is coping skills—the teens discuss various coping skills, including those they are using and which ones are helpful.

When not participating in large or small group activities, camp-ers participate in "activity time" including canoeing, fishing, game playing, and horseback trail riding. Campers also spend time after the Sunday memorial service and before leaving camp in group games and other activities. This is a time for the teenagers to just be teens and to spend time with their new friends.

The Camp Erin Model

In reviewing the framework for a bereavement camp, the fol-lowing material prepared by The Moyer Foundation's Camp Erin program presents a succinct outline of desired outcomes and key program elements. Like other bereavement camp programs, a major emphasis of Camp Erin is to provide an opportunity for children and teens to experience bonding with peers who have had similar life experiences. All Camp Erin locations work towards the following desired outcomes: normalize the grief process through bereavement education and support; decrease the camper's sense of isolation felt while grieving; provide a framework for campers to process their grief in healthy ways; build a toolbox of coping skills and resources that campers can use during and after camp; allow campers the opportunity to remember, honor, and memorial-ize those who have died; promote positive youth development; and have fun.

The Camp Erin network contains a number of consistent pro-gram elements. Camps run over a time frame of three days and two nights, most often from Friday afternoon to Sunday afternoon. The local Camp Erin partner organization selects and contracts with an accredited camp facility that offers adequate facilities for sleeping, recreation, and grief support activities. To ensure privacy and safety, Camp Erin must have the sole use of the facility for the weekend program. Campers are aged 6–17, and each camp session serves at least 50 non-returning campers. Most partner organizations exceed this requirement to increase support to their community. In 2016, the average number of campers at Camp Erin locations was 69, with the largest session having 124 campers.

Grief activities are essential to the Camp Erin experience and are key in accomplishing the desired outcomes of camp. Each Camp Erin program includes two signature activities: the Memory Board Ceremony and the Luminary Ceremony. Each local camp also identifies three to five additional grief activities, such as remembrance projects, expressive arts, and experiences that promote mindfulness and healthy coping skills. The planned activities reflect the developmental and clinical needs of campers. They are designed to be age appropriate, to utilize elements of trauma-informed care, to be strengths based, and to promote positive youth development. The camp schedule transitions between grief support and recreation activities to provide opportunities for different forms of expression, learning, and development.

In the Camp Erin model the staff positions include a paid camp director and master's level clinical director, additional paid or volunteer master's level clinical staff, and two medical staff. Volunteers include "Cabin Big Buddies" and other non-professional and professional adults who support the professional staff. Each Camp Erin location recruits, screens, and trains all volunteers in childhood bereavement and grief support in the camp setting, typically with 8 to 16 hours of training.

The Moyer Foundation facilitates a comprehensive pre- and post-camp reporting and evaluation process to ensure quality control and provide ongoing support to partner organizations. These data are compiled and analyzed by The Moyer Foundation's Camp Erin staff.

Parents receive grief education and support throughout the intake assessment, pre-camp event, parent information sessions at the start or conclusion of camp, and at a reunion event. Each camper and his or her parent are interviewed, usually in person, prior to acceptance to ensure emotional readiness for the camp weekend. Continued bereavement care services are offered to campers and their families by the local Camp Erin partner organization through its ongoing support offerings and community referrals and through The Moyer Foundation's Resource Center, the camper newsletter, a blog for caregivers, and social media (B. Gardner, personal communication, December 19, 2016).

Camp Erin—Twin Cities, Minnesota

In addition to including Camp Erin network best practices, each Camp Erin location develops its own curriculum. Following is a description of Camp Erin Twin Cities, run by Fairview's Youth Grief Services. The curriculum blends The Moyer Foundation standards with their own expertise. The camp is led by a team that consists of a director and co-director, two lead Cabin Big Buddies, two lead Sharing Circle facilitators, and the camp nurse. Sharing Circle facilitators are not professional counselors but are volunteers who have been trained and use set curricula to follow during the weekend. The leadership team arrives to camp the day before camp starts to set up and go over the plans for the weekend. Two Sharing Circle facilitators lead discussions of each Sharing Circle, help behind the scenes, and sit with the campers during meal times but do not sleep in the cabins with the campers. The Cabin Big Buddies stay with the campers at night and during most of the day but do get breaks during Sharing Circle times and team activities. All volunteers get a chance for breaks in a special leadership lounge (J. Simmonds, personal communication, January 13, 2017).

Campers participate in Sharing Circles based on age, with the youngest group called "Trees and Tents"; the next oldest group called "Compass, Canoes, and Hiking Boots"; and the oldest group of campers called "Flashlights, Backpacks and Sleeping Bags." Each age group has its own age-appropriate curriculum and participates in four Sharing Circles. The first Sharing Circle lasts about 45 minutes. It takes place on Friday evening and is called "Get to Know You," where campers introduce themselves to each other. The second Sharing Circle, "Our Unique Stories," takes place on Saturday morning for an hour and a half. Using icebreakers and pictures, campers share their stories with each other. They also use feelings cords with clothes pins to show the size of their grief. The third Sharing Circle also lasts an hour and a half, and is called "Change and Healing." During this Sharing Circle, held Saturday afternoon, campers are given a tile piece, break it, and then try to piece it back together. They discuss how their lives have changed from before the death of their person and how it looks now—represented by the pieced-together tile. The last Sharing Circle takes place on Sunday morning for 45 minutes. This is a time for campers to say good-bye to other group members and tell everyone what they appreciate about them.

When campers are not taking part in Sharing Circles, they enjoy team times such as a climbing wall for the younger campers and yoga and drum-making for the older campers. All campers make luminaries for use in a luminary memorial service on Saturday night, and all take part in therapeutic drumming. Waterfront activities include fishing, canoeing, a splash pool, and a swimming pool. One creative team time includes a digital scavenger hunt, where campers with the help of their Cabin Big Buddies take digital pictures of requested items.

Day Camps

In regard to day camps, Ruffin and Zimmerman (2010) share a curriculum that is easy to use for this type of camp setting: the Camp Good Grief curriculum. This is a five-day curriculum with 120 children and adolescents attending that blends grief activities and traditional camp activities. Using a day camp can be a cost-effective way to help children through the grief process. Ruffin and Zimmerman also point out that being able to return home at the end of the day may be comforting to the child after having spent the day sharing strong feelings, and presents an opportunity for the camper to open a dialogue with parents or caregivers about the day's grief activities. In this model, the camp is staffed using representatives of a variety of disciplines, such as hospice and school social workers, psychiatric nurse practitioners, child psychologists and psychiatrists, and art therapists. These professionals lead groups of 8 to 11 campers with the help of volunteers. Professionals and volunteers alike complete a course in grief and bereavement. Each day of camp has a theme, and theoretically it follows a combination of Fox's and Worden's tasks of mourning. The theme of the first day is dedicated to understanding and accepting that death has occurred. Younger campers use a teddy bear and older campers a talking stick while sharing in group. The second day of camp is dedicated to identifying, expressing, and normalizing feelings. Campers make masks in art therapy. On the third day, campers decorate boxes to represent a safe place to go when in need of comfort. On the fourth day, campers bring in items that remind them of the person who died, and they tell their memories around these items. On this day, they also write messages on a large shell to the person who died. They are then invited to throw this shell in a body of water. The last day of camp is family day. Parents and campers participate in dance activities before parents meet with the therapists to learn what their children have accomplished in group and get ideas on how to keep open communication going. Campers meet one last time with their new friends to say good-bye, exchange phone numbers and email addresses. Camp ends with campers performing a talent show for their parents.

In Summary

Bereavement camps share a model of a combination of grief-focused activities and traditional recreational camp activities. The combination offers a balance of fun release along with the intensity of memories and emotions evoked by grief work. All modalities offer peer bonding and normalization of feelings. Camps are varied in the number of emotionally focused sessions they hold. Most hold some sort of memorial service or activity, such as a candle lighting ceremony or balloon release. This chapter presented the Camp MAGIK model in detail and shared summaries of other models that give examples of innovative methods of reaching out to children and adolescents to help them process their grief.

Recommended Reading

Cohen, J. A., Mannarino, A. P., & Deblinger, E. (2017). *Treating trauma and traumatic grief in children and adolescents* (2nd ed.). New York, NY: The Guilford Press.

Fox, L., & Lentini, R. H. (2006). Teaching children a vocabulary for emotions. *Beyond the Journal: Young Children on the Web.* Retrieved from www.naeyc.org/files/yc/file/200611/BTJFoxSupplementalActivities.pdf

Shelby, J. (2010). Cognitive-behavioral therapy and play therapy for childhood trauma and loss. In N. B. Webb (Ed.), *Helping bereaved children: A handbook for practitioners*. New York, NY: The Guilford Press.

Worden, J. W. (2008). *Grief counseling and grief therapy: A handbook for the mental health professional* (4th ed.). New York, NY: Springer.

References

Cohen, J. A., Mannarino, A. P., & Deblinger, E. (2006). *Treating trauma and traumatic grief in children and adolescents*. New York, NY: The Guilford Press.

Cohen, J. A., Mannarino, A. P., & Deblinger, E. (2017). *Treating trauma and traumatic grief in children and adolescents* (2nd ed.). New York, NY: The Guilford Press.

Doka, K. J. (2000). Eight myths about children, adolescents, and loss. In K. J. Doka (Ed.), *Living with grief: Children, adolescents, and grief* (pp. 33–34). Washington, DC: Hospice Foundation of America.

Fox, L., & Lentini, R. H. (2006). Teaching children a vocabulary for emotions. *Beyond the Journal: Young Children on the Web*. November, 1–3. Retrieved from www.naeyc.org/files/yc/file/200611/BTJ FoxSupplementalActivities.pdf

Hammond, D. C. (Ed.). (1990). *Hypnotic suggestions and metaphors*. New York, NY: W. W. Norton.

Kaplow, J. B., Layne, C. M., Saltzman, W. R., Cozza, S. J., & Pynoos, R. S. (2013). Using multidimensional grief theory to explore the effects of deployment, reintegration, and death on military youth and families. *Clinical Child and Family Psychology Review, 16*, 322–340.

McClatchey, I. S., Vonk, M. E., & Palardy, G. (2009). The prevalence of childhood traumatic grief—a comparison of violent/sudden and expected loss. *Omega - Journal of Death and Dying, 59*(4), 305–323.

Normand, C. L., Silverman, P. R., & Nickman, S. L. (1996). Bereaved children's changing relationships with the deceased. In D. Klass, P. R. Silverman, & S. L. Nickman (Eds.), *Continuing bonds: New understandings of grief*. New York, NY: Taylor & Francis.

Perry, S. (2017, January). Prince William to grieving child: 'I lost my mummy when I was very young too.' *People Magazine*. Retrieved from http://people.com/royals/prince-william-and-princess-kate-make-memory-jars-with-grieving-children

Pynoos, R. S., Steinberg, A. M., & Wraith, R. (1995). A developmental model of childhood traumatic stress. In D. Cicchetti & D. Cohen (Eds.), *Developmental psychopathology: Vol. 2, Risk, disorder, and adaptation* (pp. 72–95). Oxford, England: John Wiley.

Ruffin, P. A., & Zimmerman, S. A. (2010). Bereavement groups and camps for children. In N. B. Webb (Ed.), *Helping bereaved children: A handbook for practitioners* (pp. 304–314). New York, NY: The Guilford Press.

Schuurman, D. L. (2000). The use of groups with grieving children and adolescents. In K. J. Doka (Ed.), *Living with grief: Children, adolescents, and grief* (pp. 165–177). Washington, DC: Hospice Foundation of America.

Shelby, J. (2010). Cognitive-behavioral therapy and play therapy for childhood trauma and loss. In N. B. Webb (Ed.), *Helping bereaved children: A handbook for practitioners*. New York, NY: The Guilford Press.

Srilekha, S., Soumendra, S., & Chattopadhyay, P. K. (2013). Effect of muscle relaxation training as a function of improvement in attentiveness in children. *Procedia—Social and Behavioral Sciences, 91*, 606–613.

Substance Abuse and Mental Health Services Administration (SAMHSA). (2014). *SAMHSA's concept of trauma and guidance for a trauma-informed approach*. HHS Publication No. (SMA) 14-4884. Rockville, MD: Author.

Worden, J. W. (1996). *Grief counseling and grief therapy: A handbook for the mental health professional* (2nd ed.). New York, NY: Springer.

Worden, J. W. (2008). *Grief counseling and grief therapy: A handbook for the mental health professional* (4th ed.). New York, NY: Springer.

7

Evaluation

He had hoped, at least, when the wind blew due East,
   —That the ship would not travel due West!
                    —"The Hunting of the Snark," Lewis Carroll (1876)

The goal of this chapter is to encourage ongoing, high quality evaluations of specialized camp programs. The chapter describes the difference between evaluation and research, offers insight as to why ethics and evidence-based practice are important and discusses the various types of evaluation. Topics include what and who should be studied, by whom, and why.

Introducing Evaluation

The distinction between program evaluation and research can be discussed around in circles depending on the point of view of the author. On one hand, Patton (2002) defines program evaluation as "the systematic collection of information about the activities, characteristics, and outcomes of programs to make judgments about the program, improve program effectiveness, and/or inform decisions about future programming" (p. 10). On the other hand, Patton defines research as differing from evaluation in that "its primary purpose is to generate or test theory and contribute to knowledge for the sake of knowledge. . . . action is not the primary purpose (p. 10). Taking the discussion further, "action research" is discussed by Stringer (2007) as a way of exploring specific programs in order to create a cycle of research, putting in practice what is learned, and then re-evaluating changes in practice. The goal is to improve services based on knowledge gained by research.

Evaluation can focus on what happened (i.e., a description), but also look further to know why it happened (i.e., an explanation). Both are important areas to be studied, but the "what" is not sufficient without the "why" if organizations want to provide the best programs. In using research and evaluation, programs can act on what is learned in order to improve the services offered to children and families.

Evaluation is an area that often is low on the priority list for people running programs. The primary focus is on the clients served and on the practical aspects of running a bereavement camp, staffing, programming, and keeping things going year to year. In programs serving bereaved children, everyone involved in the work knows they are doing "good work" for children who are in need of help. Children tell us they like camp. But, how are programs sure they are providing the best service? How are outcomes measured as these relate to the program's mission and the needs of grieving children?

Anyone who is committed to offering grief camp experiences to children would agree that these children and families are vulnerable; they are hurting and are adjusting to a major traumatic event. Children and adolescents deserve an experience at camp that will promote healing and have little or no threat of re-traumatization as they experience the deep emotions brought forth in the grief camp. Put bluntly, if a healing camp for grieving children does not know what effect it is having on the children attending, perhaps the funds supporting the camp should be used to create a traditional camp that ignores the grief issues of the child and family and simply arranges fun and relaxation.

Clute and Kobayashi (2013) searched through extensive literature for outcome studies on children's bereavement camps. In the final analysis, they were able to identify only eight studies with sufficient depth to give any indication of camp effectiveness. In concluding their analysis of camp outcomes they stated,

> Death touches everyone with profound effects. Bereaved children
> need effective support. Bereavement camps can be a valuable

resource to bereaved children and families. Camp organizers must recognize the importance of ongoing evaluation of interventions implemented so that the most effective outcomes may be achieved.

(Clute and Kobayashi, 2013, p. 55)

Why Do Evaluations?

It can be safely assumed that all grief camps want to provide quality programming for the children and families who attend. Most importantly, however, programmatic evaluation is necessary for vulnerable clients in order to do no harm. Children and families who receive the services of grief camps have suffered a major life loss and are dealing with the stressors produced by this loss. The greatest risk that camps face is raising distress symptoms in children without providing a healing component to the camp program. Children who are referred to grief camps are most often struggling with adjustment to the death of a parent or sibling. Oftentimes, school social workers or psychologists refer campers in order to intervene in school problems. Referrals might come from hospice programs, which have been informed by surviving parents or guardians of the children's adjustment problems. These children might or might not experience complex grief symptoms or meet the criteria for a mental health diagnosis. These are children and families who are in pain and need the support of programs that will help them move towards resolution of the level of distress that they experience.

A bereavement camp is a catalyst for improving mental or behavioral health for the children it serves. Often children are referred to a grief camp because they are exhibiting difficulties at home or in the community. Time, energy, and resources are valuable. If camps are not accomplishing a healing purpose, then changes that are put in place based on evaluation findings are very valuable. Clients come to camps with the expectation that they will find help. Funders, staff, volunteers, and community supporters all rally to the aid of bereavement camps on the assumption that these programs are of benefit to the children and families who attend. Mission statements and descriptions of camps are similar and often use the word "healing." For example, Camp MAGIK states its mission is "Where bereaved children and their caregivers begin to heal in a safe and nurturing environment" (Camp MAGIK, n.d., para. 2). Camp Bridges of Cornerstone Hospice and Palliative Care in Central Florida states in its description, "In this healing environment, children participate in meaningful activities relating to their loss, while also having lots of fun" (Cornerstone Hospice, 2017, para. 3).

To fulfill the desire to be healing, grief camp programs need a basis for what they do that can guide them in doing what works. Camps should challenge themselves to compare their mission and description with the evaluations conducted. Although client satisfaction is one measure of the success of a camp, this is a shallow level of evaluation on which to base a program. Enjoyment of the time at camp is a common denominator in most camp experiences. If a grief camp program aims to provide more than the outcomes that a traditional camp experience would give, there must be some empirical value of a significant percentage of the components of camp.

Although grief camps have been in existence since the 1980s, evaluation of the efficacy of these camps is relatively new (Clute & Kobayashi, 2013). If something new is started in mental health treatment, evaluation of its efficacy is needed. Grief camps are slow in doing widespread and extensive evaluations that meet high standards. When Clute and Kobayashi (2013) reviewed grief camps from 1991 to 2009 they only found eight studies that were published in peer reviewed professional journals and that gave clear information about camp evaluation. One of the goals of this book is to encourage ongoing, high quality evaluations of grief camp programs. Camps need to ascertain which components of camps are most critical to children's healing and how they are best incorporated into the camp experience.

In their book *Adventure Therapy: Theory, Research and Practice*, Gass, Gillis, and Russell (2012) discuss the importance of not assuming the efficacy of a program based on its popularity. Examples they give of popular programs that did not reach their objectives when exposed to rigorous research included the Scared Straight program, which aimed to reduce juvenile delinquency in the 1970s through emotionally charged visits by first offenders to jails, and the DARE (Drug Abuse and Resistance Education Programs), which taught schoolchildren about the dangers of drug abuse. The lesson learned from these examples is that "widely popular and interesting social programs were assumed to be effective until rigorous research uncovered hidden truths and costs of such programs on youth" (p. 286). This is a lesson of importance for those who work with grief camps. Can a program that gives a free camp experience to children, feels sympathy for the great mourning of a child who is orphaned, and watches children smile and have fun with others, not be a great program? This is a central question that each camp should be ready to address.

Evidence-Based Practice

Evidence-based practice can be defined as "the integration of the best available research with clinical expertise in the context of patient characteristics, culture, and preferences" (American Psychological Association [APA], 2016, para. 1). According to SAMHSA, evidence-based practices "integrate clinical expertise; expert opinion; external scientific evidence; and client, patient, and caregiver perspectives so that providers can offer high-quality services that reflect the interests, values, needs, and choices of the individuals served" (SAMHSA, 2016, para.1). It is the "best available research" and "external scientific evidence" that grief camps need to strive to produce. As of this writing, SAMHSA has reviewed more than 400 mental health interventions that meet its standards of evidence-based practice; however, the bereavement camp modality has not been reviewed.

Gass and his colleagues (Gass, Gillis, & Russell, 2012) have created a rubric for the assessment of evidence-based research that could be useful for the evaluation of research on grief camps. Their ten indicators of quality research are influenced by the U.S. Offices of Juvenile Justice and Delinquency Prevention and SAMHSA. The indicators include strong experimental design and statistical power, available training models with treatment/intervention fidelity, quality measurement instruments, length of treatment effectiveness, benefit-cost analysis, background literature support, results reporting, and cultural variability and replication at different sites and with different populations (Gass, Gillis, & Russell, 2012, pp. 358–361). This rubric presents high standards for grief camps to strive for.

Ethics in Evaluation

The following points come from the American Evaluation Association (2004) "Guiding Principles for Evaluators" and are reviewed here with a special stress on their relevance to evaluations of grief camps.

A. **Systematic Inquiry:** Evaluators conduct systematic, data-based inquiries.
   To ensure the accuracy and credibility of the evaluative information they produce, evaluators should adhere to the highest technical standards appropriate to the methods they use (American Evaluation Association, Section A.1., 2004).

B. Competence: Evaluators provide competent performance to stakeholders.

Evaluators should possess (or ensure that the evaluation team possesses) the education, abilities, skills, and experience appropriate to undertake the tasks proposed in the evaluation (American Evaluation Association, Section B.1., 2004).

C. Integrity/Honesty: Evaluators display honesty and integrity in their own behavior, and attempt to ensure the honesty and integrity of the entire evaluation process.

Before accepting an evaluation assignment, evaluators should disclose any roles or relationships they have that might pose a conflict of interest (or appearance of a conflict) with their role as an evaluator. If they proceed with the evaluation, the conflict(s) should be clearly articulated in reports of the evaluation results (American Evaluation Association, Section C.2., 2004).

D. Respect for People: Evaluators respect the security, dignity, and self-worth of respondents, program participants, clients, and other evaluation stakeholders.

Evaluators should abide by current professional ethics, standards, and regulations regarding risks, harms, and burdens that might befall those participating in the evaluation; regarding informed consent for participation in evaluation; and regarding informing participants and clients about the scope and limits of confidentiality (American Evaluation Association, Section D.2., 2004).

E. Responsibilities for General and Public Welfare: Evaluators articulate and take into account the diversity of general and public interests and values that may be related to the evaluation.

Because the public interest and good are rarely the same as the interests of any particular group (including those of the client or funder), evaluators will usually have to go beyond analysis of particular stakeholder interests and consider the welfare of society as a whole (American Evaluation Association, Section E.5., 2004).

It is important to elaborate on two special areas of ethics: the limits of confidentiality and issues of conflict of interest.

Confidentiality has limits. Clearly, confidentiality cannot be maintained if there are allegations of child neglect or abuse. Most professionals involved in camps or evaluation are "mandated reporters" through the laws of their states. As such, they are required to report to the local or state department of child protection any knowledge they gain regarding possible current or ongoing child neglect or abuse.

Likewise, most professionals are obligated to break confidentiality in cases of "harm to self or others." For example, if a camper tells an evaluator he or she is considering suicide, the evaluator must act appropriately, usually at a minimum sharing this information with the child's parent or guardian. The duty to warn if a person is a danger to others is rooted in the California court case of *Tarasoff vs. Regents of the University of California* in 1976. In that case, a mental health patient told his psychotherapist that he planned to harm an identifiable woman and carried out the threat when he murdered the woman. Although the Tarasoff ruling has influenced laws in many states, it is generally applied when a specific threat is considered viable by a therapist or physician. In the case of camp evaluation, harm to others is unlikely to arise, but the possibility of a child discussing self-harm cannot be taken lightly. It is important for evaluators to understand the procedures that should be followed in any situation of risk. These involve the policies of the camp, professional standards, and procedures under the institutional review board that has approved any research.

Confidentiality between children and their parents is harder to delineate. The limits of confidentiality should be explained in consents that parents or guardians sign. In addition, evaluators need to clearly explain these limits to children in language appropriate to the child's age.

Confidentiality is rarely completely ensured in small-scale evaluations, especially those that share the thoughts of evaluation participants. If one participant's opinion varies from the norm, others may be able to identify the person who has expressed those thoughts. Even if this identity is incorrect, the findings may reflect onto a participant. Although this is a problem that is most evident in qualitative evaluations where direct quotations are attributed to participants, evaluators must give consideration to protecting identity in all methods of evaluation as much as possible. Protection is especially relevant when staff members evaluate a program and negative opinions are voiced or reflected in numerical scores.

Conflict of interest carries a different difficult burden for the evaluator. Usually the evaluators or evaluation teams have a vested interest in the promotion of the camps they are studying. This conflict is common in evaluations of many programs and interventions, not necessarily limited to camps. Perhaps the most blatant situations are medical efficacy studies funded by pharmaceutical companies. Funders are unhappy if the projects in which they have an interest are shown to be unsuccessful.

Closer to the stated area of concern, grief camps are usually evaluated by those who run them, by board members, by professional associates, or by acquaintances of those who run them. There is nothing wrong with these affiliations, per se, but protection against bias must be a focus of attention in execution of the evaluation. Evaluation reports must clearly reveal and address any connection between evaluator and subject studied. This can be handled by adhering to strong evaluation methods and illuminating the affiliation in any resulting presentations or written reports. Revealing these connections is especially important if national presentations or peer respected publications are the means of sharing information about the study. Evaluation design should reflect back to the reason for research. Programs evaluate their outcome in order to increase best practices, to use resources wisely, and most importantly, to do no harm to vulnerable children. Evaluators should remain aware that their findings can influence other similarly designed programs and children and families far beyond those who participate in the specific study group.

Bias on the part of evaluators is a serious threat to the validity of any level of camp research. Most often evaluators are affiliated with the camp they are studying and have preconceived beliefs that camp is a positive experience for those who attend. The evaluation team and camp representatives need to discuss these biases in order to minimize impact on what is learned. Bias can be associated with varied aspects of camp and various methods of review. Satisfaction surveys might be important in securing camp funding, especially from small local donors, and important in encouraging referrals to camp from organizations such as hospices and local schools. Both the wording of Likert scaled survey questions (scales usually using a 1–4 or 1–5 rating) and the attention to comments in open-ended questions can shift the survey outcome. If the evaluator does not record interviews, the interviewer's recollection of the conversation may alter the reports of the outcome.

What Should Be Measured?

The central question in planning an evaluation of camp is simply, What do you want to know? Various approaches to evaluation and research design are available to anyone wishing to measure grief camp experiences. All are valuable, but it is important not to confuse satisfaction with outcome, or opinions with statistical evidence.

The success of a program can have varied meaning to diverse stakeholders, including, but not limited to, children attending camp, family members and guardians, referral sources in the community, camp staff, volunteers, funders, and program board members. The range of tools and methods used to evaluate the outcomes of camps can range from simple satisfaction surveys given to parents and campers to quasi-experimental and experimental research designs measuring children's behavior or mental health. Each camp should give consideration to the purpose of its evaluations and the resources available to accomplish an unbiased study.

Possible areas to measure are listed here, with the caution that this is not an exhaustive list, and that no program is likely to engage in evaluations of all areas.

- Satisfaction: Were children and parents happy with the camp experience? Would they come back or recommend the program to others?
- Outcome/changes in children: Behavior pre- and post-camp? Mental health pre- and post-camp? Perceptions of change by the children, their families, or the referring community? In other words, what was the outcome of camp on the children and families?
- Favorite activities or aspects of camp: What parts of camp did children like? Dislike? Suggest changes to? Suggest for future camp inclusion? What activities were most helpful or meaningful for campers?
- Components of camp: What was the quality of pre-camp orientation and paperwork? What was the quality of staff and supervision? What was the quality of the schedule of activities? What was the quality of the physical setting and food?
- As employees and volunteers: What were the most positive aspects of camp? Challenges? Level of training? Quality of supervision? Level of safety for campers and staff?

Who Should Do the Evaluation?

Evaluations can be managed by those with a wide range of training and experience, including camp staff, professors at local universities, or research groups, whether public or private, for-profit or not. Camps should carefully consider the importance of the well-being of each child with whom they work and the overall investment that is being made in each camp. Consideration is paramount to the question whether camps can "afford" *not* to understand the impact camps are having on children. It should be noted here that very minimal financial investment is needed to enact excellent evaluations. Examples of economical evaluations are given here.

At one end of the spectrum, staff or volunteers are able to efficiently conduct a simple evaluation. Counselors can conduct satisfaction surveys of children during the last hours of camp. Volunteers with little training can make follow-up telephone surveys with parents using tightly constructed Likert scales such as, "On a scale of 1 to 5, how would you rate your child's ability to talk about the death since attending camp, with 1 being worse, 3 no change, and 5 better." Office administrators can manage an analysis of cost/benefit ratio using simple information, such as an accounting of costs that includes the value of donations as related to numbers of children attending camp.

As mentioned in Chapter 4, you might include board members or interested community members, such as college professors, with talent and time to lend to the process of evaluation. The "publish or perish" stereotype of academic life is not a myth. Most schools of higher education require faculty to have a research agenda of original scholarship. In addition, many faculty members at the graduate level have student research assistants who are paid to be active in research. Professors are often searching for assignments to keep assistants occupied in a meaningful educational way. University programs in psychology, social work, counseling, and sociology may be contacted for more help. Similarly, retired professors or researchers are often seeking ways to keep their time relevant to community needs. Sympathy for bereaved children might be the catalyst for involvement in camp program evaluation.

Who Should Evaluation Participants Be?

Participants in evaluation can include elementary school–age campers, adolescent campers, parents who live with the children, volunteers who participate in the camp program, camp staff, and community members. Teachers often have intensive pre- and post-contact with children who attend camp. A combination of participants often lends strength to evaluation findings.

Several varieties of groups of participants can be found in the literature. Nabors et al. (2004) used campers, parents, and staff members to reflect on satisfaction with camp and favorite activities. Sixteen children filled out questionnaires and were interviewed at camp;

staff "recorded their ideas about what the camp meant for the children" (p. 405); and parents completed a survey before and after camp, including a six-month follow-up survey. In a more unusual study, clinicians, buddies, and parents were participants although "children were not selected for any evaluative interviews as not to contaminate their short-term in-depth therapeutic camp experience" (Farber & Sabatino, 2007, p. 391). The researchers explain that the "children's psychosocial functioning in camp was measured by . . . camp clinicians and volunteer buddies following all activities on Saturday and Sunday, and by parents at the one month follow-up" (p. 392). Approaching this from another viewpoint, McClatchey and Wimmer (2012) interviewed 19 children aged 8–17 and their 13 parents or guardians in a follow-up qualitative study in order to identify what components of a camp experience were most closely associated with the children's healing. The researchers saw children and parents separately, but at the same time, using one researcher for children's interviews and one for adults.

The outcome of camp on children who attend should be central to any evaluation and research. As mentioned previously, the mission statements and camp descriptions are invaluable in guiding the evaluation of the outcome of camp. Many camps are claimed to have an environment that promotes "healing." Some operationalization of "heal" needs to be defined. Does "heal" mean that the campers learn about natural grief reactions? Does "heal" mean that the campers learn appropriate coping skills? Does "heal" mean that the campers will have fewer symptoms of stress after camp? The meaning leads to what should be measured to determine the outcome of camp.

Any research and evaluations that will be published require permission from the participants. In those which directly involve children in questionnaires, psychometric measurement tools, or interviews, evaluators need to obtain both the consent of the parent or legal guardian and assent of the child or youth. Parental consent forms should include the purpose of the study, what types of questions and methods will be used, how the findings will be used, with whom findings will be shared, how confidentiality will be protected or limited, and the risks and benefits to the child and family of participation in the study. It should be clear that participation or non-participation in outcome studies is completely voluntary and is not associated with eligibility for services. Evaluators need to take care to write assents for children at a reading level appropriate for the age of the child. At a minimum an assent form should name the investigator of the study (this can be as simple as the name of the camp director), the purpose of the study (for example, to find out what you liked about camp, or to find out how you are feeling), an assurance of confidentiality with limits clearly explained, and that the child does not have to participate in the study and can stop at any time or not answer any question. Note that these consents may be needed for publication on websites. An example of an assent form for a 7–10-year-old child can be found in Appendix E.

Who Wants to Know?

Stakeholders in evaluations vary greatly from camp to camp, and broad categories are discussed here. Dissemination of the findings of evaluations might be done through local presentations, state and national professional presentations, websites, newspapers, local magazines, and peer reviewed professional journals.

To start with, campers and their families—clients of the program's services—deserve to have confidence that the grief camp experience will be beneficial. Although few parents, and even fewer campers, will have read or heard program evaluations of their camp, many will have looked at websites that camps produce. Pictures of children having fun and mission statements expressing a commitment to help bereaved children can be supported by brief reports of evaluations or research. Similarly, community volunteers such as camp buddies often gain their information about the value of camps from websites or through community word of mouth.

Staff and volunteers commit uncountable hours of support to running grief camps, and these people become a second tier of stakeholders. Like the families served, all those who work in the programs need confidence that they are providing a worthwhile experience. Entering into a camp environment, staff and volunteers want to know that the protocols and activities that they will be part of come from a tested intervention that is carried out reliably. When children respond emotionally with tears and heartbreaking sadness during camp activities such as balloon releases and discussions of the death of a parent, those working directly with the children want to understand the meanings of the activities and the value of the techniques that will help children deal more successfully with their grief after the camp experiences. This is true for everyone from the level of a volunteer with brief camp experience to a camp director who has committed years to the development of the program.

Board of directors members become a special level of volunteers with the organization. Not only do they commit time and financial support to the camps, but they also put forward their good names in the community. A quality, verified program enhances each member's credibility in the community. If an organization does not engage in evaluations to find out the efficacy of its program then it has neglected a commitment to its board.

Donors are another level of stakeholders. These organizations, businesses, foundations, and individuals have supported grief camps in the belief that they are participating in an important community service. Most camps that raise funds and ask for donations are incorporated as, or are a part of, nonprofit organizations. All present themselves as focused on meeting the needs of grieving children. Funders want to know that the programs they support are making a difference to individuals in their communities. Many foundation donors have specific guidelines for reporting the outcome of programs they fund.

The broad community of those who work with children are also stakeholders. These might include counselors and social workers who refer children to programs. Staff at hospices and medical settings often have close contact with families whom they hope will benefit from camp. Ministers, family friends, and others in the community might also make camp referrals. These people often have the responsibility and role of recommending treatment options for families and children who are struggling with the loss of a loved one. As such, they want to refer to a camp that is documented through evaluations to have a positive outcome on its campers.

Beyond these connections to individual families is the broad spectrum of professionals who provide treatment to children—most directly are those who run grief camps. Many camp interventions are borrowed from camp to camp. The balloon release, memorial art activities, journaling, and candle lighting ceremonies are examples. It is responsible behavior to share the knowledge of outcomes of camps so that best practices can be integrated into all grief camp programs.

Types of Evaluation and Research

Evaluation and research design can successfully follow many traditions. Creswell, in *Research Design: Qualitative, Quantitative, and Mixed Methods Approaches* (2014), has provided students, researchers, and evaluators with a comprehensive look at the variety of methodologies available. Each has its place in exploring the outcomes of bereavement camps. Qualitative explorations range from satisfaction surveys to well-designed qualitative research using triangulation of sources and paying attention to reliability and validity. Quantitative evaluations can vary from questionnaires designed by camp staff, often using simple 1 to 4 Likert scales, to psychometrically validated tools using statistical models designed to measure concepts such as

PTSD. Mixed methods can be used to clarify and enrich statistical findings by adding qualitative personal anecdotes and themes or can uncover qualitative themes that need to be explored further and quantified. Creswell (2014) describes three basic mixed methods designs (pp. 219–221). A mixed methods approach is often beyond the time and resource limits of camp evaluations. Camps want to explore a variety of outcomes. These range from understanding the most enjoyable aspects of camp, to studying camps from a positive youth development model, to the outcome of the camp experience on reducing PTSD symptoms and increasing emotional and cognitive growth.

Surveys

Surveys often give a sense of accomplishment to staff and camp sponsors. It is rare for children or parents to report unhappiness about the camp experience. Satisfaction surveys can address issues of facilities, meals, and administrative details such as pre-camp information. Additionally, satisfaction surveys can pinpoint specific activities that can be improved or eliminated. For example, one weekend camp program discovered that, on one hand, the Saturday night carnival provided by a local church was rated poorly by adolescents and "that the carnival was not age-appropriate for the older group" (Creed, Ruffin, & Ward, 2001, p. 181). On the other hand, all campers rated the campfire very highly. These reflections could save money and volunteer time in future camp schedules.

Most camp programs use some form of satisfaction survey to evaluate camp components. The danger in these surveys is a tendency to confuse how much fun campers had with the notion that the camp experience increased each child's ability to deal with the death of a loved one and use healthy coping mechanisms to move forward in daily activities and relationships. Another difficulty is determining the time to complete surveys. Camps vary on whether to ask campers to complete surveys during the final afternoon of camp or mail surveys to families later. Several camps have noted the difficulty in receiving returns of mailed surveys, and a few camps have tried using Internet based surveys with equally disappointing results. In the excitement of the camp setting, surveys done before campers leave tend to provide overly positive reflections on the camp experience. The role of surveys is best understood in two ways. Surveys serve as tools for revising some camp activities, both those with typical camp emphasis (e.g., campfires or canoeing) and those focused on psycho-educational content such as developing peer relationships based on shared feelings. They also serve to pinpoint weaknesses in elements of the overall program administration, such as pre-camp educational materials for parents.

Beyond satisfaction surveys, surveys can also be used to evaluate the outcome of the camp experience using more change-oriented questions. Just like satisfaction surveys, these surveys can be either quantitative or qualitative. Some examples of outcome-oriented questions, using a Likert scale from 1 to 5, would be "After camp I can talk more freely about my feelings surrounding my loss," "Camp helped me learn ways to cope with my loss," and "Camp helped me connect with others who have also experienced a loss." An issue is what is done with information given by a specific camper, and how does confidentiality apply, if a survey reveals serious difficulties. For example, if a statement such as "I have at least one person who cares about me" is rated, each camp needs to have a plan in place to deal with low scores that might indicate possible depression.

There are several excellent resources on survey evaluations that are worth exploring for any camp that desires to use surveys and wants to produce the most reliable data from these. Examples include *The Survey Handbook* (Fink, 2002) and *Survey Research Methods* (Fowler, 2014). Two examples of questionnaires that might be useful appear in Box 7.1 and Box 7.2. The first is an example of a quantitative satisfaction survey that could be used as a parent survey with a Likert scale to gauge satisfaction with the camp experience. The second is a qualitative satisfaction survey from Camp Chimaqua, sponsored by the Pathways Center for Grief & Loss of Mount Joy, Pennsylvania, that gives campers the opportunity to express in their own words their experience of camp. Camp Chimaqua uses the buddy system of volunteers described in Chapter 6.

Several points should be considered when using surveys. Should surveys be anonymous? If not, the evaluation runs a great risk of "response bias"; that is, the person filling out the survey could wish to give the perceived expected or desired answer. This risk increases because most grief camps are free and designed for children to have fun at camp. However, a risk of an anonymous survey is that a child or teen might disclose a serious difficulty, such as suicidal ideation, that calls for intervention, and the evaluator would be unable to respond to the need. Beyond these issues, it takes a careful design for surveys to be useful in measuring the improvement in traumatic and/or complicated grief symptoms and to answer questions about the helpfulness of camps in reducing difficulties, such as nightmares and intrusive thoughts, and improving adjustment.

Box 7.1 Camp Satisfaction Survey for Parent/Guardian

Please rank each question on a scale of 1 to 4, with 1 the lowest score and 4 the highest. If you had more than one child attending camp, please fill out a form for each child. If you do not know the answer to a question, please mark N/A (No Answer)—for example if you did not meet the camp counselors, you might not be able to answer question number 3.

	Negative > Positive				
1. My child enjoyed the overall camp experience.	1	2	3	4	N/A
2. Camp was a good experience for my child.	1	2	3	4	N/A
3. The camp counselors were caring.	1	2	3	4	N/A
4. The camp transportation met my needs.	1	2	3	4	N/A
5. The physical camp setting met my child's needs.	1	2	3	4	N/A
6. The food provided met my child's needs.	1	2	3	4	N/A
7. I would use the camp in the future.	1	2	3	4	N/A
8. I would recommend the camp to others.	1	2	3	4	N/A
9. Paperwork related to camp registration was clear.	1	2	3	4	N/A
10. I believe my child will be better able to adjust to the loss of our loved one because of the camp experience.	1	2	3	4	N/A

Please add any comments that you think we would find useful in preparing for another camp session.

Qualitative Evaluation

Qualitative evaluation has been the most widely used methodology in the published literature of camp outcomes. Qualitative data has its place in evaluation of camps, especially because of the impact of individual stories reflected in anecdotal research. Qualitative surveys, focus groups, and individual interviews can illuminate areas that

---

Box 7.2 Camp Chimaqua—2016 Camper Feedback

We were so glad you attended Camp Chimaqua! We hope this camp experience was as special for you as it was for us. It would be a big help to us if you would tell us what you thought about Camp.

1. Two (2) things I liked best about Camp Chimaqua were:
   _____
   _____

2. Two (2) things I liked least about Camp Chimaqua were:
   _____
   _____

3. I was happy when:_____
   _____
   _____

4. The hardest thing for me was:_____
   _____
   _____

5. The hardest thing for me now is: _____
   _____
   _____

6. Sharing with others was: _____
   _____
   _____

7. I think I am getting better at: _____
   _____
   _____

8. My buddy: _____
   _____
   _____

9. At the next Camp Chimaqua they should: _____
   _____
   _____

Source: Hospice & Community Care's Pathways Center for Grief & Loss, Camp Chimaqua

focus on camp activities and environment. Individual stories told in the campers' words draw support for camps from stakeholders and the general community. Strong qualitative evaluations take into account several important aspects that must be planned for. Triangulation of data from multiple sources gives credence to the information collected. For example, a series of sources strengthens the reliability of data: Interviews might be held individually with campers, journals might be kept by team leaders that reflect camper involvement in activities, and a focus group of parents might be held before and after camp. Themes reflected in all of these give a full picture of the areas being explored. Saturation is reached when themes are consistently repeated. Clearly, interviewing two or three campers will not give a full picture of the feelings of all campers; but when a larger number, such as 15, answer questions in a similar direction, the researcher has confidence that saturation has been reached. There is no set number of interviews or focus groups required to reach saturation, and occasional outliers who do not respond as the other participants do are to be expected. However, the realities of time and expense limit the number of interviews and focus groups that are reasonably possible in any project.

Another influence on the findings of qualitative research is the "positionality" of the person or people collecting and analyzing the data. This refers to the characteristics and pre-conceived beliefs of the evaluator. Perhaps the most challenging aspect of qualitative evaluations is positionality. The trap of hearing what you want to hear is difficult to avoid if the evaluator is already convinced that the camp is a positive endeavor. This can be mitigated by the use of outside evaluators who are not affiliated with the camp; however, this option is seldom feasible for timing and financial reasons, and it takes a serious focus on planning to accomplish. A common way of ensuring the validity of the data and analysis is "member checking" in which the evaluator asks several of the evaluation participants to review, in their role as part of the evaluation team, the data that have been analyzed and summarized by the evaluator. Thus, they check the data for their accuracy in reflecting the words and thoughts of the participants.

In a moving example of the strength of individual quotations used in qualitative evaluations, McClatchey and Wimmer (2014) recount part of an interview with a 17-year-old girl whose mother died of a drug overdose. Describing feelings after her mother's death, she said, "It's a lot of days that I've cried . . . just like, okay, maybe I should join my mom. You know, it's in my blood. I might as well do it." When asked what was different for her after camp she replied with happy laughter, "The difference is I don't want to end my life anymore. I don't want to stop. I feel there's, in me, I feel like there's more options than I had before. I felt like there was a wall before camp, and after, the wall is gone! And I feel like I can go anywhere and do anything" (p. 231).

As a sample of questions that might be used in qualitative interviews, Box 7.3 includes the questions used by McClatchey and Wimmer (2014) in their interview.

Box 7.3 Qualitative Camper Questions

1. What was it like when your mom/dad was still alive?
2. Tell me about how your mom/dad died and how you found out.
3. What was it like when your mom/dad died?
4. How are things different now?
5. What was the most fun at camp?
6. What was most helpful at camp?
7. What would you tell other kids about camp if they had someone die?
8. Is there anything else about camp you'd like to talk about?

Quantitative Evaluation

Evaluation using numerical comparisons with statistical analysis is not common in evaluation of camp programs. However, this method of evaluation is necessary for measuring behavioral changes and important concepts in reducing debilitating grief symptoms, increasing positive emotional and cognitive growth, and addressing mental health challenges such as PTSD. Quantitative research involves identifying an intervention (the independent variable) and a response (the dependent variable). In the context of this discussion, the intervention would be a replicable bereavement camp program, and the response would be a change in the score on some reliable and valid measurement between a pre-test and a post-test. Evaluation varies in the complexity of the design the evaluator chooses and the sophistication of the measurement instrument.

Pre-experimental designs use a pre- and post-test model to assess the outcome of the camp experience on the children who attend. Evaluators can use instruments created by the camp or established tools with known properties of reliability and validity. An example of the scale created by Annie's Hope—The Bereavement Center for Kids and used at Camp Courage and Camp Erin in Missouri is found in Box 7.4. The questions in this behavioral checklist

Box 7.4 Camper Post Survey

When you and your child/teen completed an application for camp, you rated the frequency of certain behaviors often associated with grief. Since attending camp, how often do you see your child or teen exhibiting those behaviors? Choose the numbers between 0 and 10 that best represents the frequency of each behavior.

	N/A	0 = Never	1	2	3	4	5 = Sometimes	6	7	8	9	10 = Frequently
Extreme attachment to parent or guardian												
Intense anger												
Physical fighting												
Arguing												
Failing grade in school												
Repeated illness												
Hurtful behavior to self												
Withdrawal from family												
Withdrawal from friends												
Overeating												
Loss of appetite												
Use of drugs												
Use of alcohol												
Difficulty concentrating												
Difficulty sleeping												

Source: Annie's Hope—The Bereavement Center for Kids

are answered by caregivers at the time of the child's application for camp and then again approximately four to six weeks after camp ends (for the pre-survey, the introduction is worded differently).

Quasi-experimental designs measure more than one group, with a comparison group that does not receive the intervention. In the case of children's bereavement camps, the most logical comparison groups would be made up of either siblings who did not attend camp or campers on the waiting list for the next camp session. Neither group provides a perfectly matched control group, but these do give the evaluator the opportunity to compare the campers who attended a program with a similar group of children who have experienced bereavement but have not attended camp. The use of a pre-test, post-test comparison group design can increase strong speculation about the influence of the camp experience. To make the comparison between the intervention and comparison groups more useful, Krysik and Finn (2013) point out that "although we can not assume pretreatment equivalency [in groups] we can test it to some degree by using the pretest" (p. 201) in order to see the two groups' similarities.

A true experimental design is seldom used in human services environments and use of an experimental design for social service programs is difficult. This design calls for random selection of subjects in the intervention and control groups with measurements before and after the intervention. Random selection aims to statistically eliminate differences between groups of participants who receive the treatment (i.e., who attend camp) and those who receive a different treatment (e.g., perhaps those who receive counseling). In the case of a grief camp, the evaluator would randomly select camp applicants to attend camp and the remaining applicants would constitute the non-attending control group. The difficulty of rejecting some children in the applicant pool begins to raise ethical issues. Keppel and Wickens (2004) state that an experimental design can be described thus: "differential treatments are administered to different groups of subjects . . ., and performance of some response measure is observed and recorded following the administration of the treatments" (p. 2). However, since true random sampling is unrealistic, the closest that might be reasonably expected to be achieved is a quasi-experimental design.

Ideally, evaluators choose measurement tools with an understanding of the reliability and validity of instruments. These concepts reflect that if repeated under the same circumstances a measurement tool would reflect the same findings and that the tool is in fact measuring what it is intended to measure. Quantitative research begins with a hypothesis that will be supported or not supported by the findings. Camps would most likely use a directional hypothesis in camp research. This concept can be summarized with the hypothesis that the scores on whatever instrument administered will improve (statistically higher or lower) between the pre-test and the post-test for children who attended camp. Analysis of quantitative data uses statistical procedures that are chosen based on the research question. A sample of a possible quantitative study using a quasi-experimental design and directional hypothesis is given in Box 7.5.

Box 7.5 Quasi-Experimental Research Design Example

Hypothesis: Elementary school–age children who attend a weekend grief camp will show improved scores between a pre-camp test and two week post-camp test on the Eyberg Child Behavior Inventory when compared to children who did not attend camp.

Methods: Parents whose children attend camp fill out a pre-test before camp and a post-test two weeks after camp. Parents of children who are on the waiting list for the next camp session fill out the same inventory in the same time frame. The changes in scores between the pre-test and post-test are compared using between group statistical analysis.

Mixed Methods Evaluation

Mixed methods evaluation is more involved than the other methods discussed so far, using both quantitative and qualitative research tools to derive integrated findings. Most mixed methods designs are complicated. The combination of both approaches can answer questions of what happened and why it happened. For example, quantitative data might reveal a reduction in the level of grief symptoms, and qualitative interviews might add information on what experiences were related to this outcome. Evaluators can use several strategies to collect data for a mixed methods design. For example, in an explanatory sequential approach (Creswell, 2014, p. 220) evaluators might collect quantitative data first that reflect numerical data such as a change in scores between pre- and post-tests, and then conduct follow-up interviews to clarify the reasons for the observed outcome. From another perspective, qualitative interviews and focus groups might give anecdotal information about improved coping among children who have attended a bereavement camp, but researchers might want a more objective measurement of camp outcomes and might propose pre- and post-test measures on coping, using an established instrument to be applied in future camps.

A sample of mixed methods research using the explanatory sequential approach is presented in Box 7.6.

Box 7.6 Mixed Methods Research Design Example

This mixed methods research uses a two-step approach to gain the information wanted.

The research question (quantitative): What is the impact of the camp experience on teens as exhibited in pre-test scores and one month follow-up post-test scores on the UCLA PTSD Index for Adolescents?

The follow-up research question (qualitative): Using a focus group protocol, what do teens identify as the most helpful aspects of the psycho-educational interventions at camp?

Methods

Quantitative: Time is arranged for each teen arriving at camp to take the UCLA PTSD Index for Adolescents. This is done in a non-threatening environment while refreshments are served and should take less than 10 minutes. One month later, teens are asked to complete the PTSD Index again, this time online. Teens are sent a small token of appreciation when their post-test is received (such as a $5 gift card to a fast-food restaurant).

Qualitative: Teens are invited back to a social evening held at or near the camp setting. The evening includes a light dinner or cookout and appropriate teenage activities, music, etc. At some time near the end of this evening small groups (focus groups of five to eight teens) are formed and a discussion is led by an experienced camp counselor. Questions guiding the group discussions are:

1. What did you enjoy most about camp? (a warm-up question)
2. What, if anything, at camp changed your ability to cope with your loss?

3. What was the most important thing you learned at camp?
4. What, if anything, at camp helped you in some way?
5. Would you recommend camp to other teenagers, and why or why not?

Action Research

Stringer (2007) has written extensively about action research as an approach to improving social services. He states:

> Action research is a systematic approach to investigation that enables people to find effective solutions to problems they confront in their everyday lives. Unlike traditional experimental/ scientific research that looks for generalizable explanations that might be applied to all contexts, action research focuses on specific situations and localized solutions.
>
> (Stringer, 2007, p. 1)

Action research can use qualitative, quantitative, or mixed-methods methodologies to explore an intervention such as a children's grief camp. Evaluators can create surveys; use interviews or focus groups; apply pre-experimental, quasi-experimental designs; or at the most complex level an experimental design. The benefits of action research are that stakeholders in the program provide the information that is analyzed and then findings are used to improve the program offered or agency studied. When action research is used, the research then continues in order to evaluate these improvements and continue positive changes in programs. More specifically, "community-based action research seeks to change the social and personal dynamics of the research situation so that the research process enhances the lives of all those who participate" (Stringer, 2007, p. 20).

Action research uses a "Look, Think, Act" process. Look involves identifying the research problem, identifying issues through a literature review, and collecting data. Think involves analyzing the data and considering the meaning of the information gained. Act involves creating a solution to the problem, which might mean an improvement to an existing program, an organizational change, or community development (Stringer & Dwyer, 2005, pp. 36–37). Action research calls for involving stakeholders, including clients, staff, and community partners. It also functions in a circular fashion, continually evaluating changes made and searching for expected and unexpected consequences of these changes.

One of the simplest forms of action research is the use of questions that give participants or staff an opportunity to create and change program activities. A survey at the end of camp, a mailed post-camp questionnaire, post-camp interviews, or a focus group of campers or parents might be the tool to ask which parts of the camp experience were most meaningful to the campers. In one series of post-camp interviews held for Camp MAGIK, campers from several camp locations stressed the challenge and fun of canoeing for the first time (McClatchey & Wimmer, 2012). The teamwork, trust, and self-confidence the campers described appeared to be an important element in the traditional camping components of the weekend. As a result, Camp MAGIK removed from its locations the one camp setting that did not provide a facility for canoeing. The circular process of action research then carries on with future evaluations of this and other activities so that participants actually shape the program. In thinking about designing action research the sample in Box 7.7 might be helpful.

Box 7.7 Action Research Design Example

Statement of problem: The camp does not know if the activities it engages the campers in reach the therapeutic level of helping resolve problems associated with grief issues.

Research question: How do current activities fall short in meeting the needs of campers in relation to the camp mission of "helping children heal"?

> Goal: To improve the psycho-educational components of camp in order to increase success in meeting the camp mission.
>
> Methods: A circular mixed methods approach will be used with a multi-step method of data collection (Look), outcome analysis and consideration of program improvements (Think), and program change (Act) that is then reevaluated through a cycle of data collection, analysis, and possible continued change.
>
> **Step 1: Look.** After determining that persistent complex bereavement disorder (PCBD) (as defined by the

---

PCBD Checklist–Youth Version by Layne, Kaplow, and Pynoos) is the most serious and widespread problem for children attending the camp, a pre- and post-test system design using this checklist was begun.

Step 2: Think. If findings indicated limited or no improvement in scores after camp, various therapeutic alternatives that could be added to camp are explored.

Step 3: Act. New psycho-educational or therapeutic activities are added to the camp curriculum.

The following steps then become ongoing.

Repeat of Step 1: Re-do pre- and post-testing at a following camp session.
Repeat of Step 2: Consider results and implications.
Repeat of Step 3: Change the curriculum if indicated to meet the needs of campers.

As grief camps evaluate their programs, action research seems to be the logical model to keep in mind. The goal of camp developers should be to provide the best possible services to children. Whether evaluating programs or carrying out intensively designed research, this goal should guide the use of findings.

Meeting Goals

Programs are designed around a mission, goals, and measurable objectives. These can be central to the measurement of the outcomes of each camp. For example, Birnbaum (1991) described the goals of Camp Haven: Hugs and Bugs as "providing a well-deserved weekend of fun and of facilitating the development of a social support network for the participants" (p. 26). The post-camp surveys indicated that "the goals were achieved" (p. 26). In this case, the use of brief surveys successfully met the standard of measurement tools needed to evaluate the goals. Similarly, Nabors et al. (2004) stated that Camp Great Escape had a mission "of creating a supportive environment for children to process grief experiences with peers who had similar experiences" (p. 407). Program goals were "to allow children to meet in an informal atmosphere to help reduce the sense of isolation they may feel when coping with their grief . . . [and] to provide opportunities to learn about the grieving process" (p. 404). The evaluation of camp included surveys of children and parents. The conclusion was that the mission and goals were met and "parents and children felt that the camp was a positive experience and that the children benefited from being in groups with peers who had also lost family members" (p. 403).

In a more recent and more complex study, Camp MAGIK states that one of their goals is for campers to "have healthy coping skills" (Camp MAGIK, n.d., para. 3). In a quasi-experimental design, campers attending a session completed on arrival a validated measurement on PTSD symptoms and a survey on coping skills. Campers on the wait list for a future camp session completed the same forms in the days leading up to the first camp session. Both groups then completed the forms again four weeks after the camp session. This research showed that a weekend experience at Camp MAGIK "reduced traumatic grief and PTSD symptoms" (McClatchey, Vonk, & Palardy, 2009, p. 26).

In Summary

A good evaluation is worth doing well. There is no excuse for poorly designed or executed evaluations. In designing program evaluations, the organization needs to understand the limitations of the design of the study and control for these limitations as much as possible. Awareness of the limitations of the evaluations helps program developers continue to evaluate changes they make, using the framework of action research. Control or comparison groups, previously validated measurement instruments, and the use of statistical analysis or well-designed qualitative methods add to the value of findings. Costs in money and time, ethical issues including confidentiality, and community stakeholders and consumers of your findings are all issues to consider. Repetition of evaluations leads to more confidence in the reliability of conclusions.

In brief, there are many points to be considered. First is good design, which requires exploring the use of statistical significance. Second is cost. The use of local universities, knowledgeable board members, or volunteers can help with this concern. Third, and closely related to cost, is the time a program needs to do an evaluation. The use of already existing, short, but valid and reliable, instruments can be a timesaver. It is most expedient not to create new instruments. Fourth, in considering post-tests or post-surveys, one of the keys learned by the experience of others is to use some form of incentive, such as a gift card for a small amount, to increase participation. Campers' counselors can contact campers to encourage participation as well. This may increase return rates whether you use mail-back surveys or the Internet. Fifth, ethically, carefully consider the effect on campers, confidentiality, who is paying for the evaluation, and the broad impact of positive or negative findings. Finally, consider the value of your work. Was it worth doing, to whom was it valuable, and why?

Recommended Reading

Creswell, J. W. (2014). *Research design: Qualitative, quantitative, and mixed methods approaches*. (4th ed.). Thousand Oaks, CA: Sage.
Patton, M. Q. (2015). *Qualitative research and evaluation methods*. (4th ed.). Thousand Oaks, CA: Sage.

References

American Evaluation Association. (2004). *Guiding principles for evaluators*. Retrieved from www.eval.org/p/cm/ld/fid=51
American Psychological Association (APA). (2016). *Evidence-based practice in psychology*. Retrieved from www.apa.org/practice/resources/evidence/index.aspx
Birnbaum, A. (1991). Haven hugs & bugs. *The American Journal of Hospice & Palliative Care, 5*, 23–29.
Camp MAGIK. (n.d.). *About camp MAGIK*. Retrieved from www.camp magik.org/overview.html
Carroll, L. (1876). *The hunting of the Snark. An agony in 8 fits*. London, England: Macmillan.
Clute, M. A., & Kobayashi, R. (2013). Are children's grief camps effective? *Journal of Social Work in End-of-Life & Palliative Care, 9*, 43–57. doi:10.1080/15524256.2013.758927
Cornerstone Hospice. (2017). *Children's grief program*. Retrieved from https://web.cshospice.org/programs/childrens-grief-program/
Creed, J., Ruffin, J. E., & Ward, M. (2001). A weekend camp for bereaved siblings. *Cancer Practice, 9*(4), 176–182.
Creswell, J. W. (2014). *Research design: Qualitative, quantitative, and mixed methods approaches* (4th ed.). Thousand Oaks, CA: Sage.
Farber, L. Z., & Sabatino. (2007). A therapeutic summer weekend camp for grieving children: Supporting clinical practice through

empirical evaluation. *Child & Adolescent Social Work Journal, 24,* 385–402. doi:10.1007/s10560-007-0090-0

Fink, A. (2002). *The survey handbook* (2nd ed.). Thousand Oaks, CA: Sage.

Fowler, F. J. (2014). *Survey research methods* (5th ed.). Thousand Oaks, CA: Sage.

Gass, M. A., Gillis, H. L., & Russell, K. C. (2012). *Adventure therapy: Theory, research and practice.* New York, NY: Routledge Taylor and Francis Group.

Keppel, G., & Wickens, T. D. (2004). *Design and analysis: A researcher's handbook* (4th ed.). Upper Saddle River, NJ: Prentice Hall.

Krysik, J. L., & Finn, J. (2013). *Research for effective social work practice* (3rd ed.). New York, NY: Routledge.

McClatchey, I. S., Vonk, M. E., & Palardy, G. (2009). Efficacy of a campbased intervention for childhood traumatic grief. *Research on Social Work Practice, 19*(1), 19–30.

McClatchey, I. S., & Wimmer, J. S. (2012). Healing components of a bereavement Camp: Children and adolescents give voice to their experiences. *Omega - Journal of Death and Dying, 65*(1), 11–32.

McClatchey, I. S., & Wimmer, J. S. (2014). Coping with parental death as seen from the perspective of children who attended a grief camp. *Qualitative Social Work, 13*(2), 221–236. doi:10.1177/1473325012465104

Nabors, L., Ohms, M., Buchanan, N., Kirsch, K. L., Nash, T., Passik, S. D., . . . Brown, G. (2004). A pilot study of the impact of a grief camp for children. *Palliative and Supportive Care, 2,* 403–408. doi:10.10170S1478951504040532

Patton, M. Q. (2002). *Qualitative research and evaluation methods* (3rd ed.). Thousand Oaks, CA: Sage.

Stringer, E., & Dwyer, R. (2005). *Action research in human services.* Upper Saddle River, NJ: Pearson.

Stringer, E. T. (2007). *Action research.* Thousand Oaks, CA: Sage.

Substance Abuse and Mental Health Services Administration (SAMHSA). (2016). *Evidence-based practices Web guide.* Retrieved from www.samhsa.gov/ebp-web-page

8

Outcomes of Camp Interventions

Not everything that can be counted counts
Not everything that counts can be counted
—William Bruce Cameron (1969)

The goal of this chapter is to present bereavement camp research conducted between 2000 and 2017. The chapter includes evaluations done by camps across the country, published research on camp outcomes, longitudinal research conducted on Camp Erin and Comfort Zone Camp, and the extensive research done by one of this book's authors, Rene McClatchey.

Unpublished Camp Evaluations

Many camps use some method of evaluation to learn about the outcomes of their programs. These range from satisfaction surveys to research on mental health issues. A very limited number of outcome studies has been published in the professional literature since 2000. Readers are urged to explore further all evaluations and research published since the writing of this book in 2017.

This section discusses unpublished camp evaluations that were compiled through contact with bereavement camps throughout the United States. A directory of 364 bereavement camps was compiled through an Internet search and through lists of camps published by the National Alliance for Grieving Children and The Moyer Foundation. Based on this list, 141 camp programs, many of which ran multiple camp locations or camp sessions, were contacted and asked to share evaluations or research on their camps. Seventy-six programs responded, and these are identified in Appendix F. Approximately 10% of these programs use no survey or evaluation forms, or they receive a very poor response rate to surveys that are mailed to families after camp. The majority of all camps use a satisfaction survey with campers and/or families after camp, some with a Likert scale and some with open-ended questions. Approximately 10% of the camps gather in-depth information about post-camp changes in behavior and attitudes. Although some camps indicate very low return rates on post-camp surveys, overall responses to surveys are positive.

A representative sample of camps use surveys that present information from campers, parents, staff, and/or volunteers. Camp Kita in Maine provides a program for youth who are survivors of a loved one's suicide. The program uses SurveyMonkey to gather information on camper behavior and attitudes after camp as well as questions about the camp process. Reponses are strongly positive, with 85% of the caregivers responding that after camp the campers have increased coping skills or ability to express themselves when they are upset. Camp Corazon of the Children's Grief Center of New Mexico also has an 85% response of campers who report that they experience a significant increase in their ability to process their grief after camp. Camp Chimaqua in Pennsylvania uses surveys to gather information from campers' parents, and more extensively from camp volunteers, on topics ranging from the outcomes of camp to the quality of volunteer training. Fernside's Camp Erin Cincinnati in Ohio uses multiple surveys to elicit information from parents and campers. The camp gathers post-camp qualitative survey data on the outcome of camp along with camp process data. The post-camp quotations from parents and campers indicate that campers are helped by connecting with others who share their experiences of loss and by an ability to express their feelings. These findings are typical of findings discovered by other camp surveys. The Moyer Foundation, which supports Camp Erin programs, has an extensive survey that each of the 50 camps in the network completes. Several Camp Erin sites use additional surveys (such as the one used its in Santa Cruz, California location) to gain information on the experience of volunteers.

Although most camps do not publish research or evaluations, there are some common findings shared by the majority of camps. One prevalent theme is that camp increases campers' ability to communicate about their grief. As one young camper from Camp Erin Cincinnati put it, "I learned it is okay to talk about your feelings and the person who died." Camp Stepping Stones of Hope in Arizona summarizes the evaluation returns it receives with two frequently seen themes: that talking about the death is the most helpful part of camp and that campers learn they are not alone in their feelings. An adult buddy from Camp Koala in Pennsylvania stated: "I feel like it helped listening to others tell their story. Just knowing others are going through the same thing." Frequently campers expressed that it was helpful to be with other children who had lost a parent and who really understood their grief.

Published Evaluations

A limited number of doctoral dissertations and professional journal articles published since 2000 were identified that presented research on bereavement camps for children. In this section studies are organized by type of research; in addition, it includes a summary of an ongoing multi-camp evaluation being conducted by Kent State University. The section closes with a chronological presentation of the research by Rene McClatchey, first author of this book, on the program at Camp MAGIK.

Surveys

Although many camps use surveys to evaluate their camps, only one survey could be located that was published between 2000 and the writing of this book. Creed, Ruffin, and Ward (2001) surveyed a wide variety of participants to explore the outcomes of a weekend program. This camp is unusual in that it limits campers to those who have lost a sibling to cancer or blood disorders. The program uses a weekend camp format once each fall for children aged 6–18. The goals of the camp are to "1) reduce feelings of isolation; 2) assist children with the appropriate expression of their grief; 3) educate children about the grief process; and 4) facilitate children in moving forward in their grief process" (p. 178).

The evaluation completed after the second year of camp used questionnaires for 19 children aged 6–11 and aged 12–15, seven volunteer staff members, and 12 parents of campers. The youngest group of campers responded to questions about what they enjoyed at camp by circling drawings of faces to represent their feelings about the statements, selecting among happy, sad, or no reaction. The participants ranked activities with peers and recreational camping activities such as the campfire highly. The focus of the adolescents' Likert-scale questionnaire covered activities the campers found the most helpful in dealing with grief. The children's and teens' surveys helped in understanding which activities the campers found most meaningful. Beyond this, the teen surveys reflected strong data about the impact of camp, with "Camp helped me deal with my grief" (Creed, Ruffin, and Ward, 2001, p. 180) receiving the highest Likert rating. Parents' surveys, completed two weeks after camp, indicated improved communication and a reduced sense of isolation. Staff identified "the art activity, the company of their peers, the memory book, and the memories and feelings session" (p. 180) as the most helpful parts of camp and recommended that the length of the program be extended.

Qualitative Studies

Four qualitative studies are described here. They are presented from the earliest (from 2000 publication date onward) to the most recent at the time of completion of this book. Qualitative methods described include interviews, focus groups, reviews of documents, and direct observations.

A doctoral dissertation from the University of Montana by Barrett (2003) posed two research questions to campers from A Camp to Remember in Western Montana: "(1) How can bereavement camp experiences be structured to support a child's bereavement process; and (2) What aspects of the camp did participants experience as most helpful?" (p. 4). Interviews were conducted with ten campers and one parent of each camper after a weekend camp experience. In addition, Barrett reviewed 78 summaries of routine camp exit interviews done by camp staff over two years. Themes that emerged were: 1) Value of Connections with Peers and Staff; 2) Opportunities for Remembering or Commemorating; 3) Enjoyable Experiences; 4) Natural Setting/Nature-based Activities; and 5) Freedom to Be. Barrett does not claim to have measured the outcome of camp, but concludes, "Bereavement camps have great potential to support a child's journey with grief. The camp experience is not considered a cure-all, but rather, one piece of a much larger puzzle" (p. 148).

Using questionnaires rather than interviews, Nabors and colleagues (2004) gathered data from campers, parents, and staff. They used open-ended questions with 18 children and teens aged 6–12 to learn their views. A member of the research team met with each camper at the end of the weekend camp session. Follow-up telephone calls were held with five of the children. Although the questionnaires the researchers used with children were brief and "most of the children finished answering them in about 10 minutes" (p. 405), direct quotations from the children were meaningful. Children's comments included "[Camp] helped me get my sad feelings out"; "It made me learn my true feelings"; "I need to get my crying out" (p. 406). In addition, researchers asked the campers to complete the following sentence: Because I came to camp, I think I am better at . . . Responses included "Talking about my feelings"; "Facing my fears"; "Smiling . . . not crying that much"; "Being brave and sharing with others" (p. 405). The researchers concluded that "Children provided answers indicating that they valued the peer support and counseling activities" (p. 405). Parental surveys elicited comments such as "had a great time" and "excited" (Nabors et al., 2004, p. 405). Counselors felt that the camp provided an experience to increase "emotional expression and a chance to begin to build a positive memory of the loved one" (p. 406). Overall Nabors and colleagues found that both parents and children reported a positive evaluation of camp.

Unlike Nabors and colleagues, Brown and Kimball (2012) relied on staff only, rather than the campers, to gather information. The study, titled "Residential Grief Camps: An Initial Phenomenological Study of Staff Perspectives," looked at a four-day camp experience. The researchers interviewed eight staff members aged 18–59, with multiple years of experience with the camp, which is held in the Pacific Northwest. They had varied roles at camp as cabin counselors; specialists in art, music, and staffing; adventure challenge leader; and camp director. The interview questions used were:

What is your overall experience at camp? What do you see as the benefits of camp? What are the reasons you returned to camp? What have you learned about grief from being part of this camp? What do you notice about the campers throughout the week? How has your experience of camp impacted your own grief experience (if applies)? What similar characteristics do staff members hold?

> (Brown and Kimball, 2012, p. 90)

Brown and Kimball (2012) described their findings in terms of categories and themes. The first category, Connection to Others, demonstrated themes of camp validation of emotions and through shared experience. Bereavement camp increased the understanding that "all emotions felt are legitimate" (p. 87) and provided the opportunity of "being with others who have also experienced a death in their life" (p. 87). The second category was Independence. Brown and Kimball found three themes in this category: grief is unique, personal ritual, and diverse outlets. The researchers stated that "Grief feels and looks different for everyone" (p. 87), and camp can provide the opportunity for personal rituals for coping with grief. They concluded that bereavement camps were perceived by staff to be helpful to children dealing with parental death and added clinical implications in the conclusion of their study. They stated their belief, supported by the interviews, that "suitable interventions are needed in order to provide children with the necessary tools to manage the varying emotions associated with their grief. Grief camps are a viable option" (p. 86).

From an unusual perspective, Fluegeman, Schrauben, and Cleghorn (2013) looked at outcomes of a Camp Erin (located in the Midwest) through the lens of occupational therapy. Their research questions were:

> How do the activities at [camp] impact the bereavement process among campers? How do the relationships formed at [camp] impact the bereavement process? and Is there a role for occupational therapy in community based bereavement programs such as [this camp]?
>
> (p. 76)

Ten campers completed two focus groups, one composed of children aged 6–10 and the other of children aged 11–17. Additionally, the researchers held individual interviews with four camp counselors. The central finding was that the activities at camp "were found to decrease the sense of isolation by helping the campers realize that they were not alone in experiencing the death of a loved one" (p. 77). Campers benefited by observing the coping mechanisms of their peers (p. 78) and learned new coping mechanisms through "small and large group discussions, team building activities, and journaling" (p. 78). The study found, however, that "there is a point of disconnect for the campers between what is taught at [camp] and actually applying it to their everyday lives" (p. 78). The authors suggest that the special training of occupational therapists might be useful in consulting with bereavement camps "to identify the barriers which are preventing the campers from applying what is being taught at [camp] to their home lives, and developing means for overcoming these barriers" (p. 79). The authors' point of view, as occupational therapists, was clear in the description of findings.

Quantitative Studies

Three quantitative studies looked at bereavement camps. Two of the studies evaluated camps that were affiliated with cancer treatment programs. The third was a six-site evaluation of Camp Erin. Two of the three were doctoral dissertations that did not appear in professional journals.

Packman et al. (2004) and Packman et al. (2008) described a quantitative study that uses six standardized instruments with 59 campers who had a sibling living with cancer and 18 with a sibling deceased from cancer. Both articles describe the same sample of campers, aged 6–17, who attended a one-week session in 2001. Research data on PTSD and anxiety scores are discussed in the 2004 article and data on emotional and family distress in the 2008 study. "The study instruments were administered to families in their homes, starting 4 to 8 weeks before camp for the precamp phase and 12 to 16 weeks after camp" (Packman et al., 2008, p. 44). The researchers used four standardized scales and two art-based evaluation instruments. For all campers, including those with deceased siblings, "the total PTSD severity scores and the total anxiety scores were significantly reduced. In addition, there was significant improvement in quality of life and self-esteem scores" (Packman et al., 2004, p. 210). Using art-based evaluation, in the Human Figure Drawing "both bereaved and nonbereaved siblings . . . showed significant reductions in emotional distress" (2008, p. 47). In contrast, in the Kinetic Family Drawing—Revised "the bereaved participants did not show statistically significantly improved family environment" (2008, p. 48) although the families of campers with living siblings did. The authors conclude that the findings support the effectiveness of this bereavement camp in "increasing siblings' emotional wellbeing" (2008, p. 44) and "suggest the value of camp as a psychological intervention" (2004, p. 201).

Also focusing on families affected by cancer, Nettina (2005) studied 29 campers aged 6–16 for her dissertation. She used concept mapping with pre-tests done at a weekend camp registration and post-tests done two months later. Instruments used were the Pediatric Quality of Life Questionnaire, Childhood Depression Inventory, and Kidcope. "Change from the pre- to post-camp assessment was examined on the scales of depression, coping and quality of life" (p. 34). Nettina concluded that the study supported "many assumptions about the seemingly high efficacy of the use of therapeutic camps for grieving children" (p. 51). Although there were no changes in the measurements pertaining to depression and quality of life, coping skills showed significant improvement. In addition, campers described the benefits of camp and these included themes of Attachment and Connections, Traditional Camp, Acceptance and Expression, Escape from Grief-related Stress at Home, and Kid-Friendly Environment (p. 75). As a main benefit of camp, Nettina concluded, "according to the current study children feel supported, accepted and able to express themselves at camp" (p. 50).

With a different design, Duke (2013) did a multi-site dissertation entitled "The Impact of Camp Erin on Bereaved Youth." Six Camp Erin sites participated in the study: Detroit, Michigan; Albany, New York; Anchorage, Alaska; Seattle, Washington; Kansas City, Missouri; and Toronto, Ontario, Canada. The Duke study is a multi-faceted investigation into the premise that Camp Erin improves the functioning of campers. She used a repeated-measures within-group analysis design and collected data with a pre-test, post-test, and eight-week follow-up. This was a complex study using three standardized instruments. Children in the study were aged 9–17. Fifty-five children completed all three intervals of the Children's Hope Scale, 53 the Children's Depression Inventory, and between 52 and 54 the various scales of the Self-Perception Profile. The percentage of data received from each location varied widely with the largest participation from one site providing 33% of the data and smallest from two providing only 4.4%. Although some scales did not reveal change, Duke primarily had positive findings in her results. When children's ages and the length of time since the parent's death were factors, children showed an improved score on the Children's Hope Scale. The data analyzed in the Children's Depression Inventory–Short Form revealed a decrease in depression over the pre-test to eight-week post-test time frame. The Self-Perception Profile for Children scale had five subscales: Scholastic Competency, Social Acceptance, Close Friendship, Self-Worth, and Physical Appearance. There was no difference in scores between before and after camp indicated in the Scholastic Competency subscale, the Close Friendship subscale, the Self-Worth subscale, or the Physical Appearance subscale. Campers showed improvement in the Social Acceptance subscale. Duke states that "As hypothesized, Camp Erin had a significant positive impact on campers. . . . It is evident that participants experienced some increase in hope, decrease in depressive symptoms, and increase in self-acceptance as it pertains to self-perception from Pre-camp to 8-week follow-up" (p. 92).

Mixed Methods Study

Mixed methods approaches to camp research have been scarce. Goldman (2006) did a mixed methods doctoral dissertation study with 34 campers and 18 parents. The Adult–Texas Revised Inventory of Grief was completed by the parents, the Child Behavioral Checklist was completed on the children, and A Family Interview Questionnaire, designed for this study, was used in interviews with families, including children and parents. As might be expected, the grief inventory revealed the adults' deep sense of loss. When analyzing results of the pre- and post-camp scores for children aged 7–17 on the Child Behavior Checklist, Goldman found no significant changes in the campers' behavior scores. As a qualitative aspect to this study Goldman conducted interviews both pre- and post-camp. The pre-camp interview focused on questions not related to the evaluation of camp. These interviews gave insight into the experience of the death and the coping that families faced. The post-camp interviews focused on the camp experience, and these interviews indicated themes of satisfaction with camp. In summary Goldman found that:

> Guardians and children reported that peer discussions were helpful in decreasing social isolation and allowing their children to feel less alone. The camp apparently was able to meet its mission of trying to provide an environment for the grieving families that is both fun and that fosters feelings of universality.
>
> (p. 59)

Action Research Studies

Two studies are presented as designed as action research, although camp evaluations often lead to changes in programs. Farber and Sabatino (2007) and Bachman (2013) planned their studies with the intention of exploring needed changes and then evaluating the next sessions of camp to obtain the outcome of the changes.

Farber and Sabatino (2007) designed a two-year "action-oriented" (p. 385) mixed method evaluation of the outcome of a weekend camp on children's psychosocial behavior. The campers represented 50 children aged 6–15, although the children were not directly involved in the research. Camp clinicians completed a Likert scale on children's engagement in camp activities. Camp clinicians, volunteer buddies, and parents completed the Behavioral Rating Index for Children at the one-month follow-up after each camp. The Behavioral Rating Index was added as a pre-test with parents in the second year of the study. The research questions that guided this study were:

> (1) Do camp participants evidence significant changes in their well-being over a designated camp-period? (2) Do specific group-based camp activities have a desired impact upon children's therapeutic camp experiences? (3) Do parents perceive beneficial aspects of children's camp experience at follow-up?
>
> (p. 391)

Several unexpected findings emerged. In addressing questions 1 and 2, the study indicated that some children had difficulty engaging in drumming, which was an important part of the grief expression activity (p. 394). This was an activity late in the weekend experience and was expected to have increased engagement as campers experienced increased well-being in the camp setting. A second finding noted that on average the first year's campers' "parents rated their children as experiencing slightly but significantly more problems in their children's psychosocial functioning at one-month follow-up than during camp" (p. 397). This research was designed to be an action research study and changes were made in response to the first year's findings. Several areas of change were described, including increased sensitivity regarding some children's negative reaction to drumming, improving intake assessment and parent preparation, and follow-up. Findings from the next year's camp did not reveal the same level of difficulties with post-camp psychosocial functioning.

In another study using an action research design, Bachman (2013) described the development of a new bereavement camp for children and adolescents aged 7–17. She conducted a four-year survey study of camp outcomes and used the findings in the process of planning and executing the program. Campers were enthusiastic in their responses to camp surveys at the end of camp and in follow-up mailed surveys with a 65% survey return rate over four years of camps. Surveys from staff and parents led to several changes: increased communication before camp, improved pre-camp screening, the development of post-camp groups, and a holiday reunion event in December. Ongoing evaluation supported the changes made. Over the years of camp development several issues emerged, including the question of whether to give preference to returning or new campers, the need for a more detailed camp schedule than had first been used, and the development of support groups after camp.

Longitudinal Study

A longitudinal evaluation of bereavement camps, funded by the New York Life Foundation, was conducted by Kent State University using data from Camp Erin and Comfort Zone Camp across multiple U.S. states and a few Canadian provinces. Begun in 2013, data were collected at pre-camp, at two weeks and three months post-camp, and at one year and two years post-camp. The initial sample of campers studied included 599 children and teens from 38 camps. Within the first year of the three-year study, more than 500 campers from more than 30 camps participated, making this the largest single sample to date in research evaluating bereavement camps (Richardson, Maxymiv, Freeman, Willis, & Taylor, 2014). Although any longitudinal study must deal with issues of attrition, there is value in trying to determine the long-term benefits of a bereavement camp intervention. The study used a model of Positive Youth Development (Lerner, Dowling, & Anderson, 2003) to ascertain the outcome of bereavement camps. Preliminary results indicate that attending Camp Erin or Comfort Zone Camp had a positive outcome as measured by changes in self-report scores from pre-camp to two weeks post-camp (Richardson, Maxymiv, & Freeman, 2014). Further information on this study will be published as the data collection and analysis are completed.

In addition to examining the immediate and long-term impact of bereavement camps, the Kent State University study explored the camp modality as a positive developmental setting. Freeman et al. (2015) cited eight features of settings that promote positive youth development: "Physical and Psychological Safety, Clear and Consistent Structure and Appropriate Supervision, Supportive

Relationships, Opportunities to Belong, Positive Social Norms, Support for Efficacy and Mattering, Opportunities for Skill Building, [and] Integration of Family, School, and Community" (Larson, Eccles, & Gootman as cited in Freeman et al., 2015, p. 16). They found evidence of all eight features of positive developmental settings in their site visits to camps, both through typical camp activities and bereavement-focused activities.

Yet another aspect of the Kent State University study is the inclusion of a sample of more than 100 adult camp alumni (aged 19 and older) who had attended either Camp Erin or Comfort Zone Camp prior to age 18 (Freeman et al., 2015). These alumni were asked to retrospectively reflect on how the camp experience had influenced them over time. By comparing the responses of camp alumni with responses of current campers, it becomes possible to identify which aspects of camp seem to matter not just in the short-term but over the long-run, and to compare and contrast which aspects of camp are most meaningful. Preliminary findings from the Kent State University study suggest that there are both similarities and differences between current campers and adult alumni with regard to their perceptions of which elements of the camp experience matter most (Freeman et al., 2015).

Research on Camp MAGIK

Rene McClatchey, the first author of this book, has conducted ongoing evaluations and research related to the Camp MAGIK program. Camp MAGIK, as described earlier in this book, is a weekend bereavement camp intervention serving youth aged 7–18 that is now in its 23rd year. In the research described here, data collection varies from in-depth qualitative interviews to quasi-experimental design pre- and post-camp data using standardized scales.

In 2004 McClatchey (Searles, 2004) after an evaluation of camp's outcome on grief symptoms, completed a program evaluation looking at the outcome of the Camp MAGIK interventions on PTSD symptoms. She discovered that, in fact, PTSD symptoms increased after the camp intervention. In an effort to explore the prevalence of PTSD symptoms among children and adolescents attending Camp MAGIK, McClatchey and Vonk (2005) used the Impact of Event Scale with 46 campers. Campers ranged in age from 7 to 17. Sixty-five percent of campers scored in the moderate to severe level of PTSD and 89% scored above the cutoff score for mild to more severe symptoms. PTSD was evident both in children who had experienced an expected death (such as a long illness) and those who had experienced an unexpected death. "This study indicates that a large number of children who have experienced the loss of a loved one do experience PTSD symptoms" (p. 294). The research is an important piece of work in the evolution of research on children's bereavement camps in that it illuminates the prevalence of severe mental health difficulties in children and adolescents who attend these camps.

At that time, there were no interventions related to trauma at Camp MAGIK. Using the results as action research, McClatchey extensively studied the posttraumatic literature involving children and adolescents and added PTSD interventions to the camp model. In a follow-up study published in 2009, McClatchey, Vonk, and Palardy explored the efficacy of Camp MAGIK in "reducing traumatic grief and PTSD symptoms in parentally bereaved children" (p. 19). The study used a quasi-experimental design with campers aged 6–16. A group of 46 campers participated in research from the first camp session and 54 campers from the second camp session, held two weeks later. All 100 participants completed pre-tests before the first camp session and post-tests two weeks later prior to the second camp session and again four weeks later. Measurements were made using standardized scales rating PTSD and Childhood Traumatic Grief (CTG) symptoms. The study found that the Camp MAGIK experience, using a trauma-focused weekend camp intervention, significantly "reduced traumatic grief and PTSD symptoms" among camp participants. Scores also reflected continued improvement in the post-camp time frame. This study raised the question for future research concerning components of a bereavement camp that most influenced change in the campers, that is, "what about camp make it effective" (p. 27).

Qualitative research was used to explore this question and is described in "Healing Components of a Bereavement Camp: Children and Adolescents Give Voice to their Experiences" (McClatchey & Wimmer, 2012). Thirteen families were involved in this study; the campers had attended Camp MAGIK within the preceding nine months. The researchers interviewed 19 children and adolescents aged 8–18, plus one parent from each family. Two major themes emerged from the interviews: one with information on the value of bereavement-focused camp activities and the other on the value of recreational camping activities. The categories discovered under the theme of bereavement-focused activities "were counseling sessions, memorial service, balloon release, and journaling" (p. 18). The categories of recreational camp activities viewed as most important "were connecting with other campers, canoeing, and the talent show" (p. 18). Although the latter activities were considered traditional fun parts of camp, they also promoted healing through normalizing peer connections and improving self-confidence and self-efficacy.

The themes in the qualitative research described earlier were expanded with 16 campers and 11 parents to explore "the emotional impact of coping with the death of a parent and how an intervention [Camp MAGIK] may have influenced the children's coping with issues expressed" (McClatchey & Wimmer, 2014, p. 224). The researchers recorded poignant statements on each of the themes discovered. Themes were "Sadness, Anger, Being Set Apart, Worries, Trauma, and Contemplation of Suicide" (p. 226). A 9-year-old boy expressed the theme of "Sadness" holding back tears and describing the death of his guardian grandfather as "Very sad. Very badly sad" (p. 226). The theme of "Anger" was evident in a 17-year-old girl's statements about being abandoned by her father, who died from suicide (p. 227). Sharing their stories with other children helped with healing related to the theme of "Being Set Apart"; one teenage boy stated that "there are people out there who understand me, and more importantly, who have made it to the other side" (p. 228). "Worry" often focused on the possible death of the surviving parent. Trauma "symptoms included hypervigilance, avoidance, and intrusion" (p. 229). For example, "the fear of seeing or sensing a dead parent's presence was a common phenomenon among the children" (p. 229). "Suicide" was the most distressing theme discovered and was clearly discussed concerning two girls, one aged 8 and the other 17, both of whom gave up considering suicide after camp. Although this study "does not claim that specific camp interventions changed the children's grief reactions . . . the study does provide interesting information on children's emotions before and after camp" (p. 233). The article concludes "more studies, including studies on camper re-traumatization, post-traumatic growth, and secondary traumatization of camp staff, are needed to help better understand how to help this at-risk population" (p. 233).

In 2015 McClatchey and Peters followed up with a quantitative study using the Eyberg Child Behavior Inventory that looked at "the impact of trauma focused grief education on acting-out behavior" (p. 14). Full sets of pre- and post-camp data from 33 campers aged 6–16 who attended Camp MAGIK were compared. The first research question was "Can trauma focused grief education decrease acting-out behavior among bereaved children and adolescents?"

(p. 17). Findings indicated that there was a statistically significant decrease in acting-out behavior between the pre- and post-camp scores. Although none of the children had initially scored high enough to reach a mental health diagnosis of Oppositional Defiant Disorder, an improvement in behavior can be assumed to be of importance to each family. Another research question was "What makes some bereaved youth more vulnerable to acting-out behavior after the death of a parent or sibling than others?" (p. 17). "Age, race, gender, time since loss, circumstances of death (expected versus sudden/violent), family income and guardian education" (p. 21) were explored. No clear answers emerged on this topic. The researchers found no predictors of acting-out behavior.

McClatchey's next study (in press) looked at posttraumatic growth (PTG). Five areas of possible growth were measured: "1) new possibilities, 2) relating to others, 3) personal strength, 4) appreciation of life, and 5) spiritual change" (Measurement, para. 1). Thirty-two campers aged 6–18 participated in the study. Each had attended one of three sessions of Camp MAGIK. The research questions were:

> 1) What are some possible demographic and death-related predictors of PTG among bereaved youth? and 2) Will a program that provides trauma-informed care . . . and that includes an opportunity for bereaved youth to share positive changes . . . increase PTG among bereaved children?
>
> (Outcome Studies, para. 2)

Pre- and post-camp scores on the Posttraumatic Growth Inventory for Children were used. Only two predictors of PTG appeared to have some significance in this study: older age of the child and sudden rather than predicted death of the parent. McClatchey points out that other research is inconsistent in findings about predictors and that more research is needed in this area. The results exploring the outcome of Camp MAGIK on PTG did indicate that the campers had statistically significantly higher growth comparing pre- and post-camp scores. This is a strong positive finding and might be an important area for study at other camps serving bereaved children.

McClatchey and Raven (2017) continued research in this area with a controlled outcome study of the effect of Camp MAGIK on facilitating PTG. Ninety-one youth participated in a pre- and post-camp test design using the Revised Posttraumatic Growth Inventory for Children (PTGI-C-R) with 40 in the group who attended camp and 51 in the comparison group of those who attended a later session of the same camp. McClatchey and Raven also tested participants on PTSD symptoms using the UCLA PTSD Reaction Index for DSM-5. Regarding PTG, the authors found that those children who attended camp had improved (statistically significantly higher) PTG scores at post-testing compared to those children who did not attend camp (McClatchey & Raven, 2017). Interestingly, although both girls and boys showed improvement, boys showed more improvement than girls. Although PTSD scores were lower at posttest, the difference was not statistically significant. However, camp attendees had significantly lower scores on post-camp dissociative symptoms. The recommendations of this research suggest the importance of bereavement camps incorporating trauma-informed care into their programs in order to facilitate positive outcomes for the youth they serve.

Although standardized instruments such as those that measure PTG and PTSD symptoms are important in measuring the impact of camps, qualitative research can identify the full spectrum of the meaning of camp to children, adolescents, and families. Continuing with qualitative research, McClatchey (2017) interviewed fathers who were raising their children after the death of the children's mothers. Ten widowed fathers from families whose children attended Camp MAGIK responded to the researcher's call for participants. In total these fathers were raising 22 children aged 2–16, with family sizes ranging from one to six children. Findings were condensed into several themes: 1) "ways to cope" ("Ways," para. 1), which included "setting new priorities" ("Ways," para. 2), "committing" ("Ways," para. 6), and "making use of resources" ("Ways," para. 9); 2) "concerns" (Concerns, para. 1), which included "own mortality" (Concerns, para. 1), and "lonely authority" (Concerns, para. 2); and 3) "newfound respect" ("Respect," para. 1). The article includes moving quotations that highlight these fathers' love for their children and their commitment to parenting. Several of the men had changed jobs in order to have more time to meet their children's needs. Most expressed a new realization of the immensity of the work their deceased spouse carried out in day-to-day parenting. Although this research was not directly related to the outcomes of Camp MAGIK, it added to the understanding of the families who are coping with parental loss. Additionally, it can encourage bereavement camp programs that offer a parent component, such as Camp MAGIK does, to make special efforts to include and support widowed fathers.

Limitations

All evaluations and research have limitations, and in published results the authors most often describe these limitations as part of their article. Although some limitations are described here, and some such as bias on the part of the evaluator are mentioned in Chapter 7, this should not discourage the reader from engaging in evaluations or research. Farber and Sabatino's (2007) action research and Searles's (2004) quantitative study yielded findings that are clear examples of the importance of studying the outcome that bereavement camps have on children and their families.

Lack of Generalizability

Research designed with random sampling has not been carried out on children's bereavement camps, and individual evaluation and research studies cannot be generalized from the sample of a camp to the whole population. For example, the quantitative evaluation outcome of 50 campers who participate in a standardized scale or fill out a satisfaction survey cannot be generalized or thought to represent all campers who attend a bereavement camp. Qualitative research has limitations based on the restricted samples necessary for the intense depth of involvement with participants in an evaluation, such as interviews and focus groups. For example, in the study by Brown and Kimball (2012) the sample of eight individuals from one camp setting precludes any generalization of the findings.

Similarly, the findings from one camp program cannot be assumed to generalize to the unique programs of other camps, and perhaps not even to multiple sessions sponsored by the same camp organization. This variance from program to program is referred to in research parlance as a "variation in the independent variable"; that is, what you are measuring varies from camp to camp.

Participant Bias

Participation in camp evaluations is voluntary, thus excluding some campers, families, volunteers, or staff who choose not to answer questions, fill out forms, or participate in surveys. Not all camp participants respond to the surveys or post-camp instruments that are mailed to them after camp. Researchers are left with the question, "Did the people who did not respond have the same outcomes as those who chose to participate in the full course of research?" Perhaps those who responded were happier with the experience or had some other motivation for being available post-camp. A frequent concern in voluntary evaluations is response bias, defined as the tendency of participants to tell an evaluator what is perceived as the correct or desired answer. There is also the possibility that participants, such as staff or buddy volunteers, have a vested interest in the success of the camp program and therefore respond positively to surveys. Campers and their families, likewise, might wish to be invited back to camp next year, so they give only positive feedback. In addition, cultural issues or barriers such as poor English reading skills might also limit responses from diverse families if the instrument used is not available in all relevant languages.

As discussed earlier, the bias of the evaluator can also play a role in the findings of a study. One area of limitation is the bias of the evaluator in choice of participants. For example, Farber and Sabatino (2007) did not include the children themselves in their study. Some surveys include staff and/or volunteers, and other evaluations might include children but not their families. Other limitations can be the selective collection of data, leading interview questions, and skewed emphasis in reporting outcomes.

Threats to Reliability and Validity

Very few research studies involving children and families use an experimental research design. With respect to camp studies found in the literature, researchers did not choose evaluation participants randomly and they seldom did simultaneous research on children who attended camp and compared the results with similar children who did not have a camp experience. Thus, issues such as the healing impact of the passage of time, or the traumatic impact of current events such as a school shooting, are not often factored into the results of changes in pre- and post-camp measurements. In addition, most camp evaluators create their own surveys or questionnaires that have not had instrument reliability or validity established. It is the wise evaluator who remembers to say camp "might have" influenced changes in campers' behavior or perceived healing from their grief. Too many other factors impact each child and adolescent who participates in a bereavement camp experience for the credit for change to be decisively given to the camp.

In Summary

Research generated to date supports the importance of the bereavement camp experience in children's lives. Normed measures are helpful for specific aspects of camp interventions, and qualitative evidence is also needed to assess the full impact of the human experience of camp (Clute & Kobayashi, 2013). Clute and Kobayashi found value in the information gleaned from qualitative data and expressed the need for more. Regarding quantitative data they added a need for "continued work to replicate the work of McClatchey et al. (2009) on PTSD measurement" (p. 55).

Recommended Reading

In light of the ongoing evaluations of bereavement camp programs, it is recommended that readers explore current articles in peer reviewed journals. Especially of note are writings by I. S. McClatchey and by R. A. Richardson, S. Maxymiv, and P. Freeman.

References

Bachman, B. (2013). The development of a sustainable, community-supported children's bereavement camp. *Omega - Journal of Death and Dying, 67*(1–2), 21–35.

Barrett, C. (2003). *Bereavement camp: A qualitative analysis of a therapeutic program for grieving youth*. Theses, Dissertations, Professional Papers, University of Montana, Paper 9478.

Brown, T. B., & Kimball, T. G. (2012). Residential grief camps: An initial phenomenological study of staff perspectives. *The Qualitative Report, 17*(1), 78–91.

Cameron, W. B. (1969). *Informal sociology: A casual introduction to sociological thinking*. New York, NY: Random House.

Clute, M. A., & Kobayashi, R. (2013). Are children's grief camps effective? *Journal of Social Work in End-of-Life & Palliative Care, 9*, 43–57. doi:10.1080/15524256.2013.758927

Creed, J., Ruffin, J. E., & Ward, M. (2001). A weekend camp for bereaved siblings. *Cancer Practice, 9*(4), 176–182.

Duke, A. (2013). *The impact of Camp Erin on bereaved youth*. Doctoral dissertation, University of Nebraska at Lincoln, Open Access Theses and Dissertations from the College of Education and Human Sciences, Paper 180.

Farber, M. L. Z., & Sabatino, C. A. (2007). A therapeutic summer weekend camp for grieving children: Supporting clinical practice through empirical evaluation. *Child and Adolescent Social Work Journal*, *24*(4), 385–402. doi:10.1007/ s10560-007-0090-0

Fluegeman, J. E., Schrauben, A. R., & Cleghorn, S. M. (2013). Bereavement support for children: Effectiveness of Camp Erin from an occupational therapy perspective. *Bereavement Care*, *32*(2), 74–81. doi:10.1080/02682621.2013.812820

Freeman, P., Richardson, R. A., Maxymiv, S., Shanadi, D., Willis, L., & Moncrief, A. (2015, June). *Positive developmental settings: Youth camper perceptions and adult alumni reflections*. Presentation presented at the National Alliance for Grieving Children (NAGC) Annual Symposium on Children's Grief, Portland, OR.

Goldman, L. (2006). *Family bereavement and the experience of a bereavement camp*. Doctoral dissertation. Retrieved from ProQuest Information and Learning Company (UMI No. 3177416).

Lerner, R. M., Dowling, E. M., & Anderson, P. M. (2003). Positive youth development. *Applied Developmental Science*, *7*(3), 172–180.

McClatchey, I. S. (in press). Trauma-informed care and posttraumatic growth among bereaved youth: A pilot study. *Omega - Journal of Death and Dying*.

McClatchey, I. S. (2017). Fathers raising motherless children: Widowed men give voice to their lived experiences. *Omega - Journal of Death and Dying*, *76*(4). Advance online publication. doi: 10.1177/0030222817693141

McClatchey, I. S, & Peters, A. (2015). Can trauma focused grief education improve acting-out behavior among bereaved youth? A pilot study. *Journal of Human Services*, *35*(1), 14–27.

McClatchey, I. S., & Raven, R. F. (2017). Adding trauma-informed care at a bereavement camp to facilitate posttraumatic growth: A controlled outcome study. *Advances in Social Work*, *18*(1). doi: 10.18060/21239

McClatchey, I. S., Vonk, M. E., & Palardy, G. (2009). Efficacy of a camp-based intervention for childhood traumatic grief. *Research on Social Work Practice*, *19*(1), 19–30. doi:10:1177/1049731508314276

McClatchey, I. S., & Wimmer, J. S. (2012). Healing components of a bereavement camp: Children and adolescents give voice to their experiences. *Omega - Journal of Death and Dying*, *65*(1), 11–32.

McClatchey, I. S., & Wimmer, J. S. (2014). Coping with parental death as seen from the perspective of children who attended a grief camp. *Qualitative Social Work*, *13*(2), 221–236.

McClatchey, R. S., & Vonk, M. E. (2005). An exploratory study of post-traumatic stress disorder symptoms among bereaved children. *Omega - Journal of Death and Dying, 51*(4), 285–300. doi:10.2190/EA87-LDJN-LULB-VNVU

Nabors, L., Ohms, M., Buchanan, N., Kirsh, K. L., Nash, T., Passik, S. D., . . . Brown, B. (2004). A pilot study of the impact of a grief camp for children. *Palliative and Supportive Care, 2*(4), 403–408. doi:10.1017/S1478951504040532

Nettina, J. M. (2005). *A concept mapping study of the perceived benefits of a therapeutic and recreational camp for grieving children.* Doctoral dissertation. Retrieved from ProQuest Information and Learning Company (UMI No. 3185256).

Packman, W., Fine, J. Chesterman, B., VanZutphen, K., Golan, R., & Amylon, M. D. (2004). Camp Okizu: Preliminary investigation of psychological intervention for siblings of pediatric cancer patients. *Children's Health Care, 33*(3), 201–216.

Packman, W., Mazaheri, M., Sporri, L., Long, J. K., Chesterman, B., Fine, J., & Amylon, M. D. (2008). Projective drawings as measures of psychosocial functioning in siblings of pediatric cancer patients from the Camp Okizu study. *Journal of Pediatric Oncology Nursing, 25*(1), 44–55.

Richardson, R. A., Maxymiv, S., & Freeman, P. (2014). Evaluation of bereavement camps: A positive youth development perspective. *ADEC Forum: The Quarterly Publication of the Association for Death Education and Counseling, 40*(4), 6–7.

Richardson, R. A., Maxymiv, S., Freeman, P., Willis, L., & Taylor, M. (2014, June). *Understanding bereavement camps from a positive youth development perspective: A collaborative service provider-evaluator model.* Presentation presented at the National Alliance for Grieving Children (NAGC) Annual Symposium on Children's Grief, Atlanta, GA.

Searles, R. (2004). *Camp MAGIK—program evaluation.* Atlanta, GA: Camp MAGIK.

9

Former Campers Returning as Volunteers

I did not want to leave
But that was mine to do
To live with love and joy
That is yours to do

—Written at camp

The goal of this chapter is to put the reader in touch with the human ability to find meaning after devastating loss.

Personal Narratives

One measure of the impact that bereavement camps have had is seen in the campers who return later to become volunteers at camp. A number of camps contacted for this book described this phenomenon of young adults who bring their insight and dedication to camps to pass forward the help that they received. When these former campers return, as with all volunteers, it is important to vet them thoroughly, making sure that they are ready to hear the pain of others and that they have thoroughly dealt with their own grief situation.

Four former campers and two parents of former campers were interviewed for this chapter. Although their names have been changed to protect their confidentiality, they gave their permission to share their stories.

Orphaned and Thriving

Chloe was 14 years old when she was awakened by the police knocking on her door with instructions to go to the hospital because of an "altercation" between her mother and father. She, her brother, and her maternal grandparents with whom they were living after their parents' divorce, rode together to the hospital 30 minutes away. They were ushered to a private room and after a few minutes, a nurse entered. Chloe and her 16-year-old brother, Wes, were informed that their mother had been shot in the head by their father and her injuries were too extensive for the medical team to save her. Distraught, they realized that their mother's time of death was just minutes before they had arrived at the hospital. In their daze they eventually remembered to ask about their dad. They were informed that he was missing, which immediately alarmed the grandparents. In fear that their daughter's ex-husband would now attack or harm their grandchildren, they decided to return home. One of the policemen, a friend of the family, accompanied them home. The policeman searched their home to assure the family that the man was not hiding inside. While searching, the policeman received a call to inform him that the suspect had been found dead by a self-inflicted gunshot wound. Chloe overheard the call. The two teenagers were made orphans in an instant.

Following the death of her parents, Chloe stayed on with her grandparents. When Chloe's school counselor called Chloe into her office and shared the information about grief camp, Chloe was less than enthusiastic. As a matter of fact, her first reaction was "eeeooowww" . . . She lived in a small town; she felt that everyone knew her story. Nobody asked for details, much less her feelings about it, so there was no need to talk about it. However, her grandparents told her she was going, and that she had no choice. Chloe, by now 15, tried to get her 17-year-old brother to attend. For some reason, her grandparents did not push him, so she ended up on her own. Once she arrived at camp, she was surprised. Laughing, she shared,

> I think the, the biggest thing for me about it was that I went from
> an environment where I was the odd ball out and I was the only

person dealing with anything like that to somewhere where it was like, "Hi, my name's Chloe. My parents died. What's your name and who died?" You know, it was like that was very regular—that was like the conversation starter. For everyone. And, it was nice to get the change of environment and to get to talk to everybody about what they had lost and compare it to your loss. And because we were put in age groups, with people similar to our age, it wasn't like me talking to somebody way older than me, who had a completely different outlook on it. Or someone way younger than me. It was me talking to people just like me who were going through the same things.

Soon after camp it became apparent that Chloe's grandparents were too grief stricken to provide proper care for two teenagers. Chloe and her brother thus moved in with their mother's 30-year-old sister, which seemed attractive at first because of the similarities in age. Again, Chloe was disappointed. Her aunt was used to caring for toddlers and had a very tight rein on Chloe and Wes. For one thing, their aunt would not let them contact their father's family, who in the eyes of Chloe and Wes had done nothing wrong. An even harder pill to swallow was the aunt's refusal to let Chloe apply to college out of town—she insisted that Chloe apply to the local community college and remain with her. Her aunt refused to give her the money for the application to the college Chloe had her mind set on—a state university some 30 miles away. Wes, who was now at another state university hours away, saved up enough money for Chloe to apply to her university of choice. Chloe was uncomfortable applying behind her aunt's back, and, as expected, when the aunt learned of the situation, "drama" ensued: "I knew exactly how she would react if she found out about this. So the police got involved a little bit and some social workers got involved a little bit." At that time, a month before her high school graduation, Chloe asked to live with a friend. After her aunt issued an ultimatum that Chloe needed to choose living with her aunt, her grandparents, or go to foster care, Chloe moved back in with her grandparents until her graduation.

As soon as Chloe had left camp, she knew she wanted to return. First, she thought she would be back as a camper, but found out the camp did not take repeat campers. She had asked the camp chaperone on the bus home from camp if she could volunteer. When the answer was, "Yes, maybe when you get a bit older," Chloe stated, "I was like, 'NO!' I'm volunteering soon." When she returned home, Chloe looked up the camp website and filled out an application right then and there. About volunteering at camp, Chloe stated, "all the learning experiences that I had at camp . . . going back . . . taught me like, a billion times more stuff. I definitely feel like it's something that is, like, engrained in me."

At the time of this writing, Chloe has volunteered at six camp sessions and has brought her brother and boyfriend to volunteer. She attends college at her first-choice university with a scholarship, works part-time at an after-school program, and has reconnected with her father's family. She states that her reason for volunteering rests in the fact that camp has become a part of who she is. She is a vivacious, charismatic, intelligent, and prospering young woman.

Simple Procedure, Not So Simple Grief

Ella, 15 at the time, was not feeling well, so she was asleep when her mother's friend came to pick up her mother for her mother's non-surgical outpatient procedure to have a mass biopsied. They had decided the night before that as soon as the procedure was over, her mother's friend would call and they would go out for a bite to eat. The call later in the morning woke her up. She felt bad that she was not ready to go, but her mother and her mother's friend would have to wait for her. She grabbed the phone and said, "Hey, I'm sorry, I will be ready in a minute." When a long pause followed, she immediately knew something was not right. Her mother's friend told her she would come to pick her up. She drove Ella to the hospital because "something had happened" with her mother. When they arrived at the hospital there were several family members waiting, including her father, who was separated from her mother. She was sure something was really wrong, but her father was carrying a "get well soon" balloon . . . she was really confused. A doctor came out into the waiting room and a nurse ushered the family into a private room. Ella could see the doctor was crying. "Why would a doctor be crying?" She soon found out. He stated he was sorry: He had made a mistake and did not follow procedure; he thought he could do the biopsy without a camera. "She bled out, we could not save her," he said. With everyone crying, Ella handed out tissues. Her mother's death seemed unreal and she felt "absent." She walked out of the hospital and called her friend, who she was supposed to travel with that coming weekend. She said, according to her friend, nonchalantly, "Hey, my mom just died. Can I call you later?" She did not shed any tears but went inside to ask to see her mother. Her mother was covered with a sheet up to her face. She was cold to the touch. Ella was the only family member who wanted to see her. As soon as she had, she left the hospital. Some of her mother's relatives tried to embrace her, but she did not want to be touched.

Ella is bi-racial and was adopted by her mother. Her birth mother was white and her birth father and adoptive mother, married at the time of adoption, were a black couple. After her mother's death, her mother's family chose not to stay in contact with Ella—according to Ella she was not black enough and they resented her mother for adopting a white woman's child. The family did decide to come into Ella's home and clean out her mother's closets—everything was taken. They also tried to have Ella sign over her death benefits to them.

Ella has a good relationship with her father, who became her primary parent after her mother's death. He moved into her mother's home after the death as Ella did not want to move. Her father did not feel quite at home; he did not use a bedroom but slept on the couch. Ella knows he moved in for her sake and that he was paying rent on two households to do so, which she greatly appreciated.

When Ella returned to school a week after her mother's death, she found out that an announcement had gone out about her mother's death. It was Valentine's Day, and Ella had purposively dressed in cheerful clothing to pretend that nothing tragic had happened. She was irritated, but also realized that other students would wonder where she had been, especially since she was the regular voice for announcements. Two months later her science teacher pulled her aside and told her about camp, handing her a brochure and encouraging her to go. Ella put the materials in her locker with no intention of going. Why should she go somewhere to talk about her feelings when she could talk about them anywhere she wanted—or not.

When she returned home, she told her father jokingly, "Guess where my teacher thinks I should go?" When her father heard about the camp, he said, "You should go." Ella was surprised. Her father was not one to share his emotions. As a matter of fact, even though they had seen each other every day since her mother died, the two of them had shared no thoughts or feelings in regards to her mother's death. Ella was ambivalent. She admits that it was almost a relief that her father wanted her to go—she thought he might criticize her for wanting to go. When he was supportive, she was ready.

Once at camp, she felt it was "pretty much" what she expected. She shared with the other campers what she calls "the Google version." She realized at camp, especially seeing young campers, how important it is to talk about the death. She feels that the relaxation and guided imagery exercise is the coping skill that helped her the most and she uses it four years later. When she is upset, she will ask, "Will you give me a second? I am going to my happy place." She took away from camp a change in herself to look at the glass as "half full rather than half empty."

Once she returned home, she immediately missed camp and its energy. Only when she returned home did she realize how much she had connected with her fellow campers. She wanted to come back right away. She knew that camp was a one-time opportunity because of wait lists, so she filled out and submitted a volunteer application. She states that she wants to "do," not just say how she wants things to be. When she returned, she knew she was where she was supposed to be. At camp, she is instrumental in the change that she sees in the campers and feels in herself. Speaking of her "little nuggets," as she calls her young campers, she said this about being back at camp as a volunteer:

> Every time, I appreciate it, every time. I mean, I just do. I don't even necessarily remember everyone's name but it doesn't matter . . . I just remember that feeling when I was with them. I'm doing [something] good so I got to keep doing it. Yeah, I like it.

Ella is now majoring in business at a research university. She was invited to speak about her loss on a national television program and received a scholarship from the program to attend college. There was talk about a lawsuit against the doctor in whose care her mother was at the time of her death. Ella and her father were offered assistance from an attorney who delayed action for months and then told them some days before the statute of limitation ran out that he would not be able to assist. Ella's birth mother, who was addicted to drugs, was recently released from prison and contacted Ella. Ella chose not to see her. Her birth mother subsequently died. Ella has some regrets about not seeing her, but is currently working on coming to peace with her situation.

Loss One, Loss Two, Loss Three . . .

Maggie's mother died from suicide when she was 5 years old. At that time, Maggie did not know the cause because her family wanted to "protect" her from the truth. Maggie lived with her father and at the age of 9 went with him, some family friends, and her aunt on a hunting trip. Maggie woke up in the middle of the night seeing several fire trucks and police cars in the driveway. She wondered what was wrong and felt intuitively that something was. Her aunt guided her back to bed and said everything was fine. When Maggie woke up in the morning, the emergency vehicles were gone and her aunt told her they were heading back home. She was told that everything was fine, and that her father was in the hospital because he had broken a leg. She soon learned the real truth. Her father had died, leaving her an orphan with no close relatives willing or able to care for her. Her father had, however, appointed a guardian in his will "just in case"— his female friend. Maggie moved in with her and her three children. This was a big change; Maggie's older siblings had left home by the time of their father's death. Going from being the only child at home to one of four was difficult, but she adjusted.

A few months later the school counselor told her about camp and sent home the paperwork. Maggie was excited to go to camp— she had never been to a camp before and was eager to find out what camp was all about. She became a bit frightened when she saw how many campers were attending and realized she knew no one. She no longer remembers her counselors' names, but she does remember that "they made it awesome and fun and it was great."

Maggie moved out of her family friend's home when she was 17, back to the farm that she had shared with her father. She is now a homeowner. However, her losses did not stop with her father's death. Two years later while shopping at the mall, she received a text from her sister's boyfriend to call him. The day before, she had received a Facebook message from her sister that simply said, "I love you." Although her sister would often tell her that she loved her, Maggie thought it odd that she would do so out of the blue on Facebook. When she received the text, she intuitively and immediately knew her sister was dead. She drove to her sister's home, where her fears were confirmed. Her sister had died by suicide. It fell on Maggie to meet her three nephews as they got off the school bus. One of them immediately asked her, "Mom died, didn't she?" She had to answer truthfully. Maggie describes the event, "that's sad to have to tell your nephews and it was just really, really a terrible time."

Maggie's nephews' situation brought back thoughts of going to camp after her father's death. She Googled the camp and found herself pictured on the website from years ago. She decided that she was destined to contact camp and offer to become a volunteer. She claims to have been nervous about applying, thinking there would be a big interview and that she might get rejected. The camp director, however, remembered her vividly. After the regular extensive volunteer intake process and volunteer training, Maggie was officially a camp volunteer. After her initial camp volunteer experience, Maggie signed up for a second camp and this time she brought her three nephews.

Maggie describes her volunteerism at camp as "the most satisfaction you will ever feel" and as "the best time I've ever had in my life!" She states that she could volunteer and help anywhere, but grief camp has a different atmosphere and relates to her personal experiences. She also recognizes how strong the children are and how they change her life. She commented, "they are old enough to know what has happened, but not old enough to know what to do about it. That's where I can help."

Maggie now works as a server and hopes to attend culinary arts school soon. She lives on the family farm. Sadly, Maggie's losses have not ended. She is most recently grieving the death of her girlfriend, who killed herself by jumping off a mountain ledge. Yet she remains optimistic about the future.

Type I and Type II Trauma

Courtney's dad was complaining about shoulder, back, and arm pain. Her mother suggested he go to the doctor even if it was probably just a pinched nerve. Courtney, 11 at the time, did not think anything of it and continued with her regular routine. Courtney's mother took her to a Girl Scout skating event, where her mother received a frantic phone call from one of Courtney's two older brothers. She heard her mother tell the scout leader that "Tom had a cardiac arrest." Courtney knew what "cardiac" meant but did not glean the full meaning of what had happened. Before she could ask, her mother left the skating rink without talking to her child. Courtney vividly remembers standing outside the skating rink waiting for somebody to pick her up. Her mother's friend eventually appeared to take Courtney to the hospital, where she was told the news of her father's death and was able to see him.

Her father's death was a shock to her, and the loss created a strained relationship between her and her mother. Courtney described herself as a "brat." She remembers thinking the relationship was so bad between them that she wanted to leave home though she was only 11 years old. Enter her school counselor. Courtney remembers being called in to the counselor's office together with some other children. The counselor told them about a healing camp for children and encouraged the students to bring the paperwork home to their families, stressing what a good opportunity this was. Courtney was on board right away—it sounded like so much fun!

Her 13-year-old brother was not, however. Yet they both ended up attending. Her brother had a difficult first evening. One of the male counselors took him under his wing, and after that initial day, he enjoyed camp. Courtney describes the camp as fun and a really helpful place to let off steam:

> I think I was able to get the perspective. Because especially I got to talk about things, it wasn't bottled up inside me . . . it did help me a lot to talk about it. Then I didn't have to bottle everything inside.

She also realized at camp that not knowing how to express her grief feelings led to the difficult relationship with her mother. This relationship improved immensely after camp, but the renewed and close mother–daughter relationship was time limited. Four years after her father's death, her mother was diagnosed with cancer. Courtney and her 17-year-old brother became the primary caregivers. Their oldest brother was also present as he worked as an emergency technician close by. For two years, her mother was in and out of the hospital. She had been in the hospital for an extended period of time as Christmas and her birthday approached. Her mother insisted on going home because she wanted to spend the holidays and her birthday at home with her children. She had breathing problems, and was uncomfortable in her bed, so Courtney crawled in, trying to assist her the best she could. As the sunlight was filtering in through the windows, Courtney snuck away into her brother's room and asked him to get their older brother as soon as possible because her mother had difficulty breathing and needed to be in the hospital. As their older brother took their mother to the hospital, Courtney and her other brother went to get some breakfast and head to school. Courtney figured it was just another hospital event and that her mother would soon be back home. At school, however, she received a call from her brother that her mother was not expected to live through the day. Courtney's heart was broken once again.

It was also a scary time: "I was very scared because I was only 17. Where am I going to go? Am I going to be put in foster care? It was so scary to me." It emerged that her mother had asked her oldest brother to be Courtney's guardian until she came of age. However, he had just moved in with his girlfriend and Courtney felt out of place. Instead, since they had all received insurance money, Courtney and her other brother remained in their mother's house, using the insurance money to pay the mortgage and other bills. The arrangement turned into disaster. Her brother's way of grieving was to party, party, and party. Courtney was able to hang on for her last year of high school and beginning of college, even if she had to stay out of the house to study. During her freshman year she met and started dating a man who, as soon as he realized what was happening in her life, invited her to live with his family an hour away from college. Courtney lived with his family for two years until she and her boyfriend ended their relationship. She now lives in a sorority house but plans on establishing her own apartment as soon as she graduates. She admits that "it is hard," but she mostly keeps her orphan status to herself: "I try to keep it locked away until it has to come out and I have to tell someone. But I try not to tell anybody because I don't want them to treat me differently."

After her mother's death Courtney Googled the grief camp she had attended after her father's death, but since she was uncertain whether she would be eligible to return at her age, she did not contact the camp at that time. A year or so later, she came upon the camp again when she was trying to find a boy she had been enamored with at camp at the age of 11. She entered the boy's name and added the name of the camp she had attended. She did not find this former romantic interest, but she did find the camp again. In college by now, she completed and mailed in the volunteer application.

Courtney describes the experience of volunteering this way:

> I'm able to relate to them on a whole other level. Because I was a camper, and I went through the same stuff they went through. So, being able to help them the way I was helped. I think that's why I chose to volunteer. I realized how much it had helped me. So being able to help them, it's just a really good feeling. I would do it all over again. Many, many times.

It has been ten years since Courtney lost her father and four years since her mother died. After her college graduation, she plans to head to nursing school. She says it is still difficult to deal with her losses. She is reminded of her father when she is away from the city and looks up at the stars. Looking at the stars is something special she did with him. The stars make her feel sad and remind her of her tragic losses.

Lost a Son, Gained a Purpose

Robert and his wife lost their infant son 16 years ago. His daughter attended camp a year after the death of her brother. After three daughters, Robert and his wife Sheila had been delighted to have a son. The joy did not last long. Concerned about their son's jaundice, the couple brought him to the emergency room. There the doctor discovered blood in his diaper and suggested further testing. Waiting in a private room was extremely difficult, not knowing what was going on. The doctor came to explain that surgery was needed on their son and that he would be transferred to a local children's hospital. During surgery, it was discovered that their son had infections in multiple organs. Medical staff tried to stave off the infections with various medications but were unsuccessful. Robert and Sheila's baby son was dead within a few days.

Their daughter Rachel was 8 at the time and was angry that she was again the youngest child. Distraught and dealing with their own grief, Robert and Sheila were unsure how to address Rachel. When Rachel brought home a flyer on a grief camp for kids, they thought it would be a good outlet for her to talk about her own feelings surrounding the loss of her brother. Robert stated that his daughter had always had a positive disposition and although he did not notice a change in her during the loss of her brother, Rachel has shared that camp helped her in her confusion and that it prevented her from "going negative."

Robert did not seek therapy or assistance for his grief for 12 years. Sheila had some therapy, but Robert was not ready to deal with his feelings. The turning point came when a colleague at the maintenance department at his work approached him about participating in a support group of men who had lost children. Robert thought the man was asking for help with the logistics of putting the group together, so he agreed to help, but quickly found out that the colleague wanted him to be a member of the group. Together with 11 other men, Robert helped found a group in his place of employment that now meets monthly. The group helped establish similar groups within this international company in cities all over the United States to include all parts of the organization. This group has changed Robert. He has dealt with locked-up feelings about the loss, and has come to understand that those feelings are natural and that he is not alone. He is active in the group both locally and nationally.

One day shortly after having established the support group at his place of employment, Robert was sitting at his computer and landed on an article about the work of former baseball player Jamie Moyer and The Moyer Foundation. Clicking through The Moyer Foundation's website, he saw the name of the camp his daughter had attended 13 years earlier. Robert said this about finding his daughter's camp:

> I was excited that camp was still offering these services. And I thought, man that's perfect for me. That's perfect for me,

because this is where I'm at, and this is what I do now. This is part of my new normal.

Knowing this was his opportunity to help children in some fashion to go through their grief, he contacted the camp director and offered his volunteer services. After completion of a volunteer application and a background check, Robert was ready for training. His first job as a volunteer was to greet campers at bus stops, see them onto the transportation bus, and accompany them to camp. He took his assignment very seriously, "I was their first person from camp . . . I was responsible for saying this is what we're going do. I was the guy that said hey, this is who we are and . . . I wanted to make sure that they felt comfortable."

Asked what camp means to him now and questioned why he wants to keep volunteering, Robert stated:

> I have a whole different understanding than somebody that hasn't [volunteered]. I can tell you exactly what's going on with your kid this weekend . . . I can tell you what we're going to present. And I'm going tell you your child will be different . . . It is magic. It is a magical weekend. Rachel really did have the best experience, that as a parent you can hope for . . . That was a good decision by her mom and me to do that . . . A kid cannot go through a better weekend in my mind. I would like to challenge to see a better weekend.

Robert continues to work as a mechanic and being actively involved with the support groups for bereaved parents and camp. He lives with his wife Sheila and daughter Rachel in a suburban setting. He relishes his four grandchildren, who live close by with their mothers, Robert's older married daughters.

Widowed with Two Young Children and Lots to Give

Laurie, a teacher and single mother of a young son, Kris, had joined her school's baseball team with other teachers, among them a para-pro named Jess. Oftentimes, Laurie brought Kris to the games. Jess started talking to Kris when he was in attendance, and began playing with him before and after games and at team practices. Kris quickly took a liking to Jess, and Jess to Kris. Jess simply fell in love with the boy and the boy's gentle spirit. To Kris, Jess was just like the dad he had hoped to have. Jess soon asked Laurie for a date.

Neither had any idea what was about to happen. Jess fell in love with Kris's mother, too, and soon the two were married. Laurie's family was not happy about the union. Jess had cystic fibrosis and, with this life-limiting disease, everyone knew that there were not going to be any rocking chairs on the porch at old age, no happily ever after. Laurie was in love with the kind-hearted, adventurous, caring, fun-loving Jess, but she was also realistic. Although nobody's time is for certain, Laurie knew that it was almost certain that Jess would die before she did. She accepted that. She would rather have some time with him than none.

Five years into their marriage, Laurie became pregnant. The couple had barely received the news of the pregnancy when Jess's lungs collapsed and physicians thought he would not live through the night. Laurie spent the night in the hospital's chapel, praying that Jess would live long enough to see his child. He did. He lived five more years. During this time, he was an involved father with both Kris and Zev, their new young son. Jess was aware he was on borrowed time. From a young age he had decided to enjoy every day, which he did. When he eventually entered hospice, his immediate and extended family gathered in his home for what Laurie calls "a six-week party." The night he died, Laurie was alone with him. It was an expected death, but a devastating one.

Several months later, Zev brought home a note from his school counselor about a grief camp for kids. He was hesitant to go, and Laurie thought he was too young—he was only 6 years old. Sometime after her husband's death, Laurie went overseas to volunteer with orphans. That experience caused her to rethink her career: She wanted to be more involved with children in need. She was not sure how she wanted this change to look, but decided to look into a Master of Social Work program. She took the leap, left her job, and enrolled in a two-year full-time program. Once there, she heard again about the camp program that Zev had been invited to some years earlier. Many of the social work students in the program volunteered at the program. Laurie was intrigued. Her first thought was that Zev needed to attend. She inquired further about the camp and Zev finally attended. Laurie remembers that when he came back from camp he was finally talking about his father and his death. The camp opened the communication between mother and son in regard to the death of their husband and father.

Laurie heard many positive things about camp from Zev and his counselors, and thought she might want to volunteer. However, being busy with graduate school and raising two young children, she was not able to offer her volunteer services until after graduation. At that time, she contacted the camp director and was soon trained to be a counselor for her first camp session. Laurie has continued to volunteer, catching every camp session that she can. Laurie had this to say about volunteering at camp:

> It's very rewarding. It's a *long* weekend. It's a very difficult weekend . . . the sessions are hard but *necessary* . . . it's been rewarding to be on that side [counseling] of it. To be able to help the kids. . . . process it and make sure that they know that they're not alone. That this has not just happened to them. That there is hope. There is healing. And it gives them words and tools. And to cope and to deal with and to process . . . a lot of kids and adults don't get that. So, it's a blessing that they're able to get that to help them.

Today Laurie lives with Zev, who is a make-up artist and works part-time while finishing school. Kris lives close by. Laurie has limited contact with her family of origin. She is a professional social worker and remains unmarried.

In Summary

This chapter speaks to human resilience in the face of adversity. The campers and parents of campers described in this chapter have all triumphed. They have taken tragic situations and turned their sadness and grief into helping others in their sadness and grief.

In concluding this book, the authors want to end with Wolfelt's (2004) Bill of Rights for Grieving Kids:

1. I have the right to have my own unique feelings about the death.
2. I have the right to talk about my grief whenever I feel like talking.
3. I have the right to show my feelings of grief in my own way.
4. I have the right to need other people to help me with my grief, especially grown-ups who care about me.
5. I have the right to get upset about normal, everyday problems.
6. I have the right to have "griefbursts."
7. I have the right to use my beliefs about God to help me with my grief.

8. I have the right to try to figure out why the person I loved died.
9. I have the right to think and talk about my memories of the person who died.
10. I have the right to move toward and feel my grief and, over time, to heal.

(pp. 51–52)

Recommended Reading

McClatchey, I. S., & Wimmer, J. S. (2012). Healing components of a bereavement camp: Children and adolescents give voice to their experiences. *Omega - Journal of Death and Dying, 65*(1), 11–32.

McClatchey, I. S., & Wimmer, J. S. (2014). Coping with parental death as seen from the perspective of children who attended a grief camp. *Qualitative Social Work, 13*(2) 221–236.

References

Wolfelt, A. D. (2004). *A child's view of grief: A guide for parents, teachers, and counselors*. Fort Collins, CO: Companion.

Appendices

Appendix A— A Sample Letter of Proposal

Dear Mrs. Grant,

Many children experience the death of a parent. There were 140 million orphans under the age of 18 worldwide in 2014 (U.S. Government, 2016). More than 10% of these had lost both parents. In the United States approximately 1.9 million children under the age of 18 received death benefits in 2014 because of a parent's death (Social Security Administration (SSA), n.d.). This estimate does not include children with uninsured, unemployed, or undocumented parents, suggesting that the number of children who have experienced the loss of a parent is higher. In our state of Georgia, the number of children under 18 on SSA death benefits is 44,846.

The loss of a loved one, though traumatic for anyone, can be especially difficult for children and adolescents. Research has shown countless short- and long-term effects of parental bereavement in children: difficulties in school; developmental delays; higher rates of substance abuse, depression, and deviance; increased risk of mortality as youth or young adults; and numerous physiological, health, social, and psychological issues (Dopp & Cain, 2012; Ellis, Dowrick, & Lloyd-Williams, 2013; Li et al., 2014; McClatchey, Vonk, & Palardy, 2009).

There are not enough resources for these children to receive assistance guiding them through the grief process. A local grief center sees clients who are able to come to them, but transportation and distance prevent many in need from participating. Then there is Camp MAGIK, a healing camp for bereaved children. Although we serve more than 200 children each year, on average 70 children are turned away annually when our camps are full. With increased funding we could provide services to these children. As an example, at one of our sessions we were unable to admit Hanna due to this financial constraint. Hanna's father had shot her, her mother, her sister, and eventually himself. Hanna was the only survivor. When we explained that the current camp session was full and had a waiting list, Hanna's grandmother told us that she found it outrageous that a child who had experienced what Hanna had experienced would have to wait until a later camp in spite of her dire need for help.

It is our fear that those children we cannot help in a timely manner may be unsuccessful in school and look to other means of "assistance" such as substance abuse and deviance. It is our belief that all bereaved children and teens deserve support and guidance through the grieving process. That is why we want to expand on the number of campers we can accept at each session.

Camp MAGIK holds three weekend grief camp sessions a year accepting between 70 and 80 campers in each session, depending on our resources. It is our goal to improve these campers' mental health by decreasing complicated grief symptoms by at least 50% within three months, at a cost of approximately $300 per child. We bring campers who have lost a parent or sibling together for a weekend of fun camp activities such as canoeing, a ropes course, hiking, and archery, but also for six grief counseling sessions led by professional grief counselors who follow a trauma-informed and grief-informed curriculum. Aiding the professional counselors are "co-counselors" who are graduate students, teachers, and other upstanding community members. The camp environment works well for our campers, who often come from underserved and low-income families who are not able to afford grief counseling for their children or bring them regularly for weeks to counseling. It is a convenient and cost-effective solution to bring peer support and professional counseling to those children and teens who are affected by the death of a parent or sibling but whose families cannot afford professional counseling.

We feel confident that this program is a meaningful contribution to our community and Georgia. Our outcome studies show that our camp reduces trauma and traumatic grief symptoms among our campers and promotes positive behavior and cognitive and emotional growth. Camp MAGIK is unique in providing a camp setting to fulfill its mission to provide a safe, nurturing environment where children and their caregivers begin the healing process. We are also unique in that we provide professional counseling group sessions to our campers during the weekend. Like our board, our staff is diverse and highly trained. Our founder and director and professional counselors have a combined experienced of more than 100 years working with bereaved, traumatized children and teens. They have graduate and doctorate degrees in social work or counseling. Our founder and director has researched trauma in bereaved children and adolescents and effective interventions, having publications in several professional journals. In addition, she has presented at numerous national and international conferences on this topic. We also collaborate with many community organizations such as local universities, schools, hospices, health care organizations, churches, and businesses.

We have campers who need to interact with peers who have experienced similar losses, and need to process their losses with each other and professional counselors. We have campsites to hold our camp sessions for 220 campers. We also have the support of the community in the form of volunteer co-counselors, food, arts and crafts materials, and in-kind donations. What we do not have is the money for one additional campsite. The total budget for our three camp sessions is $66,000 (see the attached budget). As you can see we have secured some of our funding, but it will take another $14,000 to hold another session. However, a $14,000 investment from you in bereaved children's futures would give us what we need to pay the cost of another campsite and serve approximately 75 more children in need of our services.

To ascertain that your money is serving its purpose, we will evaluate our efforts by using a pre- and post-test for our campers, measuring traumatic grief symptoms. You will receive the results of this evaluation a few months after the camp session is held.

Your foundation's investment in our project will provide children who have lost a parent or sibling the ability to attend our camp sessions. In recognition of your generous and truly caring investment, we would like to name you as one of our sponsors on our T-shirts and on our website, and invite your board members to visit one of our camp sessions. We know that you will be proud to know that you, through a grant of $14,000, will make a needed, meaningful contribution to the children of Georgia who have been afflicted by the death of a parent or sibling. We know that you agree that no child should have to navigate the path of grief and loss alone.

Please feel free to call me at 404.555.5555 to discuss this further and to arrange a visit to Camp MAGIK at your convenience.
Sincerely,
Rene McClatchey
Chair

References

Dopp, A. R., & Cain, A. C. (2012). The role of peer relationships in parental bereavement during childhood and adolescence. *Death Studies*, *36*(1), 41–60.

Ellis, J., Dowrick, C., & Lloyd-Williams, M. (2013). The long-term impact of early parental death: Lessons from a narrative study. *Journal of the Royal Society of* Medicine, *106*(2), 57–67.

Li, J., Vestergaard, J., Cnattingius, S., Gissler, M., Bech, B. H., Obel, C., & Olsen, J. (2014). Mortality after parental death in childhood: A nationwide cohort study from three Nordic countries. *PLoS Medicine*, *11*(7), 1–13. doi:10.1371/journal.pmed.1001679

McClatchey, I. S., Vonk, M. E., & Palardy, G. (2009). Efficacy of a camp-based intervention for childhood traumatic grief. *Research on Social Work* Practice, *19*(1), 19–30.

Social Security Administration. (n. d.). *Social security beneficiary statistics*. Retrieved from www.ssa.gov/oact/STATS/SRVbenies.html

U.S. Government. (2016). *U.S. Government action plan on children in adversity—2016 report to congress*. Retrieved from www.usaid.gov/open/children—adversity/2016

Appendix B— Sample Logic Model

Example of a logic model

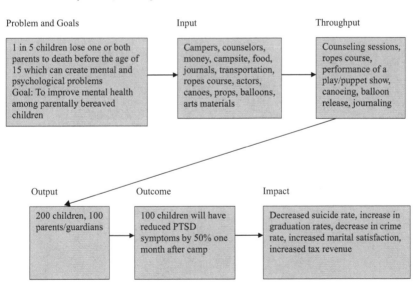

Problem and Goals

1 in 5 children lose one or both parents to death before the age of 15 which can create mental and psychological problems
Goal: To improve mental health among parentally bereaved children

Input

Campers, counselors, money, campsite, food, journals, transportation, ropes course, actors, canoes, props, balloons, arts materials

Throughput

Counseling sessions, ropes course, performance of a play/puppet show, canoeing, balloon release, journaling

Output

200 children, 100 parents/guardians

Outcome

100 children will have reduced PTSD symptoms by 50% one month after camp

Impact

Decreased suicide rate, increase in graduation rates, decrease in crime rate, increased marital satisfaction, increased tax revenue

Appendix C— Follow-up Assessment of Prospective Campers

Use these questions to promote an open conversation.

1. What was the relationship between the dead person and the child?
2. Was the death expected? Was the child present at the time of death?
3. How did the child find out about the death and how was death explained?
4. What was the child's reaction at that time?
5. Was there a funeral and/or memorial service? Did the child attend?
6. What is your family composition?
7. What are some other losses in your child's life (through death, moves, pets)?
8. Have you noticed any changes in your child's:
   a. Sleep patterns? Nightmares?
   b. Behavior at home (withdrawn, anxious, fighting, clingy, acting out)?
   c. Eating patterns?
   d. Ability to focus?
   e. Regression such as bed wetting?
   f. Cutting?
   g. Talk of self-harm/suicide? Any previous suicide attempts?

9. Does your child have behavioral issues at school?
10. Does your child complain of headaches and/or stomach aches?
11. Does your child talk willingly about his father/mother/sibling?
12. Do you talk openly about his father/mother/sibling?
13. What are your family's beliefs about death and the afterlife? Does your child understand these?
14. Does your child have any limitations that we should be aware of?
15. Is your child ready to stay away overnight in a new surrounding with unfamiliar people?
    a. How can we help make your child more comfortable?
    b. We allow our campers to use the camp director's phone to call home if he/she wishes. What reservations, if any, do you have about this?

Appendix D—
Bereavement Camp
Standards of Practice

The Moyer Foundation is pleased to lead the development of Bereavement Camp Standards of Practice ("Standards") through the generous support of the New York Life Foundation.

The Standards Committee

The Standards Committee includes professionals with expertise in camp standards of practice and overnight and day camps for bereaved youth, adults, and families. The Moyer Foundation is grateful to the following for their contributions to the Bereavement Camp Standards of Practice.

- Noreen Carrington, LMFT, FT—KP Caring Foundation
- Janette du Monceaux, LMSW—Providence Hospice and Home Care of Snohomish County, Pediatric Bereavement Specialist
- Bethany Gardner, MA—The Moyer Foundation, Director of Bereavement Programs

- Rhonda Mickelson, MEd—American Camp Association, Director of Standards
- Jenny Simmonds, MEd-Youth Development Leadership— Fairview's Youth Grief Services, Program Director
- Jason Stout—Outward Bound USA, National Outreach Director

About the Standards

The Bereavement Camp Standards of Practice ("Standards") provides MINIMUM standards of practice that primarily consider providing a beneficial, safe experience in a variety of bereavement camp settings. The Standards are suggested guidelines compiled by peers in the field; they are not a certification or license. In addition, the Standards are not a "how to" guide. In order to be applicable to many types of clinicians and settings, the Standards are generalized, minimum practices.

A revised version will be released annually following an invitation for feedback from the children's bereavement field.

Definitions

- Host organization: the organization responsible for providing the bereavement camp
- Camp facility: the venue where the bereavement camp is held
- Participants: campers, volunteers, and staff

Please contact The Moyer Foundation at *info@moyerfounda tion.org* with questions and feedback.

Fundamentals

Organization and Service Description

The host organization will establish and provide the public and participants with information regarding the purpose, mission, and scope of services of the organization; type of camp services and their goals and outcomes; and any associated fees.

Equality/Non-Discrimination

The cultural, ethnic, country of origin, gender expression, race, age, physical and mental ability, veteran status, sexual orientation, economic, spiritual and religious diversity of all campers, volunteers, and staff will be respected. The host organization will work to identify and address any barriers to inclusion.

Community Outreach

The greater community will be engaged to increase awareness regarding the benefits of bereavement camp participation. Camper and volunteer recruitment practices will reach a diverse population with identified underserved populations at the forefront of these practices.

Community Resources

The host organization will maintain an up-to-date list of community resources that address the needs of bereaved individuals and families, such as social, emotional, mental health, and spiritual needs. Resources will be provided when needs are outside the scope of services of the host organization.

Program Evaluation

The host organization will seek feedback from campers, volunteers, and staff, and will modify camp programming as appropriate in order to meet program goals and improve services.

Confidentiality and Data Protection

The host organization will develop and clearly communicate policies to all participants regarding confidentiality, social media, photography, and media involvement. All information pertaining to campers, volunteers, and staff will remain confidential within all formats and contexts, including stories shared verbally. The host organization will thoughtfully determine what information will be shared with volunteers.

Policies and procedures will be established and implemented regarding the respectful use of camper images, stories, etc., for marketing and other purposes. Releases will be obtained from campers, parent/guardians of minors, volunteers, and staff prior to the sharing of any confidential information, including data, photographs, videos, and camper stories.

Volunteers and staff will be trained to honor the integrity of confidentiality as it applies to their roles and responsibilities. All federal and state laws will be adhered to regarding the protection of confidential information and retention, as will any professional confidentiality requirements including mandatory reporting laws.

Dual Relationships and Conflicts of Interest

Policies and procedures will be established regarding dual relationships (two or more distinct relationships with the same person) and conflicts of interest (tension between self-interest, professional interest and/or public interest) to protect participants from harm or exploitation and to ensure that participants have the best experience possible.

Specific thought will be given to dual relationships and camp attendance when a prior relationship exists between staff and volunteer, volunteer and volunteer, and staff/volunteer and camper.

Volunteer & Staff involvement

Competency

The host organization will be knowledgeable and receive ongoing education regarding current literature, research and best practices related to bereavement, bereavement interventions, and camp management. All staff and volunteers will demonstrate competencies that are applicable to their roles.

Volunteer Selection and Screening

Volunteers will be selected following a formal application, screening, and reference process. At minimum, an annual criminal background check will be conducted on all qualified applicants and returning volunteers.

The host organization will identify and operate under all federal, state, and local laws, codes, and regulations related to background checks for working with minors and vulnerable populations in the program context.

NOTE: The American Camp Association provides helpful resources, including:

- www.acacamps.org/resource-library/public-policy/criminal-background-checks-issues-resources-camps

Volunteer Training

Camps that utilize volunteers will maintain the highest standards by providing volunteers with a code of conduct, policies and procedures, training, and an opportunity to evaluate their experience.

Training will be provided to all those involved in camp programming and camper supervision. Training will include at least the following topics:

- Camp leadership and reporting structure
- Staff/volunteer expectations, roles, and responsibilities
- Camp facility expectations
- Camp structure and programming
- Grief and grief support interventions
- Trauma and grief
- Working with campers
- Boundaries
- Building connection and community
- Awareness and support of staff and volunteer grief and other potentially triggered responses
- Cultural, diversity, and inclusion awareness
- Code of conduct

- Policies and procedures
- Safety, medical, social-emotional incidents, and emergency procedures
- Signs of self-harm or intentions to harm self or others
- Teamwork and conflict resolution
- Specific confidentiality

The following additional topics will be addressed when supporting children and adolescents:

- Developmental characteristics of children and teens
- Child abuse recognition and reporting
- Behavior management

Policies and Procedures

The host organization will have written policies and procedures that are congruent with their mission and values and support a safe and appropriate camp experience. Policies and procedures will address, but are not limited to:

- Recruitment, screening and retention of campers and volunteers
- Camper, volunteer, and staff requirements and expectations
- Camper, volunteer, and staff behavior management
- Safety, health, medical, social-emotional incidents, and emergency procedures
- Sexual harassment, abuse, interpersonal boundaries, and appropriate touch
- Confidentiality, data protection, social media, and media involvement
- Code of conduct
- Personnel policies
- Tobacco, drug, and alcohol possession and/or use
- Transportation
- Communication at camp
- Electronics at camp
- Referrals
- Cost of camp
- Ratios at camp

- Guests at camp
- Arrival and departure procedures
- Program evaluation
- Pre- and post-camp continued care and contact

NOTE: The American Camp Association provides helpful resources, including:

- Releases and related issues: www.acacamps.org/resource-library/articles/releases-related-issues-revisted
- Camp staff use of electronic devices and social media: www. acacamps.org/resource-library/articles/camp-staff-use-electronic-devices-social-media-some-issues-solutions

Health & Safety

Camper, Volunteer, & Staff Ratios

The host organization will develop and implement policies regarding ratios of leadership, volunteers, and campers at camp. General considerations will include age of campers, types of loss, social and emotional needs of campers, type and location of facilities; types and locations of program offerings; and the length of the camp experience. Ratios will be based on the number of clinical staff, the experience level of volunteers and the needs of the campers being served.

- Ratios when supporting minors: The American Camp Association recommends the following ratios for general programming: ages 6–8, one adult to six campers; ages 9–14, 1:8; and ages 15–18, 1:10. The host organization will determine when a greater number of adults are necessary.
- Individual engagement: Staff and volunteers will be trained to avoid 1:1 camper/staff or camper/camper engagement that is out of observable sight of others. A minimum of three participants, including appropriate supervision, should be together at all times. This policy is often referred to as the "rule of three." Individual connection is valued and can be engaged safely in a public area.
- Clinical staff and volunteers: Camp leadership will include at least one individual clinically trained at the master's level

in a relevant field and who also has expertise and experience working with the bereaved populations served. The host organization will assess the need for additional clinical staff.

- Leadership to volunteer ratio: The host organization will provide appropriate leadership support and supervision to volunteers for a safe, high-quality experience.
- Staff/volunteer to camper ratio: The host organization will identify the number of staff and volunteers needed in the program areas established.
- High-risk situations and settings: Most incidents at camp occur during unstructured program time. The host organization will identify high-risk settings or situations and develop plans for supervision and safety accordingly.
- Considerations for sleeping arrangements:
  - For overnight camps serving minors: sleeping arrangements must be evaluated for the number and location of staff within the sleeping quarters.
  - For overnight camps serving adults and families: sleeping assignments will be made with personal and family privacy in mind.

Safety and Emergency Procedures

Policy and procedures will be developed and implemented to ensure campers, volunteers, and staff are safe at camp. The host organization will consult with the camp facility in the development and implementation of safety plans. Areas to consider include:

- Presence of animals at camp facility, use of therapeutic animals in programming, and service and/or emotional support animals accompanying participants.
- Skilled facilitators for specialized activities (i.e., a certified lifeguard).
- Procedures will be established in the event that a participant is missing or an unauthorized person is discovered on the property.
- Environmental emergencies: Necessary actions will be identified in the event of unanticipated natural disasters (tornadoes, fires, floods) and/or other environmental emergencies (loss of

power, compromised water system, etc.). Staff and volunteers will be trained to know and fulfill their role in the response plan.

- Social-emotional incidents: Policies and procedures will be defined and implemented regarding acute mental health concerns that arise during the intake process, while at camp, or during post-camp follow-up. This may include, but is not limited to, neglect, abuse, harm of self or others, or other crisis situations. Programs will have at least one designated clinical staff person responsible for acute social-emotional needs of campers, volunteers, and staff and will engage appropriate follow-up.
- Accidents/Incidents: Policies and procedures should be defined and implemented regarding non-social-emotional incidents, accidents, and near misses that occur while at camp. Examples of "incidents" and "accidents" include fires; natural disasters; danger from intruders or trespassers; crises arising out of camper, staff, or rental group behavior (e.g., fighting, serious emotional outbursts, threatening others); or other situations posing serious safety threats. Examples of "near misses" and "emergencies not resulting in injury" may include lost campers, near drownings, or the use of drugs or alcohol by staff or participants.
- Guests and service providers at camp: Policies and procedures related to appropriate participation of guests and service providers will be developed and communicated. Items to consider based on the individual's participation at camp include: sign-in upon arrival; type of identifier guest must wear; escort policy; required background check clearance; and necessary paperwork (i.e., confidentiality agreement, liability release, media release, etc.). When inviting guests, camp leadership will be mindful of the vulnerable nature of the camper group and be thoughtful of the impact of guests on the campers' experience and safety.
- Communication plan: The camp will have a communication plan that includes:
  - A single spokesperson for the camp is clearly identified.
  - Communicating with guardians should a natural disaster or emergency occur.
  - Identification of an individual to contact a guardian in the event of a camper-related accident or incident.

- Identification of individuals(s) who will contact emergency personnel in various health or emergency events and collaborate with personnel to minimize the impact of the event on campers (i.e., lights and sirens off).

Camp leadership is encouraged to inform the local authorities (police, sheriff, fire department, and EMS) of the dates, location, and number of campers, volunteers and staff on-site to increase safety and minimize impact of emergencies on campers.

Medical Procedures

A healthcare plan will be developed and implemented that includes:

- The collection of a medical form as part of the camper and volunteer intake process, including a record of allergies, dietary restrictions, current prescription and over-the- counter medications, and a description of any current physical, mental, and psychological conditions requiring medication, treatment, or special considerations while at camp.
- The host organization will determine the level of healthcare provider needed during the camp experience based on the camper population, camp setting, access to additional medical support, etc. At minimum, at least one Registered Nurse, Physician Assistant, or Physician with current licensure in the state that camp is held will be on-site during the duration of the camp experience. Camp medical professionals will have current, age-appropriate CPR and First Aid certification.
- If appropriate, an initial health screening upon arrival at camp that can include temperature, signs of illness, recent exposure to any contagious diseases, etc. The review and collection of all prescription and over-the-counter medications, in original containers, will be required at this time, with the exception of items such as inhalers, epi-pens and insulin pumps. Any medication taken by a camper that day will be documented along with the next needed dosage.
- All staff, volunteer, and camper prescriptions and over-the-counter medications will be stored in a locked location, with the exception of items such as inhalers, epi-pens, and insulin

pumps. Medications will be dispersed by designated health-care providers only.

- The camp program will have a recordkeeping system documenting incidents and care provided, including:
  - Date, time, location, and name of person ill or injured
  - General description of injury or illness
  - Description of any treatment administered
  - Administration of all prescription and over-the-counter medication
  - Name and signature of persons evaluating and treating
- The camp program will establish and clearly communicate with all staff and volunteers when, how, and by whom an additional level of medical or emergency care should be contacted.
- The camp program will consider the need for standing orders from a physician for medical care provided to participants.

Transportation

When transportation is provided by the host organization or camp facility, policies will be developed that address and ensure:

- Training of drivers and driver requirements
- Verification of DMV records of drivers for past violations
- Verification of appropriate vehicle insurance
- Supervision of participants while being transported
- Safety orientation for passengers to include what to do in the event of an accident
- Mechanical evaluations and safety checks of vehicles in use
- Release form from campers or the guardians of minor campers

Camp Facility & Business

Insurance

The host organization will, in consultation with their insurance provider, the camp facility, and other vendors, evaluate the need for the types of insurance listed below.

- Liability insurance
- Professional liability insurance for those with professional licenses

- Accident insurance
- Workman's compensation for those who qualify
- Property insurance for host organization property (electronics, etc.)
- Motor vehicle insurance if any transportation is provided by the camp, volunteers, staff, or chartered
- The need to have the facility be named as a co-insurer on the camp's liability policy

Camp Facility

The host organization will have in place a signed agreement with the camp facility that includes:

- Terms of use, including dates, times, and costs
- Cancellation, minimum fees, and refund policies
- Services that will be provided by the host facility, such as food service, recreation options, program staff, transportation
- Cost and conditions for use of any recreational equipment or program services
- Party responsible for any special program activities (e.g.: swimming, challenge course, horseback riding, etc.), what is included in those activities, and the qualification level of camp facility staff related to program services provided
- Party responsible to provide first aid, emergency care, and emergency transportation
- Party responsible to supervise the camp and participants' behavior
- Required orientation to the host site regarding the site's safety procedures and regulations
- Any insurance required for the host organization and camp facility

Pre-Camp Assessment

The host organization will develop a thorough registration and assessment process to ensure the appropriateness and readiness of each camper for a safe experience in the identified camp setting.

This might include, but is not limited to, an application and additional paperwork, phone assessment, in-person interview, open house or other pre-camp event, and ongoing phone and email contact. Paperwork components will address the needs of both the host organization and the camp facility.

Consultation with other providers may be necessary. Consent and release will be obtained prior to consultation with other providers. The host organization should establish policy and procedure for determining and communicating non-acceptance to the camp program.

Categories covered in the pre-camp assessment process might include: contact and demographic information; bereavement history; social, emotional, and behavior issues; family structure and communication; coping styles; belief systems; and medical information. Forms may include: general application; consent to provide care; liability release; media consent and release; transportation release; and, in the case of minors, custody release.

During the pre-camp assessment process, campers will receive an overview of the camp experience, be informed of expectations, have concerns and questions addressed, and be informed of their acceptance status.

Camp Experience

A sense of cohesion and community will be intentionally developed in the camp program, helping campers gain a sense of belonging, respect, and trust, and to learn they are not alone. The host organization will determine any identifying items to aid in the development of cohesion, such as camp T-shirt, name badges, etc.

Camp will be structured to allow campers the opportunity to share their story, express their feelings, and receive support in a physically and emotionally safe, non-judgmental, and empowering setting. Campers will be allowed to determine their participation level in sharing, bereavement, and recreational activities. Integrating approaches such as Trauma-Informed Care and other clinical models may help promote resiliency, hope, courage, and self-esteem as campers engage their grief experience.

Volunteers will have clear methods and opportunities for breaks at camp to encourage self-care and respite from responsibilities.

Camp Schedule

Participants will be informed of the camp schedule. Attention will be given to a balance of activities and modalities that consider the developmental needs and learning and expression styles of campers. Types of activities might include:

- A variety of approaches (i.e., art, movement, music, animal assisted therapies, etc.)
- Grief education and support
- Validation and normalization
- Coping skills
- Identifying support systems
- Memorializing
- Ceremonies and rituals (i.e., opening and closing)
- Challenge, character- and trust-building activities
- Community- and connection-building activities
- Recreational activities
- Times for reflection and rest

Arrival and Departure

Policy and procedure will be developed for the arrival and departure of campers. Facilitating a welcoming and smooth process can relieve anxiety and establishes camp as a safe and reliable environment.

At minimum, check-in/out procedures will address healthcare policies, including a health screening at the start of camp and returning of medications at the conclusion. Considerations at check-in and -out when supporting minors include:

- Clear communication of drop-off and pick-up time and location
- Only designated individuals identified on the camp paperwork will be allowed to drop off and pick up campers.
- Identification verification of the guardian or approved adult
- Sign-in and sign-out sheet
- If transportation is provided, ensure that all check-in needs are met prior to transitioning camper under host organization responsibility.

- Provide emergency contact information for the parent to reach camp leadership
- Confirm emergency contact information for camp leadership to reach the guardian
- Help campers and their guardians say good-bye to one another
- Provide information sessions for guardians at the start and conclusion of camp
- Return of medications at check-out

Meal Times

Meal times are an important part of overall programming and a key opportunity for building community. Host organization should attend to these times as more than just having a meal. Special meal requests, dietary restrictions, meal times, process, and menus should be coordinated with the camp facility or food service provider. Ensure that balanced meals, snacks, and hydrating beverages are provided to participants.

Camp Rules

Facility, camp, and cabin rules will be established. All rules, enforcement policies, and consequences will be clearly communicated. Campers can be given opportunities to shape rules as appropriate.

Post-Camp Experience

Post-Camp Continued Care

The host organization is encouraged to consider the following aspects of participant continued care:

- Timely contact regarding immediate needs with the camper or guardian of a minor camper
- General follow-up related to the camp experience and bereavement needs

- A camp reunion event
- Information about ongoing bereavement programming within the host organization or other community resources
- Encouragement of campers to develop connections with other campers for ongoing support following the camp weekend, as is comfortable with the camper or guardian of a minor camper
- Volunteer and staff support, debrief, and recognition events

Post-Camp Communication

The camp program will develop and communicate policies regarding ongoing relationships, communication, and social media connection following camp between volunteer/staff to campers and camper to camper.

Appendix E— Assent Form for 7–10-Year-Old

Assent Form Used by Permission From Kennesaw State University

Research Study Assent Form (7–10-Year Age Range)

Study Title: [*Title as listed on IRB application*]
Researchers: [*List names and contact information of investigators and co-investigators*]
My name is (insert the name of the person who will approach the child during the assent process). I am from Kennesaw State University.

- I am inviting you to be in a research study about (*topic of the study in simple language*)
  Example: what kinds of foods kids usually eat and how much exercise they get.
- Your parent knows we are going to ask you to be in this research study, but you get to make the final choice. It is up to you. If you decide to be in the study, we will ask you to (*describe what the child will be asked to do in simple language that is appropriate to the child's age and maturity. If the child*

will be asked to do several things, describe each one. Explain about how long each aspect of their participation will take).
Example: talk with us for about half an hour to answer some questions about your bedtime and how you go to sleep.

- (If media recording is to be part of the study, explain that here and let the child know that you won't record them without their permission.)
- *(Describe potential benefits to the child, if any, and those to society.)*
Example: If you take part in this research study, you might learn how to choose good snacks and new games you can play outside.
- *(Describe potential risks to the child, including fatigue, boredom, pain, anxiety, etc. in simple language. Also explain what you will do to minimize those risks or handle the risks if they occur.)*
Example: We don't think anything bad would happen if you decide to take part in this research study, but some kids might get tired of sitting still while they answer questions. We will let you take a break about every 15 minutes or more often if you need to.
- If anything in the study worries you or makes you uncomfortable, let us know and you can stop. *(If relevant)* There are no right or wrong answers to any of our questions. You don't have to answer any question you don't want to answer or do anything you don't want to do.
- Everything you say and do will be private. We won't tell your parents or anyone else what you say or do while you are taking part in the study. When we tell other people about what we learned in the study, we won't tell them your name or the name of anyone else who took part in the research study.
(When relevant, the child should be informed that you must tell authorities or health professionals if you learn that the child has been hurt or might be hurt by another person, or might hurt themselves.)
- You don't have to be in this study. It is up to you. You can say no now or you can change your mind later. No one will be upset if you change your mind.
- You can ask us questions anytime and you can talk to your parent anytime you want. We will give you a copy of this form that you can keep. Here is the name and phone number of someone you can talk to if you have questions about the study:

Name (*researcher*)   Phone number (*local phone number*)

- Do you have any questions now that I can answer for you?

IF YOU WANT TO BE IN THE STUDY, SIGN OR PRINT YOUR NAME ON THE LINE BELOW:

(*If relevant: Put an X on this line if it is okay for us to record you* ____

_____   _____

Child name and signature   Date

Check which of the following applies (completed by person administering the assent):

- ☐ Child is capable of reading and understanding the assent form and has signed above as documentation of assent to take part in this study.
- ☐ Child is not capable of reading the assent form, but the information was verbally explained to him/her. The child signed above as documentation of assent to take part in this study.

_____

Name of parent who gave consent for child to participate

_____   _____

Signature of person obtaining assent   Date

Appendix F

We would like to acknowledge and thank the following camp organizations that shared information with us in preparation of this book.

1. A Camp to Remember, Montana: www.tamarackgriefre sourcecenter.org
2. Amanda the Panda Grief Camp, Iowa: https://amandathe panda.org
3. Bo's Camp, Georgia: www.navicenthealth.org
4. Camp Aloha, Georgia: www.hospicesavannah.org
5. Camp Amanda, Washington: www.wwhospice.org
6. Camp Bridges/Camp Adventure, Florida: https://web.csho spice.org
7. Camp Chimaqua/Mend a Heart, Pennsylvania: www.hospice andcommunitycare.org
8. Camp Circle of Love, Florida: http://chaptershealth.org
9. Camp Comfort, Colorado: www.mtevans.org
10. Camp Connect, Florida: https://choosecovenant.org
11. Camp Corazon, New Mexico: https://childrensgrief.org
12. Camp Courage, Iowa: https://hospiceofsiouxland.com
13. Camp Courage, Oregon: www.partnersbend.org
14. Camp Courage, Michigan: http://harborhospicemi.org
15. Camp Courage, Texas: www.hendrickhealth.org/Hospice/ hospice.aspx

16. Camp Courage/Camp Erin, Missouri: http://annieshope.org
17. Camp Dogwood, Georgia: www.wghealth.org/our-services/hospice
18. Camp Encourage, Ohio: http://stateoftheheartcare.org
19. Camp Erin, national: https://moyerfoundation.org/camps-programs/camp-erin
20. Camp Erin Cincinnati, Ohio: www.fernside.org
21. Camp Erin Lewis-Clark Valley, Idaho: http://willow-center.org
22. Camp Erin Eastern Ontario, Canada: http://cornwallhospice.com
23. Camp Erin Santa Cruz, California: www.hospicesantacruz.org
24. Camp Erin Twin Cities, Minnesota: www.fairview.org
25. Camp Evergreen, Indiana: www.centerforhospice.org
26. Camp Evergreen Hosparus, Kentucky: www.hosparus.org
27. Camp Evergreen, Oregon: www.klamathhospice.org
28. Camp Good Grief, Colorado: www.hopewestco.org
29. Camp Good Grief, Florida: www.tchospice.org
30. Camp Good Grief, Florida: www.trustbridge.com
31. Camp Good Grief of Staten Island, New York: www.campgoodgriefsi.org
32. Camp Good Mourning, Georgia: http://katesclub.org
33. Camp Hands of Hope, South Carolina: www.hpcfoundation.org
34. Camp Healing Tree, Indiana: www.brookesplace.org
35. Camp Hometown Heroes, Wisconsin: www.kyleskorner.org
36. Camp Hope, California: www.camphopeca.com
37. Camp HOPE, Wisconsin: www.camphopeforkids.org
38. Camp I Believe, national: www.gentivahospicefoundation.org
39. Camp Journey, Georgia: http://abbeyhospice.com
40. Camp Kangaroo/Camp Erin, national: seasonsfoundation.org
41. Camp Kaniksu, Idaho: www.hospiceofnorthidaho.org
42. Camp Kita, Maine: campkita.com
43. Camp Koala, Pennsylvania: www.campkoala.org
44. Camp Lionheart, Ohio: www.gentivahospicefoundation.org
45. Camp LOLO, Idaho: www.camplolo.org
46. Camp M.A.G.I.C., Virginia: http://edmarc.org
47. Camp MAGIK, Georgia: www.campmagik.org

48. Camp Mend-A-Heart, Alaska: http://hospiceofsoldotna.com
49. Camp Met, Texas: www.thecooperfoundation.org
50. Camp Millie, Pennsylvania: http://bereavementcenter.org
51. Camp New Dawn, Maryland: http://compassregionalhos pice.org
52. Camp New Hope, Delaware: www.delawarehospice.org
53. Camp Peter Charles, Michigan: www.camppetercharles. com
54. Camp Phoenix, Maryland: http://calverthospice.org
55. Camp STARS, Georgia: http://vnhs.org
56. Camp Sunburst, South Carolina: http://hospiceoftheup state.com
57. Camp Sunrise, California: www.bartonhealth.org/tahoe/ home.aspx
58. Chameleon's Journey, North Carolina: www.hpccr.org
59. Comfort Zone Camps, national: www.comfortzonecamp. org
60. Courageous Kids Camp, Oregon: www.courageouskidsore gon.org
61. Dottie Kissinger Bereavement Camp, Arizona: www.banner health.com
62. El Tesoro de la Vida Camp, Texas: www.campfirefw.org
63. Experience Camps, national: www.experience.camp
64. Grief and Growing, California: https://jewishhealingcenter. org
65. Hometown Heroes, Wisconsin: http://hometownheroes.org
66. Journey Children's Camp, Illinois: www.joliethospice.org/ index.html
67. Kids Camp, California: www.optimalhospicefoundation. com
68. New Hope Family Camp, California: www.newhopegrief. org
69. Okizu Bereavement Family Camp, California: http://okizu. org
70. Outward Bound Heroic Journey, national: www.outward bound.org
71. Shannon's Hope Camp, South Carolina: http://bridgessc. org
72. Stepping Stones Camp/Camp Labyrinth, Missouri: www. bjchospice.org
73. Stepping Stones of Hope Camp Paz, Camp Samantha, Ari zona: http://steppingstonesofhope.org

74. TAPS (Tragedy Assistance Program for Survivors), national: www.taps.org
75. Sunshine Camp, South Carolina: www.hospiceandlifecare center.org
76. Ted and Jane's Camp Courage, Michigan: www.stjoesan narbor.org

Author Index

Author Index–Authors as they appear in the content text–for work of more than five authors, only the first author is listed

249

Subject Index

Note: Bold page numbers indicate tables